Your God Shall Be My God

Religious Conversion In Britain Today

Also by Jonathan Romain

Sign and Wonders

The Jews of England

Faith and Practice: A Guide to Reform Judaism Today

Till Faith Us Do Part: Couples Who Fall In Love Across the
Religious Divide

Tradition and Change: A History of Reform Judaism in Britain
1840–1995 (with Anne Kershen)

Renewing the Vision: Rabbis Speak Out on Modern Issues (ed.)

Jonathan A. Romain

Your God Shall Be My God

Religious Conversion In Britain Today

scm press

0 334 02809 4

First published 2000
by SCM Press
9–17 St Albans Place, London N1 0 NX

SCM Press is a division of
SCM-Canterbury Pres Ltd

Typeset by Regent Typesetting, London
and printed in Great Britain by
Biddles Ltd, Guildford and King's Lynn

The book is dedicated to Matthew
who likes arguing

Contents

Preface

Six words uttered by an obscure Moabite woman have immortalized her as one of the role models for countless people ever since her time. When Ruth declared 'Your God shall be my God' she not only converted to a new religion but voiced the yearnings of all those who felt they would be more at home in a faith different from the one into which they were born. What is remarkable is that today, when religious identity in Britain is supposedly in terminal decline, the rate of conversion is as fast as ever, if not increasing. Moreover, the religious traffic is heading in all directions, with Anglicans becoming Catholics, Catholics becoming Jews, Jews becoming Buddhists, Methodists becoming Muslims, and Muslims becoming Anglicans.

For too long the swirling cross-currents of conversion have been ignored. This book seeks to bring the conversion phenomenon to the surface and examine what are the factors that lie behind it, how it affects the individuals concerned, and what its impact will be on the religious life of modern Britain. Moreover, it charts what actually happens to a person in the period leading up to their decision, during the conversion procedure itself, and once they have joined the new faith. It is the first book to do so, and is the result of numerous interviews with those who have decided to convert, as well as with their families. Its object is both to trace a fascinating development and to be a helpful guide to those directly involved or watching from the sidelines.

My own interest in the subject of conversion stems from the many individuals I have met who choose to adopt a new faith. I have admired the courage it often took to head in a new direction, and I have been intrigued by the impact that it had on so many aspects of their life apart from obviously religious ones, be it dress code or family relationships. I have been involved professionally too, having helped over a hundred people to convert in the classes I run at Maidenhead Synagogue. I am also aware that one of my own relatives – Miriam Hamilton – converted to Judaism in 1884 and had she not done so, I would not have been born Jewish.

I am grateful to the many individuals who have let me use their stories in this book. A number did not want their full name to be revealed because of family sensitivities or for personal reasons. Rather than distinguish between those requesting confidentiality and those not, I have kept to first names throughout the book, with the exception of public figures and historical characters.

I am also indebted to a number of people to whom I periodically turned for advice and to check facts. They include Zaki Badawi, Peter Brierley, George Lings and Brian Pearce. My thanks also go to John Bowden for his encouragement from start to finish of this book. I owe a lot to SCM. Above all, I am proud of members of Maidenhead Synagogue who, unlike many other congregations, have been very welcoming to those who convert, while they have also shown how much converts can contribute to a community if they are allowed to do so.

Jonathan A. Romain
Maidenhead, October 2000

I

Whose Soul Is It Anyway?

Religious changes in Britain today

At this very moment hundreds of missionaries are criss-crossing Britain in an effort to change the religious beliefs of the population. Perhaps their number runs into thousands. They give lectures in halls, deliver leaflets through letterboxes, chat on the doorstep, talk over the airwaves, accost people in the High Street, and try to set up their own TV stations. Their energy is indefatigable, with some people putting in long hours after a full day's work and others devoting their whole life to it. But even more amazing is their diversity. Some are from the mainstream churches preaching a well-known message; others are from Christian off-shoots such as Jehovah's Witnesses or the Mormons, offering a more intensive route to salvation; others are from abroad, such as Buddhists seeking to bring new teachings to the jaded West; others have a much smaller remit, such as Lubavitch rabbis with the more limited goal of re-invigorating the souls of fellow Jews; others are New Religious Movements – also known as cults – keen to make spiritual conquests, but whose religious credentials vary considerably.

The existence of this missionary zeal casts a new light on the state of religion in this country and means we have to re-evaluate the assumptions about it. It is not necessarily true, as some claim, that we are an increasingly godless and secular society that has largely turned its back on religion as a quaint relic of a bygone age, practised only by the nostalgic or the nervous. Beneath the surface picture of a supposedly calm religious life in Britain in which faith is declining quietly and churches are emptying genteelly, there is a swirling hubbub of religious activity. Religious Britain is like a river that appears to be flowing at a leisurely pace, but in which there is a series of fast undercurrents that suck others in and vie for mastery.

It is estimated that a thousand people in Britain convert to a different faith each day. They come from all walks of life. They range from sixteen-year-old black youths who have low prospects of employment to Members of Parliament three times their age and thirty times their income. For each of them religion is one of the abiding passions in their life which colours all other aspects of it. Each conversion carries a story with it. It might be about years of searching for a spiritual home, or about a moment of inspiration that caught them by surprise. Sometimes it involved the pain of breaking away from a previous path, a sense of loneliness and wrestling with doubt. At other times it was the result of a love story, finding not only the joy of a partner but also discovering a new religious home through the tradition to which he or she belonged. For many, the love story was not with another person but with God, a religious yearning that was vaguely sensed but lacked fulfillment for so long until it eventually blossomed into a wonderful all-encompassing relationship. It is seen in its most literal sense in the ring worn by a nun that symbolizes her wedding to Christ, but can be felt also by many who have human partners yet who still feel they have committed themselves utterly to God. They consider that they have contracted a relationship that is even more enduring than their earthly one, for it surpasses the sentiment 'Till death us do part' and will continue past death and into the hereafter.

For many converts, their new faith has distinctive strengths that appeal to them more than the tradition into which they happened to be born. To cite some generalizations that will be investigated more fully later: Buddhism offers a path to self-knowledge, an inner calm in an era of confusion and hype. Islam offers a sense of discipline and direction in a world that so often seems chaotic and pointless. Judaism offers communal cameraderie and personal identity at a time when family values and local ties are under siege and many feel that they do not belong anywhere. Christianity excels at spirituality and a sense of personal salvation that lift one above the limitations of the human condition. Some of these are real differences, such as between Buddhism, which is self-centred, and Christianity, which is God-centred. In many cases, though, the differences are merely perceived ones. If you dig deep into each faith, many of the characteristics of the other faiths can also be found. Nevertheless, in the eye of the searcher it is the surface differences that can make a faith appear sufficiently attractive to justify conversion.

Some of the converts have travelled exactly the same routes but in opposite directions. Thus Frank, who came from a Christian background but never felt at ease in church, has now converted to Islam and has gained a deep sense of religious conviction. At the same time Yusuf, who came from a Muslim upbringing, never felt at home in the mosque and eventually converted to Christianity where he has found the spirituality he previously lacked. They each found religious satisfaction in the faith that the other person felt was so lacking. For some people this is simply because the religious grass on the other side looks greener and they have not explored their own heritage sufficiently well to discover in it what they can see so obviously in another faith. As Rachel put it, 'I realize now that many of the things I like about Catholicism are in Judaism too – but I never took the trouble to look for them. When I embarked on my religious search, I thought I knew Judaism, but, looking back, it's clear that it was only a surface familiarity, and largely coloured – perhaps I should say prejudiced – by a couple of awful teachers at Religion School. If I had put in as much effort as an adult to research Judaism as I did Christianity – which seemed new and exciting – then I may never have left it for the church.' Non-religious factors operating in a person's life – tensions within the family, problems at work, difficulties establishing a social circle – can also determine whether a religious characteristic is seen as an advantage or a disadvantage. Thus the spirituality of Christianity that outsiders admire can seem to those within it as cold and empty; the warmth Judaism holds in the eyes of newcomers can appear oppressively suffocating to those brought up in it; while the clarity and certainty that Islam emanates to onlookers can be rigid and restrictive for those long used to it. One person's inspiration can be another person's reservation, and what appear to some as bonuses can be regarded by others as defects.

The factors behind conversion

But why is there such an explosion in the religious traffic from one faith to another? Perhaps four main factors can be identified. The first is that Britain as a society has changed from being mono-religious to multi-faith. Until 1945 it was almost exclusively a Christian country, with a small Jewish community that kept largely to itself. Since then, waves of immigration from disparate parts of the world have had a dramatic efffect on the religious land-scape:

> Within living memory every religion tended to be restricted to specific parts of the world. If one wished to see Buddhism at first hand it was necessary to travel to Ceylon or Japan. Now the Chiswick Vihara has some twenty thousand people on its mail-ing list, and saffron-robed monks walk the Sussex lanes or the streets of Wolverhampton. A Japanese peace pagoda rises on a lakeside in Milton Keynes and another is to tower above the suburbs of London. Muslims lived, then, in Arabia over-spilling into North Africa, and eastwards into Persia and India. Now among Nash terraces surrounding Regent's Park, the great dome of a splendid mosque symbolizes the presence of nearly a million Muslims in the United Kingdom. Hindus were properly the citizens of the Indian Empire. Now Leicester has the largest Hindu community, after Durban, outside India; and Birmingham and Wolverhampton, Manchester and Leeds, Coventry and Bristol, as well as dozens of much smaller towns, have flourishing temples . . . Sikhs, too, have left their ancestral homes in north-west India . . . some two hundred thousand of these 'disciples' are now settled in Britain . . . Nor should we forget the Chinese diaspora scattered the length and breadth of these islands . . . There are, too, small communities of Jains, of Zoroastrians, and of Bahais . . . (in addition) there are 350,000 Jews living in the UK.[1]

Not only is Britain a multi-faith society, but it is proudly so. Whereas in the past the general ethos was for non-Christians to 'keep their heads down' and not attract too much attention to themselves, now there are no such constraints or inhibitions. Non-Christian faiths are not ashamed to have a high public profile, whether it be the sight of Sikh turbans, or towering minarets, or halal shops or TV rabbis. In fact the Jewish community, the non-Christian faith with the longest presence in the country, provides a good example of the new willingness to stand out as different. In previous decades, religious Jews who kept their heads covered would do so by wearing an ordinary hat in public – such as a bowler or tweed hat – and thereby blend in with everyone else. Today religious Jews tend to wear knitted *kippot* and are no longer nervous at broadcasting their distinctive religious tradition. The desire for conformity has been replaced by a pride in identity. Just as it is 'okay to be ethnic', so it is acceptable to be religiously different.

This multi-faith mix is no longer new but has been present for some fifty years. As a result it has begun to affect all levels of society and permeated the lives of individuals without their having to make a conscious effort to discover it. Thus the educational system recognizes the religious diversity of the country and pursues an avowedly multi-faith syllabus. Christianity may still be given primacy, but many schoolchildren will visit a mosque, meet a rabbi, witness a Sikh ceremony and hear Buddhist teachings at an assembly. Conversely, children from non-Christian faiths will learn Christian hymns and become familiar with the New Testament. It is normative for children to be made aware of different faiths and be told that each one has its own spiritual riches and distinctive approach. It is hardly surprising therefore if, in later life, some of those former pupils do not feel at home in their birth-faith and decide to explore the other faiths to which they had already been exposed. Many others, of course, will abandon religion altogether, but some will remember religious leaders who impressed them and seek out more information, while the introduction they received will lessen the hesitation they might otherwise have felt at venturing into unknown areas.

In addition to the access to other faiths afforded by institutional developments, demographic patterns have also brought members of different religions into close contact. Voluntary ghettos may exist in certain parts of the country – Jewish areas, Sikh quarters, Muslim parts, Catholic strongholds – but many have chosen to live outside these domains, or have been forced to do so by economic circumstances. Members of different faiths live and work alongside each other, enter each other's homes, see each other's ritual objects or distinctive clothing, and are increasingly invited to each other's cycle of life celebrations. Physical proximity has led to social contact which in turn has resulted in religious familiarity. It has reinforced the general perception that there are now several religious options from which to choose. As Jane put it, 'There are many paths to God and it doesn't matter which one you take. So if ever I decide to get more religious, then I could just as well do it through becoming a Buddhist as going to church.' For some, the faith next door has become one's own. Gerry came from a lapsed Methodist background but was always interested in religious ideas and practices: 'My neighbour was a Sikh. Shortly after he moved in, he came round to ask if I had a long ladder he could borrow to fix something on his roof. It led to us becoming quite friendly and we often chatted about his religion. He explained all about the "five K's" and what they meant. I was impressed and got hold of some Sikh books to read and became quite knowledgeable on all the traditions. One day he asked me if I wanted to go with him to the gurdwara. I really felt at home there and started going by myself. In the end I converted . . . and when I'm asked about my change, I sometimes joke that I came to God via a ladder to heaven . . . and give my neighbour a big wink.' Indeed, but for a Sikh neighbour, Gerry might still be a lapsed Methodist feeling a gap in his life but not knowing how to fill it.

The result is that it is no longer even necessary to be an active seeker after other faiths to become aware of them. People previously used to one faith are now presented with an array of different religious options that were hardly thought of beforehand. The person fifty years ago who felt dissatisfied within the church but thought he either had to keep on attending services or drop out completely can now seek spiritual fulfillment in other religions that are readily available. No longer does he have to travel abroad to find them or hunt through obscure bookshops for reading material. Instead he simply crosses the road or pops into the mosque a hundred yards along from the church. A society that is used to high consumer choice in material goods finds itself equally well served in the religious sphere, with a wide range of spiritual opportunities on offer.

The second factor fuelling the number of conversions is the change in approach to religion in general. It has become much more a matter of personal choice than of inherited tradition. People do not automatically follow the faith of their family. It may be the first reference point, but if it is found wanting, then many will not hesitate to look elsewhere. As Pru put it, 'My mother didn't really believe in Christianity but would not have dreamt of leaving the faith her parents had given her and took seriously themselves. It just wouldn't have entered her head. So she did her best to keep it up and pass it on to me. But I had no such qualms. When I came to the conclusion that Christianity wasn't working for me, it was a question of "okay, I don't like this brand, what are the others like?" – a bit like trying out breakfast cereals.' Inherited religion is a fast declining concept and is being replaced by the same market forces that affect all other walks of life. It has to face the questions 'Does it serve me well?' and 'Is it the best I can get?' While many who give negative answers to such questions will drop out of religion and simply become 'a lapsed Catholic' or 'a non-practising Jew', defining themselves by the religion in which they no longer believe, an increasing number are prepared to sample other faiths and find an alternative religious product.

At the same time, religion is becoming privatized and is turning into an individual domain irrespective of the wider context in which a person operates. The old adage that 'the family that prays together, stays together' was based on the assumption that husband, wife and children all shared the same faith and that any deviance would endanger the family unit. This is no longer the case. Religion is seen by many as a private hobby that one member of the family may pursue but is not binding upon anyone else, rather like train-spotting or stamp-collecting. Thus there are no family traumas, or even raised eyebrows, if on a Sunday morning the husband goes to church, the wife to a car-boot sale, the children go fishing and they all meet up afterwards for Sunday lunch. The dinner table, not the communion table, is the family focus. Dennis is aware both of the advantages and disadvantages of such a development: 'There is a certain sadness I feel that the rest of the family does not join me at services. It would be lovely to go together. But I have to respect their disinterest, just as they accept my commitment. It doesn't make us less of a family. It's about mutual tolerance. After all, I suspect my wife would much prefer me to go car-booting with her and in some ways I'm the one causing a problem by insisting on doing my own thing and going off to church!'

The separation of faith and family is evident, too, in the growing number of mixed-faith families, in which husband and wife come from different religions and two traditions co-exist within the same household. What was once a rarity that was roundly condemned by ministers of all faiths is now increasingly common, and is much more likely to be accommodated by religious authorities. Some will not only welcome such couples into their communities but will even co-officiate at the wedding and give religious sanction to the 'double belonging'. A Catholic married to a Jew, a member of the Church of England married to a Muslim – these are marital combinations that would have been regarded as absurd, if not ungodly, only two generations ago, but are now regarded as part of the colourful religious tapestry of British life. Indeed some ministers seem more comfortable with religious differences than religious indifference, and find inter-faith dialogue a very enriching activity. Often their concern for mixed-faith couples is not so much that one partner might influence the other away from his/her faith, but that the two of them should avoid any potential religious pitfalls and maintain a harmonious relationship. It is certainly true that mixed-faith couples have to face a wide range of difficult issues, especially with regard to domestic observances and the religious identity of children, but the statistics available indicate a sharp rise in those prepared to take such risks. Only the

Jewish and Catholic authorities have researched the number of outmarriages within their flock, and they report staggeringly high figures, with 44% of Jews marrying out of the faith, while over 65% of Catholics are doing so. Hindu, Muslim and Sikh leaders speak of increasing instances amongst their members. For its part, the Church of England has been sufficiently concerned to produce guidelines to its clergy on how to deal with the rising number of mixed-faith marriages at which they are asked to officiate. But whatever the institutional reaction, the message coming from the couples themselves is that they see no problem in dual-faith households in which the partners follow their own tradition without compromising the marital relationship.[2]

Underlying these trends is a loss in the absolute authority of religion. In an age in which everything is subject to questioning, the religious certainties in which one was brought up are equally open to scrutiny. Those educated to believe 'the truth' of a particular faith may grow up to challenge its authority and question its relevance. For some this results in a religious relativism, in which the criterion for following a particular faith is not its superiority over all other faiths – which smacks of unacceptable religious imperialism – but the degree of comfort the adherent feels within it. When they search for a more satisfying faith to follow, it is for a 'me-friendly' religion that suits the individual rather than the absolute truth which the individual is obliged to follow. It was typified by Jane earlier when she said, 'There are many paths to God and it doesn't matter which one you take.' It amounts to a modern reinterpretation of the words of the New Testament. When Jesus declared that 'In my Father's house are many rooms' (John 14. 2) he meant that there were many ways to believe 'in me' and each individual could find a place waiting for them; but this sentiment has been expanded far beyond its limited context into the view that virtually all religions lead to God and none has an exclusive monopoly. Like trying on different clothes in a superstore, you choose the religion that fits you best. For others, however, they may question authority but still seek it. It is not so much the loss of authority but rather the transferability of authority. Having become disillusioned with their inherited faith, they find another religion and invest it with the same aura of invincible truth that they themselves failed to accept in their former tradition. As Ralph explained: 'I was raised in a strictly Orthodox household and taught that Judaism was the will of God and his direct command. Later on I thought "Nonsense, it's not the will of God, it's largely man-made," and I dropped out completely. When I came across the New Testament, it was like a thunderbolt and I said to myself, "This is it, this is the truth." And although I still feel that very strongly, I also realize that in some ways I am accepting the very same sense of authority that I rejected earlier in a different guise. Strange, isn't it?'

The process of the privatization of religion is summarized well by Rabbi Lionel Blue when he writes:

> With the confusion of cultures which has replaced the old isolation, has come increased emphasis on the individual, his or her personal needs, and not just those of the community, and a recognition that religious people are seekers as much as finders, pilgrims on a journey. Modern people, therefore, wander over the religious and spiritual landscape. Jewish students, in their hippy spell, journey to Nepal as well as Jerusalem, to sit at the feet of a Hindu guru, rather than a rabbi. Unlike their elders most have visited a church and sort-of-worshipped alongside other searchers. Like most searchers, their spiritual criterion is whether it works rather than its provenance.[3]

Blue's comments reflect the social fragmentation that has occured in the last half-century, led by the break-up of family life, communal authority, social certainties and national culture, culminating in a loss of identity that many people feel. In this climate, it is little wonder that they are looking for definite beliefs and guidelines in a new faith to replace those that seem to have disintegrated in the old one.

A third factor in the growth of conversions is, paradoxically, the sharp decrease in religious knowledge and experience in many households. Despite having an established church, fewer than 15% of the population in Britain today attend church every week.

Over half of those who attend at the age of thirteen will have ceased to do so by the time they are twenty. By school-leaving age very few children will claim active allegiance to the Christian faith.[4] Some people have a nominal religious identity, but many are brought up without any religion at all. They are not even 'lapsed C of E' – they are simply 'nothings'. As one Church of England vicar told an imam, 'Don't think you're the only minority faith here – we Christians feel exactly the same.' A similar pattern is emerging amongst other faiths in Britain, with second and third generation Hindus, Muslims and Sikhs becoming more assimilated and secularized. Traditional practices have been discarded by many – such as Muslims avoiding alcohol or Hindus abstaining from beef – while knowledge of the sacred scriptures is lessening. This trend is exacerbated by the increasing lack of familiarity with the languages in which the texts were written as English becomes the sole tongue of many Muslims and Hindus. For their part, Jewish leaders are constantly bewailing the decline in religious identity. As one rabbi put it, 'The decline in Jewish knowledge amongst Jews today has gone past the crisis stage – we can more or less write off the ability of some 70% of the community to pass on a meaningful form of Judaism to their children.' When the Orthodox Chief Rabbi, Jonathan Sacks, wrote a book in 1994 entitled *Will We Have Jewish Grandchildren?*, it was not a rhetorical question, but a very real fear that Judaism might be in danger of disappearing.

At the same time as this general decrease in religious knowledge, the individuals concerned still have religious needs and are still confronted by the major questions about life and death, purpose and final destination. While some can brush such issues aside, others seek spiritual answers to fill the vacuum they feel in their lives. An annual visit to a church dimly remembered from one's childhood is not enough to sustain one. The result is for many to begin a religious search in adulthood. However, rather than start investigating their roots, many assume that there is nothing to be found there and look elsewhere, turning to other faiths that appear fresh and appealing, especially as they are not tainted by past perceptions. 'It's ridiculous,' says Mark, a vicar. 'People have a few half-baked memories of Christianity from when they were angels in a nativity play and then judge the whole of Christian teaching from that. They never get past the fairy-tale stage of faith, and then reject that without having anything to fill its place.' Rabbi Joseph agrees. 'My greatest enemy in life is people's bad experiences of Judaism in childhood. However much I say "But you have to explore the faith as a mature adult," they cannot seem to shake off childish images and misperceptions. It's almost a lost cause and very few of those who were poorly educated Jewishly ever recover their enthusiasm for it.' It is to a new faith, therefore, that such searchers look and they take their spiritual needs to new pastures. This time they approach the faith with a much more discerning and sophisticated attitude, are not put off by legendary tales but see the insights they are trying to communicate, and regard the rituals not as tiresome impositions but valuable disciplines. Robert became an aetheist at the age of fourteen because 'The Old Testament miracles just seemed daft to me and totally unrealistic, while I rebelled against the Jewish laws about not being able to eat foods that all my non-Jewish friends could enjoy. I didn't understand them and they didn't make sense.' Now, however, as a thirty-six-year-old Buddhist he finds deep spiritual truths in miraculous tales about Buddhist masters and has no difficulty adhering to a strict vegetarian lifestyle. He admits that had he received a better Jewish upbringing – or had he chosen to investigate it further in adulthood rather than abandon it in his early teens – he might have found satisfaction within the faith and still be Jewish today. He typifies many who choose not to revisit the faith they felt failed them in early life and for whom it is easier to try a new religion rather than dig deeper in the old one.

A fourth factor in the growth of conversions in Britain has been the growing sense of religious awe at the approach of the millennium. Whilst this has largely been a 1990s phenomenon, it was preceded by an outpouring of messianic hopes following the unexpected reunification of Jerusalem in 1967 after the Israeli victory in the Six Day War. For the first time since the year 70, the ancient city was in Jewish hands. Prophecies that had long been put on hold suddenly took on new significance. Many excitedly

referred to Luke 21.24–27 which predicted that when Jerusalem
was rescued from Gentile domination 'then will they see the Son
of man coming in a cloud with power and great glory . . . (and)
redemption drawing near'. The charismatic movement within
Christianity developed greatly after 1967, and was then reinforced
with other 'signs' such as the fall of the Berlin Wall and the
collapse of Communism, which were taken as further proofs that
the end of days was approaching. It led to a realization amongst
church leaders that the Western world needed to be evangelized
afresh. According to George Gallup, the process has to start within the Christian community itself: 'Many of us dutifully attend
church, but this act appears to have made us no less likely than our
unchurched brethren to engage in unethical behaviour . . . We say
we rejoice in the good news that Jesus brought, but we are often
strangely reluctant to share the gospel with others. In a typical day
the average person stays in front of the TV set nearly twenty five
times longer than in prayer. We say we are believers, but perhaps
we are only assenters.'[5] William Abraham agrees entirely: 'One
of the truly astonishing facts of modern church life is that so
many church members need to be evangelized' and he calls for a
major programme of rejuvenation to teach already-committed
Christians the full implications of their faith.[6]

This evangelical impetus has been directed also to non-
believers. The closer the year 2000 approached, the more there
grew the desire for the turn of the millennium to reflect not just a
calendrical date but a vibrant Christian faith which still had a
purpose and whose mission to spread the good news was as urgent
as ever. When George Carey became Archbishop of Canterbury in
1991, he launched a Decade of Evangelism that reflected a much
more activist spirit within the church which was keen to take faith
to the faithless rather than wait for them to come and search it out
for themselves. Such was the impact of this mood of religious outreach that it crossed religious barriers and inspired Jonathan Sacks
to launch a Decade of Renewal when he became Orthodox Chief
Rabbi that same year. It was a closely modelled concept and only
differed in that it was limited to fellow Jews, whereas the Archbishop's gaze was directed to all who would benefit from receiving

the teachings of Christ. The missionary spirit was seen especially in the willingness of the Church of England to go beyond its traditional territory – church noticeboards – and venture out into wider society through a campaign of public advertisements. Not only was the church prepared to take a much higher profile, but also to speak the language of the market-place, use colloquial phrases such as 'having a bad hair-day' and consciously seek to change the perceived wimpish image of Jesus through adverts that focused on his strength of character and independence. The plan to distribute millennium candles to every household in the country, far from being a 'nice gesture', was a hard-nosed attempt to infiltrate households previously barred to them and to introduce a moment of prayer that would not be a 'one-off' but would acclimatize non-believers to prayer and make them less resistant to other efforts to evangelize them.

The sense of religious cataclysm stirred by the onward march of the calendar may have been entirely based on a Christian counting system, but it has led to an enormous amount of interest in other faiths too. A host of other groups have sprung up in recent decades or been imported from elsewhere, including the Divine Light Mission, Hare Krishna, Subud, Taoism and Zen Buddhism. Whilst they are popularly referred to as cults, this often carries a derogatory connotation which is not necessarily justified and fails to distinguish between transient groups that culminate in mass suicides and ancient traditions that are highly respected. A more neutral collective term for them is New Religious Movements, although the word 'new' means that they are new to these shores rather than all of them being new creations. They vary enormously and can be classified according to their relationship with the world at large.[7] Some are world-rejecting, attempting to have as little as possible to do with secular life and institutions, such as Krishna Consciousness and the Unification Church. Others are world-affirming, encouraging their members to realize their mental and spiritual potential but without withdrawing from the world, such as Transcendental Meditation and Nickeron Shoshu. Others are world-accommodating, not against participation in everyday affairs but preaching the ills of secular life and religious institutions, such as Neo-Pentecostalism and the Charismatic Renewal Movement.

Britain has proved fruitful territory for New Religious Movements, and it has been estimated that some four hundred have emerged in the country since 1945.[8] It means that there are more cult movements per million of the population here than in the United States, where fringe religious groups are perceived to flourish much more. Accordingly, there are 3.2 cults per million in Britain, compared to 2.3 per million in the United States. Britain also has the distinction of being the country in Europe with the highest number of Indian and Eastern cult centres and communities. Religious movements that were previously unknown or inaccessible have become familiar and available. They have also attracted very different levels of interest from that in previous decades. Whereas many of them came to Britain after long-haired students trekked to Katmandu and imported them back here, now they are supported by pin-striped businessmen who attend lunch-time meditation classes in between board meetings. This religious flourishing indicates that despite the apparently conservative nature of British religious life, with an established church that is too wedded to the state to be innovative, there are many individuals with spiritual yearnings who are prepared to seek religious answers in radically new forms.

It might be argued that the freedom to choose one's religious path should be an automatic right rather than a source of surprise. Few today would argue for the merits of indoctrination, and even those convinced of the rectitude of their own faith would wish their children to adopt it through choice rather than coercion. Brenda has no doubt whatsoever that her path is not only the best one but is God's path too and hopes that her two daughters will agree: 'God has revealed his will through his son, the risen Christ. However good the teachings of other faiths may be, there is no higher truth. You can't argue with facts. I have brought up my children to think the same, although they can't just mimic my beliefs, they have to believe it themselves. I would be mortified if they dropped out of the church, but at the same time I have to allow them to find God for themselves and establish their own relationship. I just hope they make the right decision because for me there is no second best.' The same uneasy balance between parental direction and personal freedom exists in Jewish teaching, where the rabbis comment on the first line of one of the central prayers in the the liturgy, the *amidah*, which calls upon 'our God and the God of our fathers': 'surely this is tautology, for "our God" is the same as "the God of our fathers" – so why the repetition? No, they are different. The latter refers to the God of tradition, who has been passed down through official teaching and parental influence, the God we have inherited. But that is not enough. God also has to be "our God" the God we have personally come to terms with and accepted in our own right.' The rabbinic message is clear: faith cannot just be a matter of imitation, but has to include personal endorsement. Nevertheless, the inference is that the child adopts for him/herself the parental faith. There is no encouragement to look elsewhere.

This religious pressure is compounded by the asssumption in many faiths that the religious status of children is a pre-deter-mined fact of birth. The child of a Muslim father is Muslim. The child of a Jewish mother is Jewish. The moment they emerge from the womb they have a religious identity thrust upon them. In other faiths the religious labelling is not automatic, even if parents often assume that the children follow their faith. In the church a person is not formally accepted as a Christian until baptism has taken place, although the common practice of infant baptism means that effectively the child has no choice in the matter. The insistence among some Christian denominations, notably the Baptists, for baptism to take place later, usually in the teenage years, reflects the view that membership of a faith must be a conscious decision, taken at an age of maturity and from a position of informed choice. There are intermittent calls by some clergy within the Church of England for the same practice to be adopted. However, it has never become official policy out of a combination of the desire not to upset parents attached to the tradition of infant baptism, and a fear that delay to a later age might result in a decrease in the overall number of baptisms. Despite its presumption about the religious identity of children of a Muslim father, Islam also accepts the anomaly of predetermining a child's faith. The Koran recognizes that each person is born into circumstances which are not of his/her own choosing and has the family religion thrust upon them. However, this notion – the concept of *fitrah* – does not mean that a person has the right to opt for any faith; instead it has the effect of extending the faith of Islam to every person. *Fitrah* holds that beneath the surface identity given at birth, each person is by nature a Muslim, with a natural belief in God and an inborn inclination to worship him. A parent may make a person a Christian, Jew or Zoroastrian, but inherently he is Muslim and so if he later formally adopts Islam he is not so much converting to a new faith but returning to his true origins. Thus the apparent freedom by which a non-Muslim converts to Islam is in fact merely a recognition of a hidden identity that was always present. From a Muslim theological perspective, therefore, freedom of choice is maintained but circumscribed and its potential to be an avenue away from Islam is redirected into being a path towards it.

Different terms for conversion

The issue of to what extent a person is choosing a new faith or sub-consciously returning to one's 'true faith' is highlighted by the very term that is used for changing religion. The word that is most commonly used is 'convert'. It derives from the Latin root 'convertere' meaning 'to turn' and carries the sense of changing direction. It is not specifically a theological term and can apply to any process of transformation, such as converting pints into litres or iron into steel. However, when used in a religious context, it often implies changing from a sinful or erroneous state into a better and purer one. Moreover, the process of 'turning' is a double action – turning *away* from a previous lifestyle and turning *to* a new state of being. Thus the convert is engaged in both reject-ing one path and choosing another, with both actions being equally significant. Ralph's reflections apply to many such converts: 'I suppose it was a double step for me. When I became a Christian I was taking on belief in Christ, but it was also a conscious departure from Judaism. In fact this was something that my family realized quicker than I did, and what upset them was not so much me adopting a new faith, whatever that might be, but me turning my back on the family tradition. I guess it was a case of "Hello Jesus, goodbye Moses" and by converting I was definitely making a statement about my old faith as much as my new one.' However, there are also many who, whilst thoroughly committed to their new religious identity, still have a strong regard for their former faith. When Robert is asked to talk about his Buddhist beliefs, he always mentions his Jewish origins 'because that upbringing is still an essential part of me. I often say I'm a Jewish Buddhist and I have no problem acknowledging the positive aspects I have inherited from Jewish teachings.' Some people, therefore, are unhappy with the negative implications that the term 'convert' casts on their previous religious life. Frank, now a Muslim, puts it even more strongly: 'To say I am a convert suggests either that Christianity is wrong or that formerly I was at fault in some way, when neither are true. It's just that Christianity was wrong for me.' Another objection to the term is that it concentrates on the fact that a person had a previous faith to the one to which they now adhere. 'I really object when people call me a convert', said Sally, 'as it labels me as someone who changed religion. And whilst that is true historically, in my case it happened eleven years ago and is a one-off moment long ago. Calling me a convert is to continually keep me in the past, whereas it's much more realistic to say I am a committed Muslim and have been for a long time.'

Another description is 'proselyte', which stems from the Greek word meaning a person who has come to a particular place in terms of their opinion or creed. When Shakespeare wishes to sing the praises of Perdita's beauty, he declares that 'This is a creature/ Would she begin a sect, might quench the zeal/Of all professors else, makes proselytes/Of who she bid but follow'.[9] In theory, the word is much more appropriate than 'convert' as, unlike the latter, it is purely a religious term. Moreover, it has the added advantage of emphasizing the point of arrival, the faith to which the person belongs now, rather than their former beliefs. However, it suffers from originally having a secondary meaning of someone who specifically converts to Judaism. This reflects the period when Judaism was one of the few faiths to demand exclusive obedience. The Jewish God was a 'jealous' God who insisted that Jews have no other gods (Ex. 20.5), whereas most pagan groups had a multiplicity of gods and there was no objection to a new devotee simply adding the latest object of worship to the list of other gods he honoured. Judaism alone demanded abandonment of other gods, and so it was only Judaism to which one formally changed and became a proselyte. The term was subsequently broadened and used to refer to anyone who joined a new faith, but although preferred in academic circles, it is not a popular turn of phrase, if only because it rolls off the tongue less easily than others.

The inadequacy of both the terms 'convert' and 'proselyte' may not have exercised previous generations, when Britain was predominantly a Christian country, almost devoid of religious diversity, and conversions were rare. However, this has caused dissatisfaction in recent times where there is a wide variety of faiths and considerable interchange between them. It has not only led to new expressions developing to denote religious change, but they are particular to certain faiths. Many who have become Jews, for instance, avoid the word 'convert' and prefer to describe themselves as 'a Jew-by-choice'. 'For me this fits perfectly,' said Shirley. 'It says who I am in the here and now – a Jew – and it highlights the fact that unlike those who were born Jewish and who may or may not value the Jewish heritage they had thrust upon them, I deliberately chose it and am proud to be Jewish by conscious decision.' Not all agree, and some consider that the expression is too assertive: 'It's rather flaunting things, isn't it?' counters Rebecca, 'and it's making a statement, whereas I don't think you have to wear religion on your sleeve like that but just get on with it.' Nevertheless, it is characteristic of many converts that they are enormously proud of their new status and 'Jew-by-choice' has become a fashionable term.

Converts to Islam face the same issue of being different from those born into the tradition. One expression that is used is 'White Muslim', a clear reference to the different skin-colour of British converts to those who hail from the Indian sub-continent or Africa. But apart from its potentially racist overtones, it also has the defect of being inappropriate for the many black converts to Islam in Britain. A preferred term, therefore, is 'New Muslim'. Some find that this, too, is problematic as the adjective 'new' becomes increasingly irksome with the passage of time. Another alternative is 'a Revert' – which refers to the doctrine of *fitrah* mentioned above and the notion that everyone is naturally a Muslim even though they may be born into other faiths, and so their conversion is merely a reversion to their natural state. For Christians, also, a new vocabulary has been sought. Many are baptized at birth without any understanding of the faith and although in theory they have been 'born of water and of the Spirit' (John 3.5), in practice a considerable number drift away from the church in their teens or adulthood. If, later on, they rediscover their belief in Christianity – or acquire it properly for the first time – it is not appropriate for them to convert to a religion of which they are already officially a member. Hence the emergence of the term 'born again' to denote those who were waylaid by secularism but have now re-adopted the Christian path. Nevertheless, the search for alternative terms for 'convert' does not meet with the favour of all. Hadijah speaks for many when she declares, 'Actually I don't want any special word to describe me. When people ask what I am, I say "Muslim". That's the only thing that matters. I certainly wouldn't deny that I converted to Islam – but frankly the process is irrelevant to who I am now.' Rebecca agrees. 'I'm Jewish – that's all – no adjectives. And I didn't spend months studying to become Jewish to then separate myself off from other Jews. True, I converted, but I'm not a convert. I'm Jewish.' Academics and clergy may agitate over which is the best way of describing some-one who changes faith, but for those in that situation, their object is to assimilate into their new faith and as far as they are concerned, the fewer discriminating adjectives the better. The experience of Greg illustrates the point: 'I had a great welcome from the com-munity in which I converted. Everyone knew I was a convert and that was fine. But when four years on, I changed jobs and moved to a different area and a new synagogue, I arrived as someone who was Jewish and I was accepted as such without any tags or pre-history. And that was even better.'

Gender and age

It may have been noticed that a common factor to all the different terms for converts is that they are not gender-specific. Converts come from both sexes and so a neutral expression that includes both men and women is only natural. However, this serves to disguise the fact that there is often a higher percentage of female converts to male ones. This is certainly the case within Islam where a recent analysis of those becoming Muslim indicates a 60:40 ratio in favour of women.[10] One reason is that a number of Muslim males came to Britain as single men and then married wives from the general community who converted to Islam upon marriage. However, just as important is the fact that many women are attracted to Islam because they feel it is a religion that values their womanhood. It demands that they are treated with respect, while the wearing of the *hijab* (headscarf) is taken as a sign that it is a woman's personality that counts, in strong contrast to the very different message given out by the low-cut dresses and mini-skirts in the secular world. This is not to suggest that Islam does not hold many attractions for men too, often for different reasons, as will be seen in a later chapter. Moreover, in specific cases where a person converts to Islam because of an impending marriage, a high number who do so are men. This is because Islamic law prohibits women from marrying out of the faith and so a woman attached to Islam (or whose family are still very traditional) will encourage a non-Muslim partner to join the faith. Islamic men, however, are permitted to marry women from 'the People of the Book' – Jews or Christians – providing that any children are raised as Muslims. Although many non-Muslim women in that situation do still convert, there is not the same pressure on them to do so as with non-Muslim men.

The overall percentage of female converts is even higher in Judaism, where there are five times as many women who convert as men.[11] Here, the predominance of women is to be expected for two reasons. First, the conversion process is a much more daunting prospect for men than for women; for although the study requirements are the same for both sexes, men face the added obligation of undergoing the ritual of circumcision. Normally a born-Jew is circumcised at eight days old, and the ceremony is performed in a matter of seconds and with few after-effects. For an adult, however, it can involve a full-scale operation in hospital under anaesthetic and with a recuperation period of several days. In addition to the pain and discomfort involved, there are often deep fears as to the effect on one's virility or sexual ability that are sufficient to deter many would-be converts. Second, Jewish status is traditionally passed down the female line. As a high percentage of converts to Judaism are people with a Jewish partner, this acts as a powerful incentive for females who are about to marry Jews to convert so as to pass on the Jewish heritage to the next generation. Conversely, the tradition of matrilineal descent means that there is much less pressure on the male partners of Jewish women to convert, as any children would have full Jewish status anyway. Within the church, the ratio of male-female converts is much less well defined, although it is often assumed that there is a slightly higher number of women because they have a long record of being more spiritually inclined than men and have been conditioned by history to be better at feeling and nurturing than acquiring and conquering. Some might object to this generalization and point to the predominantly male influence in the development of the major faiths, but it might be argued that while men have provided the leadership, women have sustained a more faithful membership.

The age at which people convert varies enormously. This is only to be expected, as conversion is such a personal matter and depends on a whole host of factors unique to each individual. Thus Sally became a Muslim when she was seventeen, while Frank joined the faith at sixty-two. When he was seventeen nothing could have been further from his thoughts than becoming a Muslim and he would have laughed aloud at the idea. But as the years passed, his circumstances, relationships, experiences and beliefs all changed, and by sixty-two the unthinkable had become the desirable. It is virtually impossible, therefore, to predict the optimum or most likely age for conversion, and almost pointless to talk of the average age of converts. Nevertheless, there are certain trends in conversion that mean that many converts will fall within particular age bands if their conversion was triggered by specific factors. Thus there are those who are in their late teens who have emerged from the enormous physical and emotional changes of puberty with a strong desire to seek a new religious identity as part of a general process of redefining themselves. Catrina put it suitably poetically when she said: 'Butterflies and caterpillars don't look the same and don't believe the same either. At nineteen I felt I was a new me and part of that new me was having a faith that I had consciously chosen for myself because I'd looked around and felt it was right. I didn't deliberately choose one different from that of my parents, but frankly it was almost inevitable that it would not be the one I'd been brought up in, as I had changed and moved on.'

Another group consists of those in the twenty to thirty age bracket who change their faith because of a relationship that results in marriage. As will be seen below, the conversion is most likely to occur immediately before marriage so as to obtain a 'white wedding' or a few years after marriage when the influence of one partner's faith persuades the other to join it. Another grouping involves those in their mid-forties who, having worked hard at building up a career or nurturing a family, now find themselves with more time at their disposal for spiritual needs, or who are seeking new meaning for their lives. As Gerry explained: 'I suppose I'd reached a stage in my life when I'd achieved all my original goals – job, house, family – and I was only forty-two with, hopefully, half my life still to go. I was beginning to feel a void and knew I had to fill it with something deeper.' There is also a small but definable group of those who convert in their sixties and seventies. They are prompted by thoughts of mortality, as epitomized by lapsed Presbyterian Tom: 'I always knew I'd become a Catholic one day, and it was the sound of the clicking clock that made me realize I'd better get on with it.' Alternatively, it can be the loss of a partner who was of a different tradition that causes conversion, so that both can be buried in the same manner. Of course, all these triggering effects – marriage, search for meaning,

death in the family – can come at any age and the only safe verdict
is to say that there is no such thing as a typical age to convert.

Another determinant as to the age of conversion is the faith
which the person is adopting. Certain religions seem to attract
more converts at particular ages than at others. Studies within
the church indicate that the vast majority of converts are under the
age of twenty. According to research by John Finney, they
accounted for 76% of the total number of converts in 1967 and
marginally lower in 1994. Other studies pinpoint the average at
fifteen years.[12] In most cases, therefore, they were adolescents
experiencing a crisis of identity and searching for a value system of
their own. They were influenced to join the faith that was the most
heavily advertised and readily accessible, the church. Those who
converted to New Religious Movements, such as Hare Krishna or
Zen Buddhism, were usually in their early twenties. Very often
they had tried the church but were still on a religious search for
meaning, or they had graduated to university campuses and cities
where such groups were much more in evidence than in smaller
towns or rural areas. Those converting to Islam, by contrast,
tended to be in their late twenties – one study put it at twenty-
nine. They were at an age when they were old enough to have
enjoyed secular society but become disillusioned by its excesses; or
they had experimented with alternative religious cultures but felt
the movements lacked the guidance for society as a whole that
Islam offered.[13] The highest proportion of those becoming Jewish
was in the twenty to thirty age bracket, the most common age of
weddings. A study of 1,349 proselytes to Judaism revealed that
just over half were between twenty-one and thirty years, reflecting
the fact that conversions to Judaism are largely, but not exclusively, due to the marriage-motive.[14] Lest it be thought that those over
thirty years of age lack sufficient religious inclination to seek a new
faith, it should be remembered that many luminaries did not
convert till late in life, including St Paul, St Augustine and
Tolstoy.

The generalizations above are necessary not just because of the
highly personalized nature of conversion, but also because of a
serious lack of statistical information regarding converts. This is

due to an absence of records amongst most of the faiths, either because they have no central authority or because such information has not been collated. It also reflects the fact that the importance of conversion has been grossly under-estimated. Those writers in the 1950s and 1960s who proclaimed the death of God and predicted the imminent end of organized religion have been confounded by the way in which it has survived. Even more remarkable has been the number of supposedly lapsed and lost individuals who have rediscovered religion, albeit in a faith that would probably have been totally unknown to the world of their grandparents. The religious face of Britain has changed immeasurably, as the Rt Revd Ronald Bowlby – former Bishop of Southwark – acknowledged when he declared: 'We have moved from where Christianity is a culture to where Christianity is a choice.' Membership of Protestant churches stands at only 6% of all adults, while there are more Muslims than Methodists. The assumption that people will die in the same faith in which they were born can no longer be taken for granted. Instead, there is an increasing willingness for individuals to shift their religious allegiance.

2

The Long and Winding Trail

Dissatisfaction with one's previous faith

The boost in converts has been a source of great joy to the religious leaders who have received them, but the greatest impact has been on the converts themselves. Amongst the great markers of identity inherited at birth are race, gender and religion. A person cannot change their race and, with very rare exceptions, cannot change their gender. Changing faith is a possibility, but carries with it a wide range of emotional and practical consequences. As one observer wrote:

> Just as a river may flow and flow and eventually reach the sea, so, too, may a searching soul eventually find a home . . . The course of the journey may have been rocky and difficult, winding and obscure. For some, it meant leaving family and friends, finding new paths and making new trails. For others, it was a gentle continuation of something they glimpsed from afar in their childhood, something which seemed vaguely familiar and warm. For others still, the passage was storm-tossed and tumultuous, causing wrenching changes in their lives and in the lives of others around them. For all, the journey was life-transforming.[1]

The decision to convert is usually the result of three factors: dissatisfaction with one's current state of belief, perceived advantages in the new faith, and particular personality factors that cry out for change. For some individuals, just one of those factors might apply, whereas with others it can be a combination of two of them or all three.

For many people it is the inadequacy, as they see it, of the faith into which they are born that motivates them to look elsewhere for spiritual truth. Of course, although very real for the person concerned, these are highly subjective opinions, and may be directly contradicted by the experiences of others. This is certainly evident from the comments of former members of the Church of England, all of whom left for radically different reasons. For Richard, 'Church services left me cold – there was little warmth or atmosphere' whereas Amanda, brought up in a different milieu, found that 'Every time I went to church I felt I was suffocating in all the emotional outpourings. I longed for a bit of calmness and some space for being private with God.' A similar contrast existed between Daphne and Vic. She struggled for years with Christian theology before deciding it was too illogical for her, whereas he felt his church was too rational and yearned for a sense of mystery. Marcus objected to the permissive stance of the faith – 'There are no standards anymore, everything goes, and bishops just endorse the latest fad' – whilst Geraldine resented the intolerance she came across: 'A lot of clergy are still stuck in the Middle Ages and are far too intolerant; in the end I just couldn't stick the unyielding rigidity of them all.' Even the weekly sermons were judged from opposite spectrums, with Vic complaining that his minister 'never talked about religious ideas but gave a commentary on issues that had been in the papers – and that's not what I went to church for'. In contrast, Geraldine was equally angry that her minister 'never dealt with real issues that affected us in the real world but just prattled on about irrelevant dogmas'.

There was also disillusion over particular events and the response of either the minister or fellow congregants. When Iqbal's wife left him for another member of the mosque, he was devestated. His pain turned to deep bitterness when the support he expected from others failed to materialize: 'I thought the two of them would be ostracized, but they were treated as a couple, while nobody bothered to ask how I was. There was no concern, no compassion, and I was in a state of utter despair. But for a Christian colleague at work I might have ended up an alcoholic or suicide, but he introduced me to a new circle of friends who gave me the support I needed. You won't be surprised that I began to admire the faith of such people and eventually I decided to join them in it.' It was a bereavement that prompted Gail's departure from the Roman Catholic Church: 'My husband and I went to church at regular intervals – about once every four weeks, usually the first Sunday of the month. But when he died, the priest never even came round, but just said a quick hello before the funeral service. And next time I went to church nobody said a word. I was furious. I didn't want to be fussed over, but just a tiny bit of acknowledgment would have been helpful. I was only forty-nine and decided I wouldn't waste what remaining years I had left. Looking back it was probably unfair to blame the whole Catholic edifice for the indifference of one lousy congregation, but at the time I was too hurt to be rational. I left the church, and then after a period in the wilderness, being at heart a religious person, I went looking for something more satisfying. And now I'm very happy in my new faith and I'm part of a community that values its members.' For Brigid Marlin, it was not people but God who let her down, or at least her concept of God: 'Long after I had grown up, my religion stayed at a childish level. I was a good girl; I went to church every Sunday and kept the rules. I expected God to keep to the rules too. He would look after me and make sure that nothing bad happened to me. It was not unlike the arrangement that certain shops have in New York with the Mafia. The trouble was God didn't keep to the rules. One day my life fell apart: I found that my eldest son was handicapped. Later he died . . . My shallow faith collapsed'.[2] Her search for a faith that would both restore her self-confidence and help deal with other traumas led her to explore Eastern religions and find a spiritual home in them.

Sometimes the bad experiences dated back to childhood memories that had coloured attitudes ever since. Howard recalled in vivid detail his traumatic time at Sunday school: 'It was awful. One class was taught by a sixteen-year-old – we were eight-year-olds – and he clearly didn't have a clue how to control a class. I suppose he was just doing a bit of teaching to earn some extra pocket money, but it was horribly counter-productive and should never have been allowed. The following year we got an elderly chap with a thick foreign accent and didn't learn a thing either. After that we had the rabbi who was nice enough but on a totally different planet. He might have been talking about life on Mars for all the relevance it had for us. I stumbled through enough Hebrew to learn my barmitzvah, but what I really learnt was that Judaism was not for me. Ironic really – coming of age at thirteen is supposed to be a time of commitment to Judaism, but for me it was the departure point. Not that I did anything about it at the time – I wasn't interested enough in religion to care, and anyway, being still at home with my parents, rather than cause any family rows it was easier just to go along with annual rituals and mentally sleep though them. But when I did start getting interested in the meaning of life in my late twenties, there was absolutely no way that I was going to go to synagogue to find out, and I tried knocking on other doors until I found the one that held the answers for me.' Such stories are not limited to the Jewish community, but apply alike to church, mosque and gurdwara. No doubt these children would have had a very different and much more positive experience had they attended another community within the same faith, but rather like a child who is sick on bread pudding at school and develops an aversion to it for the rest of his days, so most people never give the religion that failed them in childhood a second chance in adult life. Instead, they tend to generalize dismissively about the faith as a whole from their unhappy contact with one small aspect of it. The role of religious leaders is particularly significant in the way a faith is judged. However unfair this may be, both on the faith and on other ministers within it, a minister's behaviour is seen as an embodiment of that faith and is a critical point of judgment. Too dull or too trendy, too mystical or too superficial, too rigid or too informal, theirs is a difficult tightrope to walk and one person's ideal minister is another person's disaster area.

In other cases, the rejection of one's childhood faith is more connected with the relationship with one's parents. One of the best ways of rejecting them is to cast off their values, be it political allegiance, social etiquette or religious beliefs. 'To be honest,' Nick now admits, 'I suppose I still subscribe to many important

Christian tenets – justice, social action, charity, love your neighbour as yourself and all that stuff – so I didn't have an ideological
reason for telling my parents I wasn't going to church with them
anymore. I was fourteen and it was more a matter of asserting my
own independence. Because they went every Sunday, I wasn't
going to go. Maybe if they had been atheists, I would have
suddenly started going to church regularly! It meant that when I
went to university, I was officially non-Christian but actually still
interested in religious ideas. I started learning about Sufism and it
appealed to me enough to convert. I realize, of course, that if I have
a son, maybe he will feel "the generation gap" and try to annoy me
by being baptized. If that does happen, I reckon that part of me
will be very upset and part of me collapse in laughter.' In cases
such as these, there are two elements to the conversion. One is the
act of rebelling against the parental faith and thereby giving out a
defiant message of autonomy. The other is choosing a new faith
that is a clear statement of identity. Sometimes the choice can be
purely on the merits of the new faith, whether the result of a conscious search or the influence of a peer group. However, the two
aspects can also be intertwined, such as someone from an Irish
Catholic background joining the Church of England that the
parents regard with hostility. Becoming a Buddhist would just
puzzle them, whereas joining 'the enemy' annoys them and
achieves a double goal. But there are many others who are provided with no religious identity at all by their parents, or who are
issued with a religious label but given no education for it to have
any meaning. 'I was a genuine NOTHING,' said Karen. 'I was not
lapsed, because I never had anything to lapse from. Religion was as
alien to our homelife as pot-holing is to most people. We never did
it, never thought of it, never even thought we ought to think of it.
Yes, I knew some people went in for it – but, like those pot-holers,
you never seemed to come across them in day-to-day affairs. It was
a bit of shock when I went to Birmingham and shared a flat with
someone who was Christian. She seemed too ordinary for such an
exotic species! Well, you know the rest, I thought it might be quite
interesting to get know to more about the faith . . . and now I'm in
it myself.' Ben had the label but nothing to go with it. 'With a

name like Ben Cohen everyone knew I was Jewish, but although my parents never hid it – on the contrary they were quite proud of it – we never did anything Jewish. I never went to Sunday school and didn't have much of a home education either. If we did go to synagogue, it was only for barmitzvahs and weddings and we were just spectators. Sorry, I tell a lie, the only Jewish thing we did was to eat Jewish; you know, Jewish-style foods. So I grew up associating Judaism with apple strudel and turkey schnitzel, but not with God or spirituality. One day I walked into a cathedral and was dumb-struck by the religious feeling I got there: the uplifting choir, the magnificent architecture, the tremendous atmosphere, it was truly awesome and I realized what I'd been missing all those years. I still eat Jewish, but I believe Christian.'

Part of the problem may lie in the peculiarly English distaste for public discussion about religion. The ethos behind the saying that 'A gentleman never discusses religion or politics' represents a deeply ingrained suspicion that being too interested in, or vocal about, religion is unhealthy. A similar sentiment can be detected in the expression often quoted approvingly that 'one shouldn't wear one's religion on one's sleeve'. The desire to be religious without being fanatical often results in a casualness that descends into indifference. Abraham Carmel – an Anglican vicar who converted to Judaism – wrote how he was an object of fun as a child when he mentioned his religious inclinations: 'At school one day our English master asked us all in turn what we wanted to be when we grew up. The hasty answers he received covered the usual small boy choice: engine driver, policeman, sailor, and all the rest. When it came to my turn, however, I simply blurted out "I should like to be a clergyman". The entire class rocked with laughter, and the master joined in.'[3] Whereas many are like both Karen and Ben quoted above, who did not mind about the absence of religion in their lives and only found it by chance, others felt the vacuum very keenly. Gai Eaton did not hear the word God till he was eight or nine, and was 'a blank sheet' for many years thereafter into adulthood. In his spiritual autobiography, he records: 'And yet I needed to know the meaning of my own existence. Only those who, at some time in their lives, have been possessed by such a need can guess at its intensity, comparable to that of physical hunger or sexual desire. I did not see how I could put one foot in front of the other unless I understood where I was going and why. I could do nothing unless I understood what part my action played in the scheme of things. All I knew was that I knew nothing – and I was paralysed by my ignorance as though immobilized in a dense fog.'[4]

As well as these general factors, there are also specific reasons why some people have left certain religions and decided to seek God in a different form. Many former Catholics, for instance, blame its emphasis on sinfulness and punishment as the reason for their lack of faith. The Roman Catholic Church may have changed enormously in recent decades following the reforms of the Second Vatican Council, but for Pierre, 'The overwhelming feeling I inherited was a sense of my utter worthlessness. It was awful. Yes, the priest also spoke about the God of love, but the predominant message was a world of darkness and sin, in which I was writhing under a crushing weight of guilt. It haunted me for years, till one day I suddenly said "I don't have to believe all this," and then that was it. I wasn't a Catholic anymore. That's when I felt free to look for the real God of love that I was sure did exist.' Joanna had a very negative experience at a convent school. Regular lectures about the perils of the world and the hellfire that awaited sinners left her nervous and mistrustful. Suffering was exalted as a gift to atone for one's sins, while death was portrayed as something to be desired rather than feared. 'But I was a little girl of ten who didn't want to suffer or die. It was only years later, once I was married and a young mother, that I could shake off the feelings instilled in me, and then I was so angry at what they had done and how they had poisoned so many young minds. I had stopped going to church long ago, but now I wanted to give my children a religious background – although one that would nourish and enhance them – and so I began attending classes on Islam and now the whole family is Muslim.' Another commonly cited factor for defections is Catholic teachings on sex. Shelley was someone who valued her faith and took it very seriously, 'But I became increasingly concerned about sexual ethics. It seemed horrendous to ban impoverished families from using contraceptives – bad for them individually and disastrous on a global level – and that was so obviously wrong that I began to question other aspects of church teaching, such as on divorce and celibacy. I gradually realized that I still believed in God, but not the Papal version of it, full of its taboos and preoccupations. I wanted something much more life-affirming and in touch with reality as I saw it. I started re-reading the Old Testament and reckoned that Judaism had God without the hang-ups, and so began a spiritual trek there.'

It should be noted, of course, that for others it is precisely the strength of Catholic teachings on family life and sexual ethics that has led them to convert to Catholicism from other denominations which they regard as lacking moral vigour. Indeed, many of those who transfer from the Church of England castigate the 'wishi-washiness' of its teachings and its tendency to 'be all things to all men'. Jack was someone who felt that 'morality was constantly being re-defined. What was a sin yesterday is okay today. I grant that in some cases these were necessary changes, but overall there was a real sense of drift and I found I couldn't tell what was right and wrong anymore. It wasn't that the goalposts had moved – they were so far apart, I couldn't even see them! And although there are some things in Catholicism that I find hard to accept 100%, by and large I do feel I am part of a faith that has standards which I respect and am prepared to live by.' The issue of women's ordination is another oft-quoted reason for Anglicans to switch allegiance. A succession of high-profile figures became Catholics in the wake of the Church of England's decision in November 1992 to ordain female priests. Well-known politicians included Anne Widdi-combe and Sir George Gardiner, although perhaps most signifi-cant was John Gummer, who had been a leading member of Synod and a lay preacher. For them, and many others, the decision to leave was accompanied by dissatisfaction with the church on a range of other matters – ranging from 'happy-clappy' services to radical bishops – but whereas those could be tolerated as tempo-rary aberrations or local variations, it was the fundamental change in doctrine that led to their departure. Those who had no hesita-tion in serving a woman Prime Minister felt unable to take communion from a woman priest. The ordination of women also opened up an almost unbridgeable gulf between the Church of England and the Roman Catholic Church, and dismayed those who had been hoping for a reconciliation between the two. For Sandra, 'I always considered myself to be a Catholic who happened to belong to the Church of England, which was a sort of English branch version that would one day link up again with the mother church. With the ordination of women I realized that I couldn't maintain the fudge any longer and I had to decide in which camp I really was. It was a short journey in a double sense – the Catholic church was literally fifty yards down the road, while in many respects I'd belonged there all my life.' Not all who made that journey found it so simple; for others the leap of faith was much greater, as Anne Widdicombe declared when the vote to ordain women was announced: 'I found myself in a denomina-tional no-man's-land. I knew what I was rejecting, but not what I was going to.'[5]

There are also those who felt that seeking refuge in another denomination within the church was not an option for them as their discomfiture lay in the very roots of Christianity itself. The same sense of mystery that attracts some repels others, with many attesting that although they were firm believers in God, they could not believe in the Trinity. 'I don't want to sound rude,' said Sammy, 'but the whole Father, Son, Holy Ghost, and Virgin Mary bit makes more sense as a TV soap opera or cartoon strip than as serious religion.' Derek is more circumspect but equally adamant: 'For years I mouthed all the prayers and accepted the Trinitarian concept. But the more I thought about it, the less plausible it seemed and in the end it was such an obstacle that I felt I couldn't go to church any more. So I looked for a faith that had God as the central concept and in a much purer form, which is what led me to Islam. I feel much happier there, because I can hold on to Jesus as an inspired individual, to be respected as a prophet and a wonderful preacher, but not have to believe that he was the Son of God who died for my sins.'

Those who left Judaism for another faith also had specific reasons propelling them away from it as much as attracting them to the new one. For some, it was the apparent rigidity of rabbinic thinking and the constant emphasis on rituals. 'Yes I'm sure dietary laws were very important in earlier centuries when hygiene was minimal or the Black Death was raging,' explained an exasperated Sharon, 'but how can you define faith today by whether you have a ham sandwich or not? Don't get me wrong, I didn't leave Judaism so that I could indulge in pork – if it was just that, I could have stayed a lapsed Jew – it was that I was looking for a religion that put belief at its very centre and where the minister preached every week not about legalistic do's and don'ts but about our relationship with God.' Another common factor that made Judaism unattractive to some born into it was not so much the religious tenets but the social consequences. 'I just hated being different,' said Danny. 'I was bullied at school for being Jewish. Later on I wasn't allowed to go out with non-Jewish girls. At college there was a whole culture that I wasn't part of. At work I sometimes felt ideas and projects I suggested weren't taken up because it was a Jew suggesting them. Even if that was nonsense, it was certainly how I felt. There was nothing about Judaism *per se* that I could put my finger on and blame, it was just being Jewish. So you can understand that I wasn't exactly keen to practise anything much. I got to the stage where I wanted to get Moses off my back, and so when I came across a belief-system that not only made sense to me but would also mean saying goodbye to Judaism, well, I just leapt at it.' The disadvantage of minority status applies to members of many other faiths too, but many born into Islam or Hinduism in Britain today have a skin-colour that immediately marks them out as different from the white majority. Jews, however, are largely white and can therefore assimilate into general culture much more easily, and are only held back by the religious difference – a distinction that can be jettisoned by those who so wish. Some Muslims and Hindus might echo Danny's complaints, but would find it impossible to stand out less simply by relinquishing their religious faith. Indeed, by joining a predominantly white church they might be exposing themselves to 'being different' in yet another arena rather than minimizing their sense of isolation.

Attractions to a new faith

For many converts negative factors concerning their former
faith are far outweighed by positive ones connected with the new
faith. The classic route is the experience of St Paul – a sudden and
unexpected calling. His conversion to Christianity on the road to
Damascus has been replicated down the centuries in the lives of
thousands of ordinary people. As with Paul, it can be a vision of
Christ that is so powerful that it transforms their lives forever. As
one believer described it: 'We are like someone who has been
awakened out of a deep sleep, we are converted from darkness to
light, and have experienced the firstfruits of the age to come.' For
others, it is a moment that leads to God, as happened to Thea: 'I
was sitting in the library, having just finished a piece of research
for a book on chimney-pots, when suddenly there was a rushing
noise and I was engulfed by what I can only describe as a dazzling
darkness. I felt a presence that was so real it was physically there. I
say "it" because there was no body or voice, but this amazing
sensation. Then it was gone. For a moment I was very confused,
and then I had this feeling of utter certainty come over me, like
warm blanket enveloping me, and I realized that I had experienced
God. From being a complete disbeliever who thought those who
did were emotionally challenged, I knew I had to acknowledge
Christ.' Such moments of religious awareness are not limited to
Christianity. One day Imama woke up and said out aloud, 'I am a
Muslim,' and from then on she was. With barely a second's consciousness, she just knew it to be true and had merely blurted out
an inner reality. Not all are so compliant. Brian fought hard to
resist the call: 'If Jews had patron saints, then mine would be
Jonah; I know exactly what he went through. It always amazes me
when people speak of God as being just. Where on earth does that
come from? God isn't fair, and if there is such a thing as free will,
then it's no more than free-ish, because free means take it or leave
it, and that isn't even on the table. God had no respect for the fact
that I didn't want him. It didn't matter that I said "no" a thousand
times, or turned away when he called. In the end I was a wreck,
admitted defeat and phoned a rabbi about becoming Jewish.'

There are many others, though, for whom the biblical character Ruth is a much more potent symbol than Paul. For Ruth there was no decisive moment of drama, bringing instant enlightenment in a blinding flash. Instead, there arose within her a gradual realization that the tradition into which she was born no longer held any meaning for her and she now felt attached to a different faith. We never find out what had started this process – perhaps Ruth herself could not pinpoint it. She had been married to a Jewish husband, but he had not been particularly religious and had even chosen to move away from the land of Israel and settle in non-Jewish parts. It was only after he died and when her mother-in-law Naomi was about to leave that Ruth realized how much she now identified with Judaism and how it was an integral part of her. It was then that she uttered the words that have resonated down the ages and that so many others have had cause to say: 'Your people shall be my people, and your God, my God' (Ruth 1.16). It reminds us that conversion is often not so much a matter of change but a coming home. It is a recognition that the religious values and aspirations that some people have always felt but never found a satisfactory way of articulating, can now be given full expression in a particular way. Certainly many are led to a faith not by dramatic visions of the Deity but through everyday contact with laity. Sometimes this can be friends whose lifestyle one admires and seeks to emulate for oneself. Judy recalls how she realized that her friends fell into two groups: those great for a evening out and those whose advice she valued, and that the latter were all churchgoers. 'It made me think about what counts in life and where I should be heading. I decided to ask one of my Christian friends if I could go to church with her, got involved in her Bible study group and became a regular worshipper myself. I can't honestly say I was ever "called to God" but I was indirectly shown the path.' Shirley is even more direct: 'The strange thing is that I didn't come to convert through religion. I liked a lot of Jews, and then found I was liking Judaism. It wasn't so much the faith that attracted me at first, but the people in it.'

For others, the reverse applied; it was not the introduction of friends, but the search for friends that prompted interest in the faith. 'I lost touch with most of my friends when I went off to university, and then lost most of them when we all graduated and went our separate ways. I found I had a great job that kept me going between nine and five, but evenings and weekends were a disaster area. I knew the Christian Union had a reputation for offering a really warm welcome at university, so I thought I would see if there was something similar at the local church. Maybe I just struck lucky, but there was a special graduate group and I got involved.' Once contact has been made it can be any one of several different aspects of a faith that lead a person to adopt it for themselves: the experience of services, the teachings of the faith, powerful figures in the past who become role models, charismatic living individuals with whom the person identifies, the rituals, home practices, or sense of community. Sometimes it is the romantic image that the faith conjures up in a person's mind, such as the renewal of Jewish life in Israel after the Holocaust or the unswerving tolerance of Bahais despite the persecution they have suffered. The convert has to adopt the tenets of the faith as a whole, but the particular point of entry can vary enormously.

There are also some faiths which are more likely to attract adherents from particular faiths because of the special relationship between them. Very often this is when one is portrayed as a fulfillment of the other. Thus some Muslims who no longer feel that Islam provides the answers to their needs find a home in the Bahai faith, which sees itself as the latest revelation, incorporating the best of all three previous monotheistic faiths and honouring the teachings of Moses, Jesus and Muhammad alike. In a similar vein, some Jews resolve that Christianity is the new Israel and that the New Testament has indeed replaced the Old Testament. Some convert outright and others take a more circuitous route via the Jews for Jesus movement, which holds that the coming of Christ has fulfilled the prophecies of the Hebrew Bible and established a new covenant on earth. For Vanessa, 'what amazes me now is that it took me so long to see the light. I suppose that's because I never read the New Testament till a friend at university encouraged me. You just don't find it in a normal Jewish home. But when I did read it – wow! – everything seemed to tie together so naturally. Jesus was the Messiah that Isaiah foretold and I couldn't avoid facing that truth. If only other Jews would not be afraid to read the Gospels for themselves and open their eyes.'

The converse can also apply, whereby members of a later faith can feel drawn to 'the ancient trunk from which it stems'. It can lead Christians, for instance, to decide that the church has departed from its true roots and that in its attempt to spread monotheism to the pagan world it developed too many ideas that were alien to the worship of the one God. Charles was one who felt that 'it was only when I started reading the Old Testament for myself that I realized how far we had strayed from the God of Moses. The Virgin Birth, the Trinity, the notion of God dying in human form – I began to find them totally unacceptable and felt more and more uncomfortable attending services. One Sunday the vicar preached on how Jesus had shown the light to the Jewish world engulfed in darkness, and something inside me cried out "No, the light was there already and is still shining brightly." The following Saturday I walked into the local synagogue and I've been there ever since.' Whether the journey is from an earlier faith to a later one, or vice-versa, another element in such transitions is the familiarity factor. Jews and Christians, for instance, both share a large range of Bible stories, while they have a common series of religious reference points – be it the Garden of Eden or the Flood or Mount Sinai. Many of the rituals also correspond, even if they are invested with different meanings, such as wine and bread on a Friday evening symbolizing sustenance and joy for Jews, whilst at Sunday mass they signify the body and blood of Christ for Christians. It means that if a Jew or Christian changes from one religion to the other, they feel much more at home in the new tradition than they would if they converted to Hinduism, which has no shared history. The existence of rituals that hold both warm resonances and fresh meaning can be very important for converts. The same applies to Jews and Christians who become Muslims and thereby adopt many new traditions yet still maintain attachment to Moses and Jesus as prophets.

For some, the connection is close to home, as contact with the faith is through a member of the family, such as an uncle or cousin who had either converted themselves or who had originally come from a different tradition. As Seema explained, 'I had read a couple of books about Islam and was quite interested in knowing more, but I would never have had the courage to go to a mosque by myself. When my older sister married someone whose sister had converted to Islam and I got to know her, I thought "this is my chance" and asked her to take me to a service. Even so, it was still pretty daunting going in for the first time, and if it wasn't for her I might still be on the outside looking in.' In many cases, though, the person was the child of a mixed-faith marriage, a situation which often resulted in two trends. One was for the child of that marriage to be brought up in the faith of one parent, but in later life decide to opt for the religion of the other parent. Although it meant that there was easy access to the new faith, it was not without other problems: 'Actually I had wanted to convert to Catholicism years and years ago,' said Janice 'but I felt it would upset my mother and be seen as identifying with my father more than her. He and I had always been closer, and although that was not the reason for changing faith, I had to be really careful it didn't cause a rift with her.' In cases where parents have divorced and there is a real sense of rivalry or bitterness between them, it can be even more difficult for a child, however adult in years. The act of converting from the faith of one to that of the other can be seen in highly emotional terms – as a 'betrayal' or 'going over to the enemy' – and can either cause a great degree of friction or even lead to the conversion being kept secret. Anne did not tell her mother that she had converted to Judaism for four years because 'we lived a hundred and fifty miles away from each other and there was no point in having a row every time I saw her. It was only when children arrived and questions began to be asked about christenings that I had to break the news.'

The other trend is for the product of a mixed-faith marriage not be brought up in either faith, but later wish to seek out his/her religious roots. Denise had a Jewish father and an Anglican mother, both of whom were non-practising and she was brought up without any religious instruction. In her thirties, however, she began to feel the pull of roots: 'It was very strange. I had one or two

Jewish friends who took no interest in their religion and just wanted to be like everyone else, whereas I felt a deep yearning to explore the Jewish part of my heritage. I knew that on my father's side I came from a long line of Jews and they seemed to be beckoning me, urging me to keep the tradition going. When I asked him about it all, Dad wasn't able to tell me much and was surprised that I was interested. I read voraciously, becoming more and more certain that this was the path for me. He was so nonplussed that he wouldn't even take me to synagogue, so I had to go by myself. But once there, I knew that's where I belonged.' In some cases, the pull of roots seemed misplaced, as with Jason who had always felt interested in things Jewish and at home with Jewish people. He was keen to read news about what was happening in Israel and whenever he was on a business trip and had time left over for sight-seeing, he would visit the local Jewish quarter. Although this attraction puzzled him, he still considered himself a nominal member of the Church of England and had a church wedding. It was not until he was forty-three that it emerged that his maternal grandfather had been Jewish but that all connection with the family had been cut off when his mother had married his father. 'It was a bombshell – although a welcome one; suddenly everything fitted into place, and whereas I had felt beforehand that it would be almost presumptuous to convert – why would they want to have me as one of them? – now I felt I had a right to it and it was more a matter of reclaiming my heritage.'

Jason's situation is unusual but not unique, for with the gradual rise of mixed-faith marriages in Britain since the 1930s, there are many who have found, to their surprise, that they had a religious heritage in their family tree of which they were unaware. In certain instances, it was only a death in the family that brought it to light. A death-bed plea by her father to be buried in a Jewish cemetery shocked Sophie, who had always considered him to be as staunch a Baptist as she was. Jean's father never told her his secret, but it came to light in old family papers that she discovered when clearing out his house. In both cases, it triggered a quest to find out more of their past – perhaps also a way of honouring their father and seeking to recapture something of the person they had loved and lost. To the dismay of her former church, Sophie converted to Judaism, while Jean is currently on a course of instruction. Of course, not all react this way. Sophie had two sisters who were equally surprised by their father's revelation. However, for them it was purely a matter of historical interest. As far as they were concerned, it did not require any response from them or lead to any re-appraisal of their life. As one of them stated at the time, 'It was as if he told me that he had played with meccano toys when he was a boy. It was just a piece of information, interesting but nothing to do with me, and I wouldn't have rushed out to buy meccano either.' Clearly, such news is only of significance if it corresponds to a religious inclination – already felt or unconsciously present – in the person concerned, in which case it can have a dramatic effect and lead to radical changes in one's religious orientation. Nevertheless, children of mixed-faith marriages are more likely to change faith than those from a same-faith marriage, whether because they are aware of religious options from an early age, or because the parents have a more relaxed attitude to religious differences, or because there is a less binding sense of family tradition, or because they have direct contact with a faith other than their own. As Janice put it, 'A lot of my friends grew up assuming you had to keep to the family faith – the only choice was how and whether you did it fully, partially or nominally, but if you dropped out then you'd still be a lapsed Catholic or Jew or whatever. I grew up knowing that the world was a religious supermarket in which I already had the pick of two faiths and could add as many as I liked.'

There are other family situations which can propel an individual to conversion. One is where a person has an obviously ethnic or religious surname from his father's side which is at variance from the religion in which he is brought up. According to Tim, 'It was never a problem when growing up. We were a Methodist family and that was that. It was only when I went to public school where we used surnames that I got strange looks and everyone assumed that as Cohen I was Jewish. I got so fed up that I traced the family tree and found that I had a Jewish great-grandfather. Although I never met him he seemed to dominate my life. Things came to a head when I was at Oxford and won a rowing blue. I got phoned up by a reporter from the *Jewish Chronicle* who wanted to run a story about me! I decided that if the rest of the world was going to take me for a Jew then I might as well find out about it. I didn't rush into it, but slowly found out more and got involved in a few Jewish events. Having the name Cohen began to help for a change! Twelve years on, I'm about to take the plunge, although I'm now so much at home in it all that it feels more like I'm just getting the religious paperwork sorted out rather than going for a major transformation.' For Amos, it was assumptions based on his colour that led him to Islam. He came from a long line of Christians in Pakistan who had devoutly kept to biblical names and who had sometimes experienced danger because of their loyalty to the church. When he came to Britain at the age of fourteen with his parents, he expected his family to be lionized in a Christian country for upholding the faith. Instead, he was devastated when he was treated as a 'Paki' and assumed to be a Muslim. He became used to being teased at college for eating pork – 'does Allah know what you're nibbling?' – and the object of racial abuse based on the colour of his skin. 'What hurt most was that so-called Christians just stood by. The fact that I was a fellow-Christian seemed to count for nothing. And even if I wasn't, the whole ethos of the New Testament is to love your neighbour as yourself, and they certainly didn't. The only ones who did befriend me were some of the Muslims. To cut a long story short, I got very embittered and disillusioned, and decided that Christ had always stood up for the oppressed and the underdog, and so maybe it would be more Christian to become a Muslim. And that's what I did. My parents were upset, but as I said to them, it was Christians who deserted me, not the other way round.'

For those who are adopted as young children, and who later are keen to trace their origins, religious identity can be a powerful element. Thus Bradley was adopted from Muslim parents as a baby and brought up by a Jewish family. It was only in his late teens that he was told about his adopted status, and it led to a hunt for his real parents which culminated in him becoming a Muslim. As he himself admits, the decision was partly a way of rejecting his adopted parents, with whom he had always had a troubled relationship, but it was primarily a search 'for the real me. It wasn't that I identified totally with everything that Islam stood for, but more that I knew that's where I belonged. It was a bit like being a Manchester United fan – which is one of the main passions in my life – I don't always agree with some of the team selections or new player purchases that Alex Ferguson makes, but that doesn't stop me being a United fan through and through. Same with Islam. It's me, and I take the rough with the smooth.'

As was seen in the statistics in the previous chapter, marriage to someone of a different faith was a powerful motive that led many to convert, although the circumstances can vary enormously. For some it was a simple matter of establishing domestic unity, with it often being the wife who joined her husband-to-be's faith as a simple act of uniting with him in this part of life as with all other aspects. As Tara explained, 'I suppose it just made sense really. We moved into the same house. We set up a joint bank account. And I adopted the same religion as him. I reckoned that if we were going to be together, it should be in everything, including religion. So I became a Catholic.' For others, it was not just a matter of principle but of practicalities, particularly when marrying some-one from a faith that had a strong domestic tradition. 'I knew that when we set up home together, Dave would want to keep the food laws and to do the special Friday night ceremony; and then there'd be the festivals, most of which seem to take place in the home as much as in synagogue. I'd liked what I'd seen of Judaism so far and as I wasn't particularly attached to my own faith, I thought "well, if I'm going to keep it up for him, I might as well do it for myself as well and become Jewish".' For many, it was a longer-term issue that they were considering and the advent of children. 'I think it is so important for children to have a stable background,' said Jackie, 'and that has to include religion. You can't have parents pulling in two directions at once; it would leave the kids in a hell of a mess, not knowing who they are or where they belong; and anyway it wouldn't be good for the parents either, fighting over who has control and whether the kids were getting their fair share of each faith. I know some people say "we'll give them the best of both", but I can't see it working.' Still, not all think that far ahead, and the concern can be much more immediate and the wedding day itself. As one bride-to-be put it: 'Because of our different religions we could only have got married in a registry office, but I wanted the romance of a traditional English event, a big religious service followed by a proper reception with all my family and friends. I needed all this to really feel married.'[6]

The desire for a 'white wedding' can be a very powerful one, not just a matter of the ceremony itself and the surface glitter, but a powerful feeling that the couple wish their union to be blessed by God – or at least by one of God's representatives on earth. On what is the most important day in the lives of most people, there is a deep-seated need for a sense of consecration, both to give the wedding greater authenticity and to provide the marriage with an added layer of protection. Needless to say, there are also those for whom this does not apply and who prefer a civil ceremony, but whereas this is an option open to all, a religious service is often limited to members of the same faith. The 1949 Marriage Act, for instance, only permits synagogue weddings if 'both partners profess the Jewish faith', while other traditions expect the bride and groom to adhere to the faith's precepts. A mixed-faith couple who wish to have such a ceremony can only do so if one of them converts to the faith concerned. Sometimes the conversion is an act of love rather than a practical move, as in the case of Hadijah: 'I knew Abdul would never ask me to convert, but I was equally certain that he would be delighted if I was to take his faith. That was my main reason really – to please him. It was my wedding present to him.' Others pre-empted that stage and, like Justine, began thinking seriously about conversion long before marriage plans were discussed. 'I could see where the relationship was going and knew that we had a long-term future. I wanted to find out as much as I could about him and the things that made him tick. His Hindu background was obviously an important element, even though he was quite assimilated, and I began attending classes without his knowledge. He was very surprised when a friend of his told him he had seen me at the temple, and although he said it wasn't necessary I knew it meant a lot to him.' In Fiona's case, an element of strategy can be detected and she admits that 'once I had decided he was the man for me, I started learning about Islam – and letting him know I was – so as to be more acceptable to him. All his brothers had married fellow Muslims and I reckoned I didn't stand much of a chance unless I was one of the faith too. After three months I told him that I was interested in converting. He smiled and said "That'll make things a lot easier" Bingo!' In complete contrast was Tina, who came into contact with the faith for the first time through her Muslim fiancé and took a liking to it. However, she did not want to feel pressurized either by his hopes or his family's expectations, so she went to the mosque of her own accord and took lessons without telling him. 'One day I came home and said "By the way, I became a Muslim this afternoon." He was stunned; also a little cross that I had not told him what was going on. But he understood that I had to make sure I was doing it for me, and with hindsight it was the best way of achieving it.'

There are also many cases where conversion was not just a good idea but a requirement of the relationship: 'Jonathan and I were deeply in love and nothing made me happier when he proposed to me. But no sooner had I accepted when he said that we could only go ahead if I converted to Judaism. Saying it like that now makes it sound as if I had a gun to my head – and I suppose I did – but I wanted to marry him and was happy to accept that condition. So instead of going off to choose a ring we went to find a rabbi!' Others, such as Alison, were less amenable: 'When he asked me to convert I was furious. It seemed really wrong to make it a condition of marriage. Either he loved me or he didn't. And I was doubly angry in that he had never said anything about it when we were going out together. If he wasn't religious then, how come he could get religious now? And if I was okay as I was as a girlfriend, why did I have to change to be his wife?' Whilst conversion was often for the sake of the partner – requested or not – it was sometimes more for the sake of the family. 'We had this strange conversation,' said Terry, 'where she started saying how much she loved me and how much I meant to her. I knew she was getting at something else and asked her to come out with it. She just burst into tears and said we could never get married unless I converted. Her family wouldn't accept me otherwise and she couldn't go against their wishes. I think she was terrified of me saying no and of her losing me. I just laughed and said, "Well, if that'll keep them happy, why not?" I've always been an easy-going bloke, but I can imagine a lot of others objecting.' Rick was one of them: 'I was flabbergasted. In fact at first I felt let down. How could she ask that of me, when she knew I wasn't religious and when I didn't even know her family, as they lived the other end of the country. It was only then that I realized that was precisely the reason why she'd never taken me home. It wasn't even that I was the wrong faith, just a different faith, and their family life and culture and religion were so bound up together that they were inseparable. And even though we might be living two hundred miles down south, it was still important for them to feel that their daughter and future son-in-law shared the same religious culture.'

Amid all these instances, there are also those who genuinely became interested in the faith of their partner for its own sake once they had been introduced to it. Martin freely admits that he thought being Buddhist was only if you wanted to be a monk in Outer Mongolia, and was quite surprised when he found that he was going out with one. 'I was even more surprised once I learnt a bit about its teachings and discovered it made a lot of sense. We began to go to meditation classes together and I became even more involved than she was. Even if we'd split up, I would have continued with Buddhism, because I knew it was right for me'. The same is true for many others, for whom the partner was a catalyst that led to the new faith rather than the direct cause of the conversion. Perhaps there are also those who are attracted to someone of a different faith precisely because they are interested in it and the relationship is an indirect way of exploring it further. Evelyn is sure that this applies to her, albeit on a subsconscious level: 'I never said to myself "Oh great, he's a Muslim, so I'll date him and get him to show me the Koran" – I was attracted to him because he was good-looking and vivacious, but at the same time I am sure that it was being a Muslim that was part of the attraction. Only the other day I remembered that when I was a ten-year-old and saw *Lawrence of Arabia* I wanted to be a Muslim bride, so maybe it goes back much deeper.'

The question of which partner is the one to convert depends on a number of factors. Most obviously, it is the one with the lesser faith, particularly when they have long lapsed and are happy to follow the other partner. That is certainly the case for those couples who have decided it would be wisest to unify the family faith as a matter of principle. In this respect, religion is just one of a series of tasks that are divided up, consciously or by default, within a marriage. One partner tends to take the lead in super-vising the household finances, or looking after the garden, or arranging the annual holiday, depending on their level of interest. When the decision to convert is dictated more to please one partner's family, it is often the family of the partner who belongs to a minority faith, where ethnic ties are still stronger. Most Hindu families, for instance, would prefer their offspring to marry a fellow-Hindu as much for cultural reasons as religious ones. Of course, religious Christians also wish their children to marry believers and can feel a sense of hurt if they do not, although they too may be described as a minority compared to the vast majority in the country who classify themselves as 'lapsed C of E'. Alterna-tively, status issues regarding the children may be the determining factor, such as a non-Jewish woman converting so that any children will be born Jewish; alternatively, religious law may play a role, such as Muslim women being allowed to marry only another Muslim. At other times, it may be cultural factors that decide, as when Corinne, a non-practising Methodist, married a Hindu: 'From a strictly religious point of view I didn't need to convert, as the Hindu faith is so tolerant of others, while his family were largely in India and the few over here were quite laid-back. But we both felt it was the right thing to do, given the way he lived his life and the circles in which he moved.'

The discussion between the couple about the subject of con-version can range from the sensitive to the excruciating, and from the prolonged to the monosyllabic. Sometimes it can be a straight-forward chat, businesslike in character, dealing with one of the issues that face them in a matter-of-fact way. At other times, particularly when one partner wants the other to convert but is hesitant to put on any pressure, it can result in spasmodic half-hints that are left undiscussed but which leaden the atmosphere. This happened to Jill: 'It was awful, it was like there were all these unexploded time-bombs in the air. After a while, I stopped being upset and got angry and said "Either drop all the innuendos or come out with it." By that time, of course, I knew he wanted me to convert, but I resented the way he was going about it.' It can prove an agonizing dilemma for the person who wants the other partner to convert to their faith: do they suggest conversion and be seen to be pressurizing the partner, or do they say nothing and risk the other partner thinking it's not all that important? They also have to contend with feelings of hypocrisy – or resist the charge of hypocrisy – if they themselves have not displayed great religious fervour up to that point in the relationship yet know they are still deeply attached to their faith and desperately want the partner to share it too. As Jonathan said pithily, 'I may be a pork-eating Jew but I'm still very Jewish. I know it came as a shock to her when she realized how Jewish I felt. It took me quite a while to get her to understand that being religious and being Jewish aren't neces- sarily the same thing. And just because I don't go to synagogue much at the moment doesn't mean one day I won't want to take my children to synagogue and bring them up with all the traditions in the same way I was.'

Some couples manage to resolve the issue quickly and amicably, but for others it lingers on painfully. Alison is a prime example: 'We've been together for nine years, living together for eight of them. There's no doubt we would be married by now but for the conversion question. It took me a long time to calm down after he tried to insist I convert. In fact I dismissed it out of hand to begin with and wouldn't talk about it. It was only when I was sure that he loved me enough not to call the relationship off that I began to wonder why it was so important and be a bit more sympathetic to the idea. It's meant a lot of heartache and anguished discussions, but we'll get there in the end – just.' Other couples found they were engaging in a religious power play. Georgina recounts how 'we had talked about conversion a little midweek and then to my amazement he told me he wanted to pop into the gurdwara over the weekend. He had never even mentioned the word in three years, let alone go there. And then he started bringing home Sikh books to read and casually leaving them around the house. "Stuff you," I thought, "we'd talked about conversion, but not which one of us would convert," so next Sunday I took myself off to church and told him to have Sunday lunch ready by the time I came back. It was very silly really, but I didn't want to be pushed around religiously. Actually I was so bored in church that the following two Sundays I just pretended to go and went to a friend's house instead. I can smile about it now, but at the time it felt like war. In the end I couldn't keep it up – I think he was beginning to wilt too – and we sat down and talked it through.'

If there is such a thing as 'conversion etiquette' and how one partner should broach the subject with the other, the guidelines might be as follows:

Don't tackle the subject via innuendos and hints.

Do introduce it in an honest and straightforward way.

Don't ask your partner to convert as part of a birthday wish-list, in front of others, when you are about to go out, or during sex.

Do talk about it when you are alone, have time and are not doing something else.

Don't say: I will only marry you if you convert.

Do say: I love you and want to marry you, although I have to be truthful and say it would please me enormously if you converted, so can we discuss it at some stage.

Don't say: If you don't convert, we will have to split up.

Do say: Let me explain why conversion is so important for me.

Don't say: My parents insist you convert.

Do say: We have a long-standing family tradition that I would like to share with you.

Don't get angry if your partner says they are not sure.

Do say: Okay, let's leave it for a while and discuss it again when you have had more time to think about it.

Don't say: I have bought some books on the faith that I want you to read.

Do say: If you want to read some literature on it, let me know and I'll get some.

Don't say: I will make an appointment for you to see a minister and he will be able to persuade you.

Do say: If you think it would be helpful to talk to a minister, we can go together some time.

In all of the above, the common theme is to remember that conversion has to be the free-will decision of the other partner, and that the more pressure that is brought to bear, the more likely they are to resent matters. Encourage rather than bludgeon. Even if pressure brings short-term compliance, the discontent will erupt at a later stage. Ultimately the best convert is the one who feels that they are being asked to share something special rather than being bullied into something alien.

Whilst the variety of marriage-motives for conversion are clearly very compelling for the individuals concerned, they may be of less appeal to the ministers who are asked to oversee those conversions. Trying to please partners or in-laws may be very noble, but have little to do with religious conviction, while the desire for a 'white wedding' is even less likely to impress those who take the faith seriously. For some ministers such motives, or lack of motives, present a major problem and they are unwilling to give any religious instruction unless a reasonable degree of personal sincerity is displayed. This results either in a certain amount of subterfuge, with the prospective convert falsely enthusing over religious values, or going to a more accommodating minister. Tara chose the former path: 'I knew I couldn't go along and say I wanted to convert for my husband's sake, so I said how much I shared his religious values and wanted to adopt them for myself. It wasn't 100% true, but it's not as if I actually disagreed with them, so I reckoned it was okay really.' No doubt many ministers are fully aware of the mixed-bag of reasons that bring engaged couples to their door seeking conversion and choose to ignore them in the belief that what is important is turning a mixed-faith couple into a same-faith couple. Even if the convert is less than ideal, the assumption is that it will help the other partner maintain the faith and ensure that any children are brought up in the tradition.As one imam, Zaki Badawi, put it very frankly, 'Cupid is the best preacher!' It is the characteristic of ministers to think not just in terms of immediate events but of future generations. Those schooled in the Bible and God's promise to make his descendants as numerous as the stars in the sky and sand on the seashore (Gen. 22.17), or in the prophecies of Isaiah, tend to operate in the long-term. Others take a more sanguine view and disregard the whole question of motives. As Rabbi Joseph put it: 'To me, it matters not why a person wants to convert – because they're in love, or read a book, or heard a voice, whatever – it's not the route that counts, but the destination. If they have come to find a home in Judaism then I am happy to help. I'm fully aware that many people come to Judaism through a Jewish partner and but for them they would not be approaching me. I never ask "Are you converting 90% because of him or her?" I take it for granted that they are! So long as there is something in it for themselves – even if only 10% – then that's fine by me. The worst that can happen is that someone converts and becomes a lapsed Jew. Well, we've got enough born lapsed Jews already, so one or two more won't make any difference! I'd much prefer to be taken for a ride by some like that, than be so strict that I lock out those who are genuine.'

The list of reasons for converting to one's partner's faith is long and powerful, yet, as was seen in the previous chapter in the case of some faiths, such as Judaism, even more convert after marriage than beforehand. It arises because many people do not wish to change faith for the sake of a marriage – usually for one of four reasons: because they have a faith to which they are already attached, or because they lack any religion and do not wish to take one on, or because they do not know enough about the faith to decide either way, or because religion is simply not an issue in the couple's lives at that stage. In the case of the first two categories, marriage makes little difference to their opinion, and they remain attached to their belief or disbelief. In the latter two categories, however, married life can effect a change in their attitude. Mary is a good example: 'Frankly we never discussed religion when we were dating and it was only after getting married that I began to see Sikh family life at close quarters. Although his family didn't dominate us like some in-laws do, I got to know his mother and sisters very well and began to admire their way of life. No one put any pressure on me – as I was a policewoman they had to watch their step anyway! – but gradually I understood more and more and started doing little rituals around the house and at mealtimes. One day my husband said half-jokingly, "Are you trying to become a Sikh without telling anyone?" and I realized how part of the religion I had become and decided to make it official. I think we must have been married about six years by then. But if you'd asked me beforehand if I would ever convert and I would probably have said "No way". Funny how things change.' Sheila would agree but for an entirely different reason. Like so many couples, religion was not one of the issues with which she and her husband were concerned when they got engaged: 'A registry office marriage was all we wanted irrespective of the religious differences. Close family and a few friends and not too much fuss. Our minds were more on a mortgage and job changes than anything else. I suppose I had religion somewhere in the back of my mind as one of the things that couples ought to discuss, but it was so far down the list of priorities that it got relegated to "one day – when we win the lottery and have got time to sit and think". Then I got pregnant and started reading all those mother and baby books, and realized we had to make some decisions.'

The imminent arrival of children means that mixed-faith couples are faced with a range of religious questions about their childrens' future, including what religious identity to give them, as well as the separate issue of what religious education to provide them with. Even more urgent are decisions about initiation rites: if one partner is Jewish or Muslim and a baby boy is born, do the parents circumcise him or baptize him, or neither, or both? It is often at the stage when children are contemplated, or have arrived and are beginning to ask questions about God, that one partner decides to unify the family faith and convert. Sometimes it is the partner who needs to convert for the sake of the children's status – such as a non-Jewish woman married to a Jewish male who has agreed to bring the children up Jewish and because of the law of the matrilineal line in Judaism, it is she who has to convert. However, this does not always apply. Jeff was not Jewish, while his wife was. Before they had married they had decided to bring any children up as Jewish, although there was no need for him to convert as they would have Jewish status anyway through their mother. This seemed a satisfactory arrangement until children actually arrived: 'It was only then that I began to feel strange about the decision. For a while I couldn't work out why as I didn't object in principle, and then I realized that I was worried about me being the odd one out in the family and somehow different. As I didn't have any strong beliefs of my own and I agreed with most of what Judaism stood for, it wasn't too difficult to convert. It was certainly the right thing to do, and I feel we are a stronger family unit because of it.' There are also those who convert not so much for the sake of the children but thanks to them. Margaret had agreed to bring up the children as Muslim but did not want to convert herself: 'I was happy for the children to follow his faith, but didn't feel it was right for me. I wanted to play my part fully, rather than leave it all to him, and used to read them childrens' books on Islam. The strange thing was that the more I told the children, the more at home in Islam I began to feel. In the end I was buying adult books for myself. By the time the oldest was six, she had a Muslim mother!'

In addition to the above, a variety of other circumstances can attract one to a new faith. Adopting the majority faith of the country can be a way of someone from a minority ethnic group integrating within it. As the German writer Heinrich Heine explained when he abandoned Judaism for Lutheranism in 1825, 'Christianity was a passport to European society.' The same applies to many Muslims in Britain today, according to Zaki Badawi, who become Christian in order to assimilate socially and economically. Sometimes they will deliberately seek out Christian wives so as to ensure that their children are born with the right credentials rather than have to acquire them. This process can also apply to other religious minorities, although less so to Jews, for whom this may have been an issue in previous decades, but who have now assimilated sufficiently into general society to be accepted as they are rather than under a religious flag of convenience. Sometimes the inverse takes place, where a person from a minority faith seeks a partner from the Church of England as a

way of gaining cultural acceptability, but then asks her to convert to his faith. It is a clash between ambition and roots, between
social aspiration and religious tradition that is exemplified by
Hussein, a successful businessman whose wife converted to Islam
on marriage but acutely analysed their situation: 'I know he loves
me dearly, but I am also aware that when we were going out part
of my attraction was that I was a sign that he had "arrived". I
was virtually an unofficial advert for the business, as if to say:
respectable Christian girlfriend, this man is obviously going
places. The irony was that the moment he proposed, that side of
things lost all their appeal for him, and he wanted me to be like his
mother and sister, a good Muslim wife.'

For some, conversion goes far beyond social integration and is a
form of marriage market or even sexual gratification. Linda openly
admits now what she failed to tell the rabbi who converted her:
that she wanted a Jewish husband – 'Jewish men have a reputation
for being rich and successful, but also good husbands and fathers.
Well, that's what I wanted, and I decided that rather than hang
around bars and discos, I should become part of the local Jewish
community. In fact, it worked even better than I hoped. There I
was, every male Jew's fantasy of a blonde bombshell, but 100%
kosher with it. I was spoilt for choice. As for the religious side,
lighting candles on a Friday night and going to synagogue every
now and then is a small price to pay for an adoring husband and
financial security.' Although it is impossible to quantify how many
other Lindas there are, with the high rate of Jews marrying out of
the faith it is not necessary for would-be spouses to convert to gain
a Jewish partner and the likelihood is that hers is a rare situation.
Barry represents what is probably another uncommon motive,
albeit one that cannot be ignored, based on sexual yearnings: 'As a
teenager I was engrossed by the fact that whereas Jewish women
observed menstrual laws which kept them apart from their
husbands twelve days in every month, sometimes more if there
was the slightest trace of blood remaining, Christian women did
not have such rules. It stayed with me into adulthood and I just
knew I wanted sex every night and that having it in blood would be
even more of a turn-on. Of course, I didn't have to convert to get

that, but somehow going to church – "enemy territory" – and getting baptized made it all the sexier. Forbidden fruit and all that. Don't misunderstand me – I love my wife otherwise I wouldn't have married her, but I knew that whoever I married had to be a Christian and I wanted to be one in bed too.' For the opposite sex, fantasies about circumcised Jewish or Muslim males are some-times factors that make a relationship with them seem all the more desirable and that in turn can lead to conversion to secure the marriage. As one person on the receiving end of such admiration recorded: 'There are – thank God – a small breed of women who seem to think that Jewish men are blessed with special sexual talents. Indeed, when I asked Lara what the difference was between going out with Anglican men and Jewish men, she said, without a moment of hesitation, "Jewish guys make more sensual lovers."' Conversion can be a way for some to turn lovers into husbands.

Divorce can be another trigger for conversion, particularly amongst women. Every year a small number convert to the faith of their former husband. Sometimes it is because they are now the sole parent bringing up the children, and if the children belong to a different faith, it is an incentive for the mother to convert so as to consolidate the family unit. Alternatively it can be a way of justify-ing the person's continuing place in a church or synagogue circle which they shared with their husband before the divorce. If he has now abandoned the family, their point of contact with the com-munity is in danger of being severed unless the wife joins the faith and becomes a member in her own right. In some instances, the conversion is a method of spiting the former spouse, either because it is something he had long wanted and she had always been unwilling to do; or it is a way of occupying a space on what was previously his territory and thereby letting him know that she would not be conveniently disappearing into the sunset. In Liz's case, there was a much more specific motive: 'I knew that one day he would marry the other woman and this was the only synagogue in town. It was also a place where we had taken the children to weddings and barmitzvahs over the years. I couldn't stop him getting married elsewhere but I was determined that it would not be locally, and if he knew he was likely to bump into me here then he would think twice about showing his face or bringing her.' There are also those who take the opposite route and who, following a divorce, convert to a different faith to their former partner. This can either be as a deliberate act of separation, trying to cut off every possible common link, or in an attempt to establish an entirely new social circle. Needless to say, such cases do not prove healthy grounds for conversion, and rarely sustain long-term devotion to the faith. Moreover, they must have taken some effort to mislead the minister who instructed them and, at very least, failed to establish a relationship of trust.

Entirely different are those who convert after their partner has died. This too can be from a variety of motives. For some, it is a form of guilt that they had never done so when the person was alive and they attempt to rectify matters. At seventy-two, therefore, Alec took up conversion lessons to Judaism because 'although she never ever asked me to convert, somehow I'm sure it would have given her a lot of pleasure if I had. Well, now I'm on my own and I feel it's the least I can do for her. I just hope she's looking down and can see what's going on!' For others, it is a form of holding on to their partner's memory, trying to reach them beyond the grave, and showing how much they still love them. By immersing themselves in the deceased's tradition, reading the books he/she would have read, going to services that he/she might have enjoyed, it is a way of cheating death and overcoming the separation imposed on them. 'We always belonged to different churches and for thirty-seven years it never bothered us,' said Deidre, 'but now he's gone, it's very important to me to do what he would have done.' For yet others, it is with thoughts of their own death and the desire to be buried in the same religious cemetery as their beloved.

There are many instances, though, where very different circumstances operate. Requests for conversion are a common phenomenon in prison. Here, too, the motivation varies enormously. For some it is because of a genuine religious experience, the culmination of remorse for past misdeeds and a desire for a new future. As Kenny put it, 'I was at rock bottom. I despised myself and reckoned that most of the world despised me too. My family had long disowned me, and most of those I called "mates" were villains of one sort or another. I thought about suicide. I had briefly considered going to one of the chaplains to seek repentance, but I decided that not even God would want to have much to do with me. And then one day in my cell, with nothing special happening, I suddenly felt this aura around me, as if I was being physically lifted a few inches off the ground and held tightly. And I just knew that it was Jesus and that he loved me and would always be there for me. It was Day One of my recovery and I've never looked back since.' Others meet God halfway, so to speak, for one of the problems in prison is the long hours with nothing to do. Rod was just one of several who opted to break the boredom by attending the Bible study classes the chaplain ran for an hour each week. He expected to be mildly entertained but instead found himself riveted: 'I had never gone to church in my life and just picked up a bit of Christian teachings from RE lessons at primary school. Reading the Bible as an adult was a revelation – no joke – and I thought, "This makes a lot of sense." When I asked the padre if I could convert, he suggested I wait till I got out, but I kept on putting in requests to the Governor and eventually they said okay, do it inside.' The caution of the authorities was not unique to Rod's case, but is standard practice owing to the high percentage of conversion requests for ulterior motives. Sometimes it is because prisoners consider it will enhance their chances of gaining parole if they are known to be Christians, and clergy are reluctant to be used a means of early-leave. For other inmates, it is because they perceive conversion will bring certain perks, particularly conversion to Judaism, in which case they can insist on being supplied with kosher food, which is generally prepared outside prison and brought inside in special sealed dishes, and is considered to be of a higher quality than the standard fare. For those looking for an excuse to avoid prison duties, the excuse that they cannot work on the Jewish Sabbath and festivals is also attractive. There is also the hope that, once released, they are more likely to receive practical support and even financial backing from religious organizations, a supposition that is not necessarily the case but for some is enough to warrant a conversion on the off-chance it may produce results later on.

Guilt of another kind motivates some individuals. When a person is particularly sensitive to the injustice that his/her religious group has perpetrated against another group, it may lead to joining that group as an act of atonement. That can be most obviously seen in German Lutherans who have converted to Judaism as a way of identifying with the victims of Nazi atrocities and the complicity of most German churches by failing to protest. As Helga explained, 'I was born after the war and don't have any personal guilt, but I always felt uneasy with the unwillingness to confront the past that I found in Germany, even in my own family. That's one of the reasons why I came to live in England. And although the church wasn't involved directly in the mass murders, without their passivity Hitler would have found it very difficult. I can't bring the six million Jews back, but what I can do is take the place of one of them by becoming Jewish myself. In a way, I'm turning the clock back and trying to undo what happened all those years ago.' Similar principles prompted Gerrard to become a Buddhist: 'When I started reading history and it began to sink in that the best the Christian West could do was drop a bomb on Hiroshima and kill thousands upon thousands of women and children, I thought that thirty years on, the least I could do was renounce the church and show solidarity with those who had survived. I know it won't bring them back to life or change current nuclear policy, but it helps me live with myself and feel that ordinary people count too.'

The wider context can also apply when a faith carries a political message as well as a religious one. This can be seen in Latin America in the 1970s where the Roman Catholic Church's identification with liberation theology gained it many adherents who saw joining the church as a way of establishing a new political order. At the same time in the Soviet Union, many brought up as atheists found that the Baptist Church offered them both a chance for personal salvation and a means of resistance against the tyranny of Communism. It means that the same religion can have a very different impact when political circumstances are different. This applies to the Baptist Church, which has struggled to maintain its membership during the same period in Britain. The faith that is vibrant and pioneering in one country can be staid and unadventurous in another, and attract few newcomers as a result. Faiths can also go through different stages in the same country and acquire a change of image within a relatively short period. In Britain, for instance, Islam was seen almost exclusively as the religion of immigrants, while Catholicism was largely limited to members of long-standing Catholic families. In the 1990s, both perceptions changed rapidly, with it becoming 'macho' for many white Britons to adopt Islam, while becoming a Catholic was considered 'chic' in the upper echelons of society. One became part of an admired minority that combined the whiff of the exotic with a strong sense of identity. There are many factors that lead to this transition, including the cultural acceptability of the faith (epitomized by the Prince of Wales' visit to a mosque or meetings with Muslim businessmen), the emergence of a religious leader who commands wide respect (as in Cardinal Basil Hume), the disappearance of previous stigmas (seen in the election of Muslims as MPs and their appointment to the House of Lords), and the retreat of the established faith (the steady erosion of the appeal of the Church of England).

Personality traits

If dissatisfaction with one's current religion and perceived advantages in the new faith are two critical aspects that lead to conversion, there is a third factor: particular personality traits in the individual concerned. Much derives from the upbringing a person has as a child. Where there has been a stable and happy home life, in which children are nurtured and valued, it is likely that they will have positive associations with the religious symbols and beliefs that were part of that childhood. Many will follow in the faith of their parents, having come to endorse it in their own right. Going to services – or observing home rituals – are as natural for some as holding their fork in their left hand and knife in their right. It is an essential part of their identity and in which they feel very comfortable. Of course, the pattern is not uniform, and there are those who had an equally positive childhood but who developed in different ways religiously in adulthood, be it abandoning the faith or changing to a different one. But as a generalization, those with an untroubled early home life are less likely to convert for personality reasons unless an external cause impinges, such as marriage.[7] Conversely, those who suffered from some form of neglect or repression when growing up are much more likely to wish to exchange the faith of which they have negative images; alternatively, if they had no faith upbringing, they may seek to use a new faith as a way of escaping some of the ills that have shaped their life. The bad experiences need not be directly connected with religious life to cast their shadow on it. Rick remembers being beaten every time he came home from Sunday school with a bad report and, not surprisingly, developed an antipathy to all things Christian. Ken, though, was regularly beaten by a father who often came home drunk. When they went to church every other Sunday at their mother's insistence, Ken could not understand why the vicar could greet his father in such a friendly way and felt let down by the God who should have known better. 'I think I expected God to tell the vicar what was what going on in our house – to act as some sort of policeman – and for the vicar to tell my father off and get him to mend his ways and stop hurting me. Seeing Dad singing away with gusto and then shaking hands with everyone afterwards made me sick. If that was God, he wasn't doing his job very well. I never got over the fact that he failed me when I needed him most.'

The aberrant role of fathers can also be influential if they are absent or weak, in which case the person is often likely to identify with a strong father figure. A psychological study of converts to Christianity showed that a high proportion of them came from homes in which their father was not present or played an inactive role. Conversion to Christianity and aligning themselves to the Father and Son was often a way of leaving the dependency on their mother and creating more balanced forces within their lives.[8] For others, the need for a strong male figure leads to enthusiastic support for a charismatic leader within the major faiths – such as the Lubavitcher Rebbe or Ayatollah Khomeini – or to a self-proclaimed guru in small sect.[9] In some instances the attraction of a particular faith is not just because it is different from the world of one's childhood, but because it offers a direct antidote to the traumas suffered in it. Thus when Ken sought a new religious identity in reaction to his drunken father, one of the reasons he chose Islam was precisely because it banned the consumption of alcohol. In similar vein, Gaye had desperately unhappy memories of her parents getting divorced and even worse ones of being abused by her stepfather. One of her first acts on leaving home was to convert to Catholicism, largely because of the church's rejection of divorce and its emphasis on family life.

Those who are attracted to the collection of minor cults and offshoots that have sprung up in modern times – known as New Religious Movements – seem to be especially likely to have come from disturbed homes. A study of forty converts from various groups – born-again Christians, repentant Jews, Hare Krishna devotees and Bahai converts – along with a control group of thirty non-converts, found that the converts characterized their childhood as unhappy more often than the non-converts. One half of the converts described their childhood as extremely unhappy, with only six recording a normal or happy childhood. Among the traumatic events they reported were early parental death, witnessing a parent attempt to commit suicide, violent fights or recurrent mental breakdowns of parents.[10] It is significant, therefore, that whereas the popular perception is that psychological impairment is caused by membership of cults, in fact it usually pre-dates it and pre-disposes them to join such movements. A study of Sufi converts revealed the astonishing fact that 78% had experienced a major trauma of this nature prior to conversion.[11] Those who had previously been involved in the drug culture are often likely to be amongst those engaged in religious conversion. Sometimes this is a means of escaping the clutches of the drug circle in which they move, by both establishing a new social group and using the religious disapproval of drugs to reinforce one's determination to kick the habit. Donna was one of many who 'knew I couldn't do it by myself, but where to turn for help? One day I was walking past a church and looked up and saw Jesus on the Cross. I just melted. I knew He was my way out. Now I'm hooked on Bible study and prayer groups, but believe me it's a lot cheaper and you get to live longer.' Others are attracted to certain religions precisely because they are used to altered states of consciousness and wish to maintain such experiences without drugs and their concomitant dangers. The Divine Light Mission has a disproportionately high number of former drug users who find it offers them a drug-free 'high'. Similarly Sufi converts have a significant record of previous drug use. They were consciously looking for mystical experiences, but realized the drugs were unhealthy and sought to replace pyschedelic experiences with meditation-led ones.[12]

In other instances, conversion is not to counteract parental hurts or substance-abuse, but to provide an answer to a sense of sinfulness. It can reflect deep neuroses that torment the individual with his/her own sense of guilt. The answer is to find redemption, and so those faiths that emphasize the sinfulness of mankind and the salvation that is on offer through them prove the most attractive. Whereas for some the mere act of conversion is sufficient to alleviate the perceived sin, in most cases it needs to be supplemented by various punishments – such as vows of abstinence – or by regular confession. The church, with its roots in the Fall of Adam and its climax in the death of Jesus for the sins of the world, is immensely attractive to those in this category. It also has much to offer those who feel overwhelmed by a sense of worthlessness. Carole is adamant that 'There is nothing worse, absolutely nothing worse, than going around feeling totally unloved and useless, and that no one gives a damn whether you're there or not. Yes, it must be pretty awful losing a leg or something in a car accident, but if you still go home to someone who loves you, then it matters much less. But having two legs and no one to notice, that's got to be worse.' Jesus was the answer. 'To know that Jesus loves me, to know that He accepts me as I am, and that however bleak things seem I am never alone, that transformed my life. In fact, it made life worth living in the first place.'

The success of such conversions in eradicating the person's problems is variable. Sometimes, the very act of decisiveness can be a means of heading in a new direction and casting off one's previous despondency. In the case of Carole, for instance, being loved in heaven resulted in finding love on earth when she met her husband-to-be at a church committee meeting. For her, it was not so much the introduction to a new social circle that counted but the new confidence to shine in the company of others. 'In the old days, I didn't love myself very much – in fact I despised myself – so there was no reason for anyone else to like me either. Once I had a friend in Jesus, I knew I counted for something and started being much more out-going and sociable.' Others find that conversion can have a positive effect on their lives not because of its therapeutic value but because it changes the frame of reference under which they operate. Reza felt that life as an insurance salesman was constant stress, 'either in keeping up sales targets or in keeping up with the lads at weekends. It was superficially very good but absolute murder in practice. Then I started to get interested in Islam and began to see everything differently. Priorities changed. Allah was the real goal. Sales charts and pub parties weren't even listed. Now I do the same job, but in a much more relaxed way and I mix with people who I'm not in competition with all the time.' There are other problems, though, that cannot be overcome so easily. Deep-seated phobias, violent temper, or self-destructive tendencies do not disappear simply because the owner of them has changed faith. Whilst some converts are lucky enough to solve some of their problems through a new faith, others simply take their misery with them. In some instances, it leads the convert to lapse, feeling that the faith has failed to help them in the way they anticipated. In other instances, it makes the tendencies slightly more bearable, and at least holds out hope that prayer and repentance will lead to a better life in the world to come even if they cannot solve the problems of this one.

Analysing the full range of personal problems that are the motivating factors that lead many converts to seek a new faith, Snow and Phillips put them into five categories:

1. *Spiritual problems* including meaninglessness, lack of direction and purpose, a sense of powerless and poor self-image.

2. *Interpersonal problems* including marital problems, child-rearing problems, parental problems and other relational problems.

3. *Character problems* including drugs, alcohol, self-centredness, and various personality problems such as uncontrollable temper.

4. *Material problems* including unemployment, job dissatisfaction, finances and school-related problems.

5. *Physical problems* including headaches, nervousness, chronic illness, obesity and lack of energy.[13]

What all the individuals involved have in common is a need to find friends and gain salvation; and although that is shared by many people, most of them have plenty of alternative routes open to them, whereas the above groups feel that conversion is often their best option, or even their only one.

Chance

If there are complex reasons for conversion that lie deep in the human psyche, there are also much simpler factors at work, including pure chance. Yasmin insists she was quite happy as a Muslim and although not ultra-religious, regarded Islam as her natural home. Walking to a friend's house one day in the summer, she was caught in a sudden downpour and, having neither umbrella nor coat, she decided to take refuge in the nearest building, which happened to be a church. 'I went into the foyer for a bit, but as it was still raining very intensely, I decided to wander around inside while I was waiting. I had been to a church before as part of a school lesson, so I knew what to expect, but this time I had this incredible sensation that I ought to kneel down and pray. I must have spent a while at it, because the sun was out again by the time I emerged. My friend was shocked when I explained why I was late – she was also a Muslim – but I went back the next day. It wasn't a revelation or anything like that. I just felt a real sense of prayer and spirituality. I didn't actually convert for another six months as I wanted to be sure that it wasn't a temporary fad. The only thing that did change was that from now on I always carry a pocket umbrella in my bag!' No doubt it could be argued that Yasmin was ready for change even if she was not aware of it, or even that God had directed her steps towards the church, but without the shower she would not have entered the building and discovered Christianity at that stage in her life.

The same applies to Gavin who occasionally took his lunch-break in the local park where he ate his sandwiches and read the paper. On one occasion he noticed that someone had left a book behind on the bench. It was a Koran, and although he only had time to flick through it, he was sufficiently interested to take it home (despite feeling somewhat guilty at stealing a religious text). The result was that 'I felt this was really for me. All I had known about Islam before was media stories about gun-totting extremists, but here was a faith full of wisdom and with application to virtually every aspect of ordinary life. I was enormously impressed and keen to find out more.' He admitted that had it been a copy of the Adi Granth left on the parkbench, he might now be a Sikh rather than a Muslim, but added that chance was a normal part of life and he had no quarrel with it. Marianne, a non-practising Methodist, could echo the same thoughts. She came to Judaism thanks to a friend who had brought a video over to watch together. After the film had finished, the friend had been flicking through the television channels on the remote control when she alighted on a programme on Jewish life in Britain. Marianne was fascinated and when the friend tried to move on to another channel, insisted that she switch back. 'Somehow it caught my imagination – the history – the rituals – the family life – the survival despite the terrible things that had happened to them. I wondered if other people were allowed to become Jews and went to the library to get some books on it. Eventually I summoned up the courage to go to the local synagogue, they said I could attend services if I wanted, and I got more and more involved.' In these and many similar cases, chance encounters were the trigger for conversion, and can be said either to have brought forward a transition that would possibly have occured at some time in the future, or to have initiated a change that might otherwise never have taken place.

In complete contrast are those who came to faith through the deliberate influence of others. This can range from friends who invited them to services or social meetings, to complete strangers who knocked on their door or accosted them in the street. For Harvey, it was the former: 'I belonged to a football team that used to play on Friday evenings – nothing serious but just a way of staying fit and letting go after a week in the office. One of my teammates was continually badgering me to come to a study group he went to. I kept fobbbing him off and said he'd have to wait till the end of the season. Sure enough, after the last game, he asked me again. I'd run out of excuses so I went along just to get him off my back. Actually, it was quite interesting and I started going regularly.' Kerry was brought to Jesus through a friend who invited her to a Billy Graham rally: 'I'd heard about him, and although I wasn't interested in churchgoing or anything, I wanted to see what all the fuss was about. Boy, did I find out! He was amazing. And when he asked people to come forward, well, there I was, trotting down the steps. My husband thought this might be a five-minute wonder, but what I received then has remained ever since and now I'm a churchwarden and pillar of the community!' For Sara, it was a knock on the door that changed her life. 'I couldn't believe my eyes. A Jehovah's Witness. I knew all about them going from house to house in search of converts, and now they had actually appeared in the flesh. It was quite spooky, a bit like being called up for jury service out of the blue. I pointed out that I was Jewish, but they said that was no problem and started telling me about the faith. As it happened I was on my way out to get some money before the bank closed, so when I explained that, one of the ladies gave me a magazine to read and said she'd call back next week. Despite being very suspicious, I did take a look at it and liked what I saw, although it left me with lots of questions. When she came back, she came inside and we discussed things for hours. After that I started going to meetings and eventually did home visits myself. I'm not so involved anymore, because the local branch dwindled and closed down, but I still think of myself as a Witness.'

Whilst the above examples can be categorized as people being keen to share their faith, there is a thin dividing line between encouraging others to join them and pressurizing them to do so. Perhaps one criterion for distinguishing them is the level of intensity in which it is done. Another is the extent to which the individual being targeted is allowed the option of saying 'no' or backing off once introduced to the faith. Gemma was a lapsed Jew who considered herself a 'citizen of the world' and open to truth wherever it was to be found. When she became involved with a group of people who were members of the Baghwan group, she found herself being pulled in to an alarming degree. 'Talking about it now makes it sound like some kind of CIA plot, with smiles up front to get you into the car and then the heavy brigade waiting to pounce once you were inside, but that's exactly what happened. They were really laid back and cool to begin with, saying I was welcome to join the commune for a few days and see what it was like. But the moment I was there, they took my clothes and gave me a robe to wear. They also gave me a new name – my spirit name, they said. Personal possessions were taken to an office – "for safe-keeping" – and suddenly it was hard to remember any of the old me. To be honest, I liked most of the lectures and meditation sessions, but just felt a bit uneasy about the fast pace of it all. When I asked to go out for a while to see to things at my flat, I was told that someone would do that for me. Part of me resented the lack of freedom I had, but it was also a great relief as the longer I stayed on the commune the more I felt nervous about facing the outside world on my own again.'

The physical imprisonment that occurs amongst some sects is paralleled by the emotional entrapment practised by others. Kent attended a Christian House Church study weekend at the invitation of a friend. 'It was amazing. People who I'd never met came up to me and said how special I was. Others told me that they were always there for me. By the time I'd left I must have told my whole life story to at least five separate people There was nothing sexual – in fact you couldn't get a more prim and proper lot – but I was made to feel king of the world and that they loved me very dearly. It was wonderful really and I couldn't wait till I could see them all again. As it turned out, I broke my leg a couple of weeks later, had to go up north to stay with my parents and lost touch with them all.' Much as Kent may have been valued in his own right, any newcomer to the group would have received exactly the same response so as to ensure that they felt overwhelmed by warmth and wanted to come back for more. This technique – 'love-bombing' as it is sometimes known – also has an insidious aspect, to make the individual feel that only in the group is he appreciated fully, and that outside the group lies an uncaring world which he should reject in favour of his 'new family'. It would be wrong to assume that such techniques are only successful when applied to those who are without purpose in life or who are emotionally inadequate. The techniques can also be very appealing to those who are full of goals but who cannot necessarily achieve them or feel frustrated by others. To be told one is wonderful is a statement that few people are reluctant to hear, while it can be hard to resist the soothing message that the struggles in the outside world do not count and what is important is to be found in the faith-group alone.

While many of the instances of conversion cited so far have involved a firm decision to proceed within a short space of time, not all happen in this way. There are also many cases of soul-searching, with those concerned bombarding themselves with a host of questions: Is it the right path to take? Are my motives all that they should be? Am I being influenced by others? What effect will it have? How will my family react? What if I feel I have made a mistake? Sometimes the process takes a considerable period. Carla took six years before she became a Muslim: 'I had been nervously edging towards Islam for ages. It seemed such a momentous decision that I had to take it very slowly. I read, I talked to Muslim friends, and slowly became sure that converting was the right way for me to go.' Pauline was held back more by worries of the reception that she would receive: 'I desperately wanted to go to the mosque but felt caught by the fear that they might reject me because I did not know enough and I would make a complete fool of myself. But, then, without going, I wasn't able to get to know what it was really like, so I was caught in a web of my own fears.' Like children going to a swimming pool who know that they want to splash around with all the others there, but are nervous of

actually stepping into the water, so too do many converts circle the
object of their desire for a long time before daring to knock at the
door to be let in. This is also the case if one not only has to overcome one's own hesitation but defy the disapproval of family.
Gerald knew his father would 'go beserk' if he forsook Judaism for
the church, so he attended services for many years without becoming baptized. 'It wasn't just to spare his feelings, but also to give
me time to work out whether converting would be worth the
furore it would unleash. At one point I thought I would wait till
after he died, but that seemed a bit macabre, while I wasn't sure I
wanted to wait that long.' The road to Damascus, a sudden
moment of unexpected exhilaration for some, can be a long and
hesitant trail for others.

3

Different Routes

Why choose one particular faith over another? It has already been seen that attraction to a faith can be due to a variety of personal circumstances: a chance encounter, the encouragement of a friend, easy access, or the perceived solution the faith holds to a problem with which the person has long wrestled (such as alcoholism). Alongside these subjective aspects are more objective criteria in the form of the distinctive traits of the faiths which result from the emphasis they place on certain beliefs or practices. The major religions are now examined in alphabetical order.

Buddhism

Buddhism is not by nature a missionary faith and conversion does not play a significant role in it. It is seen as a path that is beneficial for an individual, but truth and harmony can be derived from other sources too. Buddhist leaders are willing to teach the wisdom of their faith, but only to those who wish to receive it. It is neither limited to the select nor obligatory for all. The position is epitomized by the story concerning Upali, a millionaire who was a well-known and prominent supporter of Jaina Mahavira. Mahavira was the founder of the Jain religion and differed with the Buddha in his teachings on the subject of Kamma, and he dispatched his disciple to the Buddha in order that Upali might defeat the Buddha in argument with him on the subject. In fact, the opposite took place and Upali became convinced that the Buddha's point of view was right and he asked the Buddha to accept him as one of his lay followers. Instead of welcoming him, the Buddha urged him to withdraw his request and take time to reconsider the whole issue. This surprised and pleased Upali, who commented that other religious groups would usually acclaim the arrival of a famous convert by hoisting flags and beating drums. When he re-iterated his desire to follow the Buddha, the Buddha asked him to continue to respect and give alms to his former teachers, the Jains (*Majjhima Nikaya*, Vol. I, p. 372). In another episode, the Buddha warns lest anyone interpret his teachings as being designed to wean people away from their existing faith and increase the number of his own followers. He gives direct instructions that 'Let him who is your teacher be your teacher still . . . Let that which is your rule be your rule still . . . Let those points in your doctrines which are wrong and reckoned as wrong by those in your community, remain so still for you . . . Let those points in your doctrines which are good and reckoned to be good by those in your community, remain so still for you' (*Digha Nikaya*, Vol. II, p. 56). Moreover those who do convert to Buddhism are not obliged to deny their past religious allegiance. On the contrary, it is through penetrating deeply into Buddhism that they can understand their former faith better and derive insights from it. It would be wrong, though, to categorize Buddhism as totally tolerant of other faiths, for although it recognizes their validity, it is also adamant that the mainstay of most of them, belief in God, is incompatible with Buddhism as it directly contradicts the Buddhist vision of Reality. The actual method of conversion is the Going for Refuge, a declaration of acceptance performed in front of a monk. It involves repeating the three-fold formula, usually in Pali or Sanskrit:

Buddham saranam gacchami
Dhammam saranam gacchami
Sangham saranam gacchami

To the Buddha (enlightened teacher) for refuge I go
To the Dhamma (body of teachings) for refuge I go
To the Sangha (community of monks) for refuge I go

It could be said that, unlike the Western concept of conversion in which a person swaps one faith system for another, conversion to Buddhism involves undergoing a shift in one's very experience of the world. It is a 'turning about' at the deepest level of consciousness; not merely a new theology but entering the stream of enlightenment in a total re-orientation of one's life. Buddhism can seem very attractive to those who felt let down by Judaism, Christianity or Islam, and who are reluctant to try what they consider to be a rival version of the same product. Instead of claims and counter-claims as to who is the true prophet of God and who has the most authentic revelation, Buddhism directs the centre of attention away from a Deity and on to the individual. Instead of focusing on the demands of God, it concentrates on the needs of the soul, offering paths of awareness rather than ritual commands and articles of faith. That was certainly the attraction for Martin who felt that 'it put me in the driving seat of life. You realize that everything is an opportunity for you to grow and expand, and live as fulfilled a life as possible. And if things go wrong, you can't blame other people or the outside world. You have to bring changes within yourself and that will lead to changes in the outside environment. It's enormously liberating, although it can also be quite scary just how much your own energy can change.' Equally attractive is the use of meditation and chanting, unlike the heavy reliance on words in other faiths. Such techniques can often articulate inner emotions and aspirations far better than set liturgies.

There is a popular image of Buddhist converts as predominantly being hippies – a picture perhaps derived from memories of the veneration of the Beatles for the Maharishi in the 1960s and the generation that 'dropped out' and preferred 'flower-power' to conformity. However, the gap between this and the reality of the situation serves to indicate how much has changed in the perception and position of Buddhism. Certainly it was first taken up in significant numbers by those looking for an alternative lifestyle. Many made contact with Buddhism in their early twenties whilst on the trail to Katmandu in a bid to 'find themselves'. Many adopted Buddhism full-time, becoming monks or lay teachers. Today, Buddhism is no longer seen as counter-culture or eccentric. This is partly due to the passage of time, with it becoming more known about and acceptable; and partly because many of the hippy generation have grown older and become part of the establishment, bringing Buddhist concepts into everyday life with them. To this must be added the role of the current Dalai Lama, whose dignified defiance of China has made him a heroic figure. By upholding the hope of a free Tibet, yet maintaining Buddhist principles of pacifism and persuasion, he has become one of the few religious leaders of world renown. Those that convert to Buddhism are more often people in their thirties, who have already worked hard to obtain qualifications, and occupy demanding jobs and positions of responsibility. They are looking for meaning to life beyond the stress that high-powered work brings. Many – although certainly not all – come from middle-class backgrounds who have the luxury to be engaged in such intellectual quest, or who have the resources to attend retreats. The appeal is to both men and women alike. It is estimated that there are some 40,000 Buddhist converts in Britain today, in addition to 100,000 ethnic Buddhists. So great has been the spread of Buddhism, that the Western Buddhist Order has been established to cater for the needs of indigenous Britons who have adopted the faith, yet who lack the historical memories and geographical roots of ethnic Buddhists. They also bring different cultural assumptions to the faith, as well as their own personal agenda, with the result that a form of 'Western Buddhism' is beginning to emerge that reflects the background and needs of the converts. This has been assisted by the decentralized nature of Buddhism, with it long being acceptable for various different forms to exist in the East, while teachers who establish themselves in the West are given the freedom to adapt the context of their message and teach in ways that appeal to Western audiences.

One remarkable aspect has been the number of Jews who have converted to Buddhism. They have formed a disproportionately high percentage of the membership. In the United States, where figures are available, the Jewish population of the country is 2%, but they account for between 10% and 30% of Buddhist groups. They are even more prominently represented in the upper echelons of the movement, serving as spiritual leaders, organizers and teachers.[1] Their heavy presence – a feature in Britain too – has led to them being affectionately referred to as a 'Jew-Bu' or 'Ju-Bu'. Most Buddhists are not former Jews, but many former Jews are Buddhists. The appeal of Buddhism is due to a coalition of reasons: they, like others, are looking for spirituality, having failed to find it in the faith in which they were brought up. However, they are much less likely to turn to the church because of ingrained Jewish antipathy to doctrines of the Trinity and Virgin Birth that render it semi-pagan, as well as their consciousness of the church's long history of antisemitism. At the same time, concern for the survival of the State of Israel has usually resulted in long-held wariness of the Arab states and so made conversion to Islam a much less attractive option than for others. To those brought up on pure monotheism, the plethora of gods in Hinduism makes it seem virtually idolatrous. Buddhism has far fewer negative associations and many positive aspects. The stress on ethics in Buddhism echoes one of the main characteristics of their Jewish upbringing, but without the theological overlay or excessive ritualism. It means it contains elements that are simultaneously both novel and familiar. As Robert put it, 'Judaism told me to "love my neighbour as myself", but Buddhism showed me how to actually do it and gave me the techniques to put it into practice.' For many former Jews, therefore, Buddhism gives a spiritual dimension to the practical concerns they have, and they would endorse the view of Marc Lieberman that 'I have Jewish roots and Buddhist wings.'[2]

Christianity

Christianity has never been anything other than strongly missionary. Jesus' opening words to his disciples were 'Come after me and I will make you fishers of men' (Mark 1.17), while 'the great commission' was spelt out by him unmistakably: 'Therefore go and make disciples of all nations, baptize them . . .' (Matt. 28. 19). The world was divided into Christians and non-Christians, with unbelievers often being synonymous with sinners. Having faith in the Gospels was not seen as a beneficial option to be chosen by those who so desired, but a compulsory obligation for which the alternative was suffering eternal destruction (II Thess. 1.8) and being cast 'into lakes of fire and tormented forever' (Rev. 20.10). The duty to evangelize was not just incumbent on the leadership of the church, but on every member. To be a Christian was to be a witness to the divinity of Christ and to take upon oneself the duty of continuing the ministry he started (Eph. 4.11). For his part, Paul charged all who followed Jesus to 'preach the word, be urgent in season and out of season' (II Tim. 4.2).

In the past the church has been quick to take advantage of major world developments to promote its message as new areas of population became accessible: travelling wherever the Roman legions went after the conversion of Constantine, gaining more souls after the discovery of the New World, opening up Africa in the nineteenth century, and surging into Eastern Europe after the collapse of Communism. In the West today, nominally Christian but with large numbers indifferent, it still invests enormous efforts to convert the godless using a variety of methods: from local cream teas to national advertisement campaigns, from outreach programmes in areas of urban decay to ministries targeted at those at university, from open-air services on street corners to door-to-door distribution of leaflets. It has been estimated, however, that 80% of people become Christians not because of these attempts, but through existing contact with friends or acquaintances who are members of a church.[3]

In some quarters, the missionary zeal of the church is undiminished, with evangelical groups in Britain as keen as ever to convert those of other faiths or no faith. They are painfully conscious of the large pockets within the country that do not consider themselves Christian, while they are also concerned that even many churchgoers do not have a personal relationship with Jesus. Modern evangelists are urged to be passionate advocates for Christ:

> They need to be shepherds who know where their sheep are and can find them without driving them further from the fold. They need to be news announcers who get the message straight and

who make it known clearly to the nations without resorting to the sensationalism of Madison Avenue advertising techniques. They need to be lawyers who can argue their client's case with integrity, good humour and grit. They need to be midwives who can help nature and grace bring children of God to birth through the pain of repentance and the joy of faith. They need to be physicians of the soul who can link the lost and weary with the healing medicine of the kingdom. They need to be mothers who bring their little ones to be bathed in the waters of baptism, to be fed by word and creed at the breasts of mother church, to be nourished by the bread of life and wine of heaven, to be drenched in the gifts of the Spirit, and to be equipped with the oil of prayer and fasting.[4]

However, many Christian institutions have largely lost their sense of mission. On coming into office in 1991, the Archbishhop of Canterbury declined to give his patronage to Christian Mission to the Jews – the first incumbent to do this – on the grounds that it was no longer appropriate and conflicted with his extensive inter-faith work. It was a sign of the major theological change within the Church of England and showed that proselytization was no longer one of its top priorities. The same can be seen in the role of Christian chaplains on university campuses. Whereas once they had a strong missionary role and considered it part of their duties to convert non-Christians, now that would be regarded as highly offensive and beyond their remit, which is instead to minister to their own flock and work towards cordial relations with others. The Methodists have lost their revivalist impetus and are in sharp decline, while the Salvation Army achieves good works but makes few converts. This is partly because Christianity has been part of the fabric of society for so long that it is assumed that the job of evangelization has been completed. Energy is instead directed at promoting social action, supporting church schools, and maintaining Christian institutions. Reconverting the country would be a huge admission of defeat. In addition, a new ethos of inter-faith dialogue has challenged many of the assumptions of mission. If the validity of others' faith is accepted, then the need for mission is obviated. Indeed, it is a precondition of dialogue that neither party seek to convert the other.

Among the changes introduced by the Second Vatican Council in 1965 – and which quickly permeated into the British churches – was admission that 'Relations between Christians and Jews have been for the most part no more than a monologue. A true dialogue must be established . . . The condition for dialogue is respect for the other as he is, for his faith and religious convictions. All intent of proselytizing and conversion is excluded.'[5] When, in 1990, the Church of England's newly appointed Director of Evangelism, Bob Marshall, declared that one of his goals would be converting Muslims, the resultant furore in both Muslim and Christian circles forced him to drop the project and concentrate on lapsed Christians. There was also an outcry when the Council for Christians and Jews – whose Presidents include the Archbishop of Canterbury, the Cardinal Archbishop of Westminster, and the Moderator of the Free Churches' Council – issued a Code of Conduct in 1996 under which a person who engaged in proselytization could be expelled. There were objections by evangelical groups within the church who accused church leaders of conniving at a ban on missionary activity and denying the right to preach the gospel to Jews. The Council did not relent, though, nor did any of the Presidents withdraw their support, and the incident was a stark indication that they preferred inter-faith harmony to canvassing new souls. Such incidents have led to attempts to re-assess the mission of the church in the light of new trends in inter-faith dialogue. One answer is to speak not of evangelism, the conversion of individuals, but of evangelisation, permeating society at large with gospel values, such as through engaging in welfare work or promoting business ethics. Another response is to redefine traditional terms, seeing evangelism – sharing the Christian faith – as perfectly acceptable, whereas proselytism – manipulating people into the Christian faith – is totally improper.[6]

One of the most successful groups at conversion today are the House Churches. The story of Piers Du Pré is instructive as it represents an experience common to many others. He relates how two close friends came to stay at his house for the weekend. On

Sunday morning they suggested that he join them for worship at their fellowship meeting and, after twice turning down their offer, their persistence paid off and he eventually agreed to accompany them. The modern single-storey council building in which prayers were held was very different from the beautiful church to which he was accustomed. He was even more disconcerted to find that instead of hymn books or prayer books, there were only printed sheets with songs, while the music came not from an organ but from someone playing the guitar. At the end of the service he was ready to leave immediately.

But you can never escape unnoticed. Bob Woollard, the pastor of the fellowship, was by the door and introduced himself. When I told him who I was he said, 'Oh yes, we've been praying for you for months.'

My pride rose within me. How dare anyone even think I needed prayer?

'How nice of you. Thank you,' I replied through gritted teeth. After a few more moments of conversation he just looked at me and said, 'Why don't we pray together, right now?'

And then it happened. I burst into tears. A chair was found for me but I couldn't stop crying. A number of people were saying 'Hallelujah' and 'Praise the Lord'. Bob asked me if I would like to give my life to Jesus. I said, 'Yes.'

That night, on the way home in the car, I suddenly realized that I was praying out loud, something I had never done before. The moment we returned to Birch House, I found Mum's Bible. I began reading the New Testament. I couldn't put it down. For the first time I could clearly understand what I was reading. What I previously knew as religion was fast becoming a vibrant relationship with God through His Son, Jesus. I hardly slept that night.

Later when he told his mother what had taken place, she said:

'You seem to have such a deep relationship with Jesus. You seem to have an assuredness. I don't.' She faltered and her lovely, big hazel eyes began to fill with tears. 'In fact, I don't think I have ever given my life to Him in the way you have. I need to. Will you pray for me?'

. . . I knelt with her and encouraged her to tell Father God how she felt. I led her in a prayer of commitment.[7]

The account illustrates the assertion earlier that most conversions occur through the contact of a friend who is already a Christian, while it also highlights the fact that many of those converted are already officially members of the church, but who lacked a deep personal experience. Both aspects applied also to Piers' mother. Much less common – although perhaps more associated with Christianity – is direct revelation from Jesus, as epitomized by Hugh Montefiore's experience:

At the age of 16, sitting in my study one afternoon, and indulging in an adolescent muse, I saw clearly a figure in white (although the figure was and is still clear in my memory, I doubt if it would have shown up on a photograph). Although I had never even read the New Testament, or attended a Christian service of worship, I knew immediately that the figure was Jesus, and I heard the words 'Follow me' . . . Many explanations of such visions of Jesus have been attempted, but, so far as I am concerned, it was an incursion of the Transcendent into my life . . . My conversion was as simple and as momentous as that . . . In the morning I was a Jew, and by the evening I was a Christian.[8]

For many converts there are specific appeals held by Christianity, especially its promise of the forgiveness of sin and its guarantee of a place in the world to come. These are powerful attractions, particularly for those who feel burdened by a lifestyle that they feel is sinful or worthless. The Muslim Yusuf 'was walking by a church noticeboard which had a poster saying "Jesus Died For Your Sins" and I just burst into tears. I went in, bowed before the altar, and told God I would be His servant.' Coming from an entirely different tradition, Indarjit explained that in his eyes

Sikhism was a religion full of rules and Christianity a religion full of God. 'As a Sikh I was taught that I should do good, and the more good I did the better. But one can never achieve everything one should, and when I came into contact with Christianity I realized what was missing: that you needed to have God's grace and without that it was all in vain.'

The success of the various efforts at mission is shown in the fact that an estimated 78,000 people joined the church in 1992 – which amounts to 200 new Christians every day. Moreover, as can be seen in the chart below, by far the largest increase was registered by the Pentecostal churches. This is due not only to their energy, but also to their clear vision, strategy of church planting and constant emphasis on evangelism:[9]

Denomination	Number joining	Percentage increase
Anglican	33,000	1.8%
Pentecostal	12,000	7.1%
Catholic	8,500	0.4%
Independent	8,300	2.3%
Baptist	6,000	2.6%
Presbyterian	5,800	0.5%
All others	4,400	0.5%
Total	78,000	1.2%

Hindusim

There is some debate as to whether Hinduism can be described as a missionary faith or not. On one level, the answer is an emphatic 'no', as it does not seek to persuade people to adopt a particular belief, nor worship the plethora of gods that it reveres. Unlike the monotheist faiths which zealously insist that the true path is only through their particular version of the deity, Hinduism is far too aware of the different manifestations of the divine spirit to object to systems of worship that do not correspond to its own. Yet at the same time, it holds that conduct is far more important than creed and is keen to spread its notion of upright living to those who differ from it This primarily applied to converting pagan tribes in previous eras, whereas members of mainstream faiths today are regarded as morally acceptable. There is therefore no religious objection in principle if a Hindu intermarries with a Jew or Sikh, even though parents may worry about cultural differences. Nevertheless, the Hindu way of life is still on offer to those who so desire. The number of those in Britain who become Hindu is small, estimated at around a hundred a year. Most of them do so not via local Hindu communities, which are largely concerned with maintaining the religious identity of existing adherents. Instead, the growth is primarily through the Hare Krishna movement, which has specialized in taking the message of Krishna consciousness to the public at large, most famously through its street processions with drums and chants. Gaura felt that it provided him with 'a path towards enlightenment. But whereas lots of faiths try to do that, Hinduism acknowledges your weaknesses and works with them and through your own endeavours.' Roopa was much more ecstatic: 'It's a way of finding eternity. That's pretty wonderful isn't it, and nothing else counts.' Whilst those who choose to become Hindus are welcomed, the community's greater concern is with those of its own members who it feels are being enticed away. This applies especially to unmarried Hindu girls who become pregnant and are rejected by their family, or young Hindu males who run away from home. In both cases, it is alleged, Muslim missionary groups target such individuals and urge them to turn to Islam and find a new home within it. Yet this is not so much a religious war of supremacy, but a sociological pattern whereby those who fall foul of tightly-knit ethnic communities find that they have lost both their family circle and religious home at the same time, and need to seek refuge elsewhere. On another level, Islam can also be attractive to Hindus who object to or suffer from the caste sytem. Although such divisions have lost much of their force in the Hindu community in Britain, they can still operate in some circles, especially in expectations of marriage. Whilst Judaism and Christianity could also offer a home to Hindus seeking a faith without a caste system, those from ethnic backgrounds can find it easier to assimilate into the Islamic community, which is multi-ethnic and far better at integrating those from a different racial and cultural milieu.

Islam

If one faith can be singled out as attracting the highest number of converts in Britain, it is Islam. This is doubly surprising. First, because Britain, for so long dominated by the church and where conversion was largely a matter of a person switching from one Christian denomination to another, is finding that another faith is making inroads in its midst. Secondly, because Islam has been accustomed for centuries to existing in countries where it was the dominant, if not exclusive faith, and therefore had lost much of its missionary zeal. Now, however, it is finding itself in the unusual position of being both a minority faith and being attractive to an entirely new range of population. Da'wa – the call to others to join Islam – has always been a strong component of the faith, and the early centuries were spent in both territorial conquest and religious conversion. The call is rooted in the Koran and the injunction to 'Invite all to the way of your Lord with wisdom and beautiful preaching' (16:125). The verse declaring that 'It is your duty to enjoin good and forbid evil because you believe in Allah' (3:104) was taken to mean spreading the message of Islam to non-Muslims. Early attempts at such a task in Britain date back to the 1880s and the Islamic Missionary Society established in Liverpool by William Quillam, an English lawyer who had come across Islam during travels in Arabia and tried to import it back to Britain. Despite isolated successes, the real growth in conversions has only come in the last decades of the twentieth century once a substantial Muslim immigration had taken place in the post-war years and had begun to make its presence felt in society at large. Estimates of the number of converts vary, especially in the absence of central records, but a general consensus is that there are up to 10,000 Muslim converts in Britain.[10]

Despite both the command to proselytize and the high numbers that have converted, there has been little organized attempt to conduct an Islamic missionary campaign. This is due to a number of factors: lack of co-ordination between the disparate Muslim groups scattered across Britain; such groups are often more concerned with internal rivalries than reaching out to society at large; a shortage of articulate English-speakers capable of presenting Islam favourably to the wider public; a legacy of antipathy to the imperialist West means that attitudes amongst Muslims are not conducive to bridge-building; an emphasis on preserving the faith by maintaining cultural and linguistic identity makes it hard to adopt Islam without adopting ethnic characteristics too; the fact that many Muslims are coloured, immigrant or 'ex-colonials' and therefore have a sense of deference to the white indigenous population. In addition, much of the preaching efforts of Muslim religious leaders is targeted at their own community in an effort to keep existing believers within the fold and resist the temptations of secular society. This is especially aimed the younger and British-educated generation, who are much more vulnerable to the lure of the Western world.

In the absence of overt missionary activity, most of those that have come to Islam have largely converted of their own accord. One study charted their route as follows:

Conversation with Muslim friends	37%
Reading Islamic literature	23%
Travelling to Muslim countries	23%
Marriage to a Muslim	14%
Influence of family members	3%[11]

For many of them the attraction of Islam is that, in Gavin's words 'it offers certainty and stability and continuity in a world of constantly moving goalposts'. It appeals particularly to those who find society a moral whirlpool and are looking for a clear set of standards to which to anchor themselves. Its opposition to alcohol, drugs and sexual promiscuity can make it seem far superior to the church in whose backyard such problems have flourished and which seems unable to control such trends. This puritan quality certainly appealed to Catherine who would often drink considerable amounts of alcohol. She was conscious of it being a problem, but felt she lacked any incentive to change. On one occasion she had had several drinks before going to church for Mass and her Muslim boyfriend had said, 'How can you pray when you're intoxicated?' His question shocked her profoundly and led to a decision to investigate Islam, to which she later converted. For others, too, the desire to bring about a change in their personal habits can lead to adopting a new faith which offers an external support for that attempt. Unlike Christianity, Islam also offers a comprehensive framework of public and personal rituals – prayers five times a day, food laws, regulations about personal hygiene – that those from Christian backgrounds find appealing. As Reza put it: 'As a Christian I didn't have to *do* anything. Just go to church once a week and be good inbetween. Islam makes demands on me every day. It intertwines the spiritual with the mundane: eating, washing, praying. It forces me to be constantly aware of my relationship with Allah and my role in society. It's enormously powerful having that discipline and back-up.'

It could be argued that a similar combination of rituals and morals, and with an even longer tradition, can be found in Judaism. It also has the advantage of being even more familiar to those from Christian backgrounds and without the same cultural leap to being part of a largely immigrant community. Despite this, Islam is still more attractive, for a number of reasons: it is much more of a world-wide religion and is not seen as a clique; nor does it have the association of being a faith with victims, with centuries of antisemitism culminating in the Holocaust; nor is it associated with the failure of the Judaeo-Christian heritage to prevent the emergence of a decadent society; it is much more open to converts than Judaism, both in principle and in ease of actual conversion; it is also seen as new and fresh and vibrant. Islam has also been able to appeal to several different constituencies in Britain at once. For women it is seen as highly protective of their femininity, giving them a defined role as homemaker and mother, yet also with the ability to have an active job and a position of responsibility, providing these duties are fulfilled. Thus they can devote themselves to the home as an honoured and honourable profession, but also pursue a career if they so wish. The veil is seen not as a means of excluding them from society but of avoiding sexual competition, and gives them the freedom 'to be myself and not have to preen for the sake of others or be an object of ogling by people I don't even know,' said Evelyn.

At the same time, Islam appears to many men as being a more 'masculine religion' compared to 'wimpish' Christianity. For them, whereas the latter concentrates on love and grace, the former preaches discipline and pride. The underlying message of worshipping God and living ethically may be the same, but the wrapping in which it comes can seem very different. The male-dominated leadership of mosques (and also of Islamic states) serves to emphasize this image, while the decision in 1992 to ordain female priests in the Church of England has reinforced that divide. As Gavin explained: 'There's no doubt that Islam has a "macho" quality about it. It's a tough religion, with definite expectations and hard demands. Of course we believe in mercy and forgiveness, but the accent is on duty and living up to expectations.' This aspect may be particularly appealing to males who feel disenfranchised in society at large, where women's involvement in almost all areas of life has made deep inroads into the previous ascendancy of males. For some, it has restored old certainties about roles and 'where people stand'. The ability of Islam to be attractive to both males and females has been paralleled by its popularity across the racial divide. Most English-born converts are white, but it has spread amongst the black population too. Whilst the former tend to relate most to its religious message, for the latter it also holds political significance. Whereas Christianity is associated with the imperialism of the past and the racism still evident in parts of Britain today, Islam is seen as valuing every individual irrespective of race or colour. Whilst black churches may be very successful, their separation from mainstream churches speaks volumes about the welcome they have received by the Christian community. Islam is perceived as genuinely colour-blind. The unexpected experience of the American black activist, Malcom X, whilst in Mecca represents the feelings of many ordinary blacks in Britain:

You may be shocked by these words coming from me. But on this pilgrimage, what I have seen, and experienced, has forced me to re-arrange much of my thought patterns previously held, and to toss aside some of my previous conclusions . . . Never have I witnessed such sincere hospitality and such over-whelming spirit of true brotherhood as is practised by peoples of all colours and races here . . . For the past week, I have been utterly speechless and spell-bound by the graciousness I see all around me by people of all colours . . . America needs to under-stand Islam, because this is one religion that erases from its society the race problem . . . During the past eleven days here in the Muslim world, I have eaten from the same plate, drunk from the same glass, and slept in the same bed (or in the same rug) – whilst praying to the same God – with fellow Muslims, whose eyes were the bluest of the blue, whose hair was the blondest of the blond, and whose skin was the whitest of the white. And in the words and in the actions and in the deeds of the 'white' Muslims, I felt the same sincerity that I felt among the black African Muslims of Nigeria, Sudan and Ghana.[12]

Despite being a religion that appeals to many because of its concern with everyday realities, Islam has also attracted those seeking a more mystical approach to life and who have come to it through Sufism, which seeks to offer direct experience of God and deeper insights into the meaning of existence. Both Judaism and Christianity have mystical traditions, but they are often hidden from view and available only on request. Moreover, both faiths are slightly wary of those pursuing a mystical path lest it lead to heresy or personal tragedy. An ancient rabbinic story, for instance, tells how four friends started studying mysticism, the result of which was that one went mad, one committed suicide, one lost his faith and only one emerged unscathed. Jewish tradition has long insisted, therefore, that only those who are over forty years old may study mysticism. The assumption was that this limited mysticism to those who were married, had children and were used to earning a livelihood. The object was to ensure that mysticism was made accessible only to people who were thoroughly rooted in

everyday realities and were less likely to be led astray by its powerful effects. However, it is often those in their twenties who are
most keen to explore such avenues and they can be frustrated by
the restrictions. Sufism, by contrast, welcomes those engaged in a
quest for hidden truths whatever their age or status, and is happy
to share its wells of wisdom.

The path undertaken by Gai Eaton typifies that of many other
searchers:

> I began to read books on mysticism . . . The reason for this
> should be obvious. If you are unwilling to accept anything on
> hearsay, and quite unable to believe in God simply because you
> are told that you should, then personal experience and spiritual
> insight are the decisive factors . . . The more I read the more
> certain I was that I at last had some understanding of the nature
> of things and had glimpsed, if only in thought and imagination,
> the ultimate Reality beside which all else was little more than a
> dream.[13]

Eaton's mystical leanings led him to find fulfilment in Islam and
become one of its leading exponents. The success of Islam in
recent years in attracting so many new adherents has in turn led to
a new self-confidence in a religious leadership previously diffident
about promoting the faith outside the existing community. This
has been compounded by the emergence of a new generation of
Muslim leaders who are British-born and who lack the wariness of
the immigrant generation who felt obliged not to create 'too much
of a stir'. The new generation is keen to be proactive in raising the
profile of Islam as befits its size in Britain today. They have also
learnt to imitate Christian missionary techniques, and are now
printing literature in English, arranging public lectures at
mosques, holding seminars on university campuses, and produc-
ing videos and cassettes about the faith. Less defensive and more
assertive, Islam is growing rapidly in Britain today.

Judaism

Judaism, too, is making gains, although on a much lesser scale and more because of other people's interest in it than any efforts of its own. In its original biblical form, Judaism was an avowedly missionary faith, forcibly converting tribes it conquered and with an entire book taking as its heroine the Moabite Ruth, whose declaration 'Your people shall be my people, and your God my God' (Ruth 1.16) became the rallying cry of subsequent converts. Moreover, there could be no higher signal of the honour due to a convert than the fact that David was her direct descendant and that from her stemmed both the most successful king and the messianic line. It was little wonder that Matthew complained that the Pharisees were so imbued with a missionary spirit that they would 'traverse sea and land to make a single proselyte' (Matt. 23.15). However, external circumstances rather than theological developments caused a major revision to this policy. With the conversion of Emperor Constantine to Christianity around 313, the church changed overnight from a minority sect to the official religion of the most powerful empire in the world. It also led to a series of edicts protecting the church, which included punishing those who converted a Christian to Judaism. Missionary activity became dangerous not only for the individuals concerned, but also for the Jewish community at large resulting in fines and arrests. The position was similar in Islamic countries, for although the Jews did not experience the same persecution that they suffered in Christian lands, converting a Muslim was banned under pain of death. The effect of this enforced brake on missionary activity led a change of attitude within the Jewish community, seeing it initially as unsafe and then as undesirable and ultimately as un-Jewish. It was also underpinned by the view that Christianity and Islam were forms of monotheism, and so, unlike the pagans in biblical times, did not need to be converted. According to rabbinic interpretation, 'the righteous of all nations have a place in the world to come', and while Judaism was seen as a faith chosen by God to reveal his existence to the world, there was no concept that only Jews were assured of divine favour.

By the time British Jewry was readmitted to England in 1656 after being expelled 400 years earlier, it was so nervous of public criticism if anyone converted that it became routine to refuse all applicants, and any that insisted were sent abroad to convert so that at least it took place on foreign soil. An additional justification for rejecting candidates was that unless a convert observed Jewish law 100%, it was considered better that they remained non-Jewish. This negative legacy has remained a hallmark of the British rabbinate, with a new objection to conversion being that it is a backdoor to intermarriage, and that a less rigorous stance will result in Jews marrying non-Jews who have officially converted but in reality are indiferent to the faith. Thus the former Orthodox Chief Rabbi, Immanuel Jakobovits, declared that during his term of office in the 1970s and 1980s, he was faced with 400–500 applicants for conversion a year, but only accepted 1% of them.[14] The figure, which he quotes with approval, would horrify many a Christian leader, who would be more likely to have welcomed the other 99% too. It is only in the Reform and Liberal movements that a more positive approach is slowly emerging, and whilst there has been no return to actively seeking converts, those who enquire of their own accord are often accepted. Even they, however, have to go through a lengthy and demanding course, usually involving a programme of study for a minimum of a year and requiring circumcision for males. It is based on the view that a conversion is not just a matter of changing beliefs, but joining a people and adopting a culture. Like learning to drive a car, a convert to Judaism has to acquire a range of new skills never previously encountered. Candidates then have to appear before a *Beth Din* – an examining board of three rabbis – so as to justify their request for acceptance and prove both their knowledge and sincerity. As Brian noted, 'To say the process is off-putting is the understatement of the year. First, you are turned away, then when you persist you are told to read some books, then when you come back you are grudgingly let on to a course, then after a long study period, you are sent off for an exam – it's one series of hurdles after another and plenty of chances for failing or just dropping out. The only good thing is that when you finally pass, then you really feel that you achieved something worth having.'

Despite the obstacles put in the way of converts, there are still those who find Judaism attractive, particularly those brought up in the Christian tradition who find that although they believe in God, they cannot accept other parts of Christian theology. As Charles explained: 'I faced a real problem. Christianity meant a lot to me, but I could not accept doctrines such as the Virgin Birth or the Incarnation. I admired the teachings of Jesus enormously, but found worshipping him hard. I suppose I wanted God without Jesus. That's exactly what Judaism offered – the faith and ethics free of all the doctrinal overlay.' For others, again from a Christian background, it is the sense of roots that appeals to them. Anne had often been told at Methodist Sunday school how the church stemmed from Judaism and 'I developed a yearning to be part of the ancient trunk and not just perching on one of the branches. So twenty years later I plucked up the courage to walk into a synagogue, and although I suppose it could have been a disastrous experience, as it happens I found it was exactly what I had hoped for, and I have stayed ever since.' However, the vast majority of converts to Judaism come not as a result of a religious search, but thanks to a relationship with someone Jewish, with the vast majority of converts involved in an impending or existing marriage to a Jew. Within this figure, the motives can vary greatly: for some conversion is a way of mollifying prospective parents-in-law who object to their son/daughter 'marrying out'; for others it is a way of achieving a 'white wedding' in a synagogue rather than settle for a registry office one; for others it is to unify the family unit so that they are both 'heading in the same direction' and can provide a stable religious background for children; for others it was because, having come into contact with Judaism by chance through a partner, they then found that it appealed to them and wished to adopt it for themselves without any pressure being brought upon them.

The fact that marriage is the main trigger to conversion to Judaism is not surprising in view of the absence of a strong missionary impulse over the better part of the last two millennia.

The historical background makes it almost inevitable that it is more a matter of non-Jews coming to Judaism than Judaism reaching out to them. Moreover, it is a paradox that many rabbis seem to prefer a conversion because of marriage to one motivated purely by religious factors. As Rabbi Joseph explained: 'Someone who marries into a Jewish family automatically has a support group, with a spouse and in-laws who can involve him/her in Jewish home life and festivals. It's a major advantage and helps you integrate within the community. A person who comes to Judaism alone has to start totally from scratch and has no guidance. Remember, it is very much a home religion and a family faith – the domestic rituals and celebrations are designed to be shared, and it can be very lonely lighting candles by yourself and singing alone. I am always much more wary of accepting a convert who comes out of faith than one who comes with a Jewish partner in hand. The former may be more sincere, but the latter has much greater chance of feeling at home within Judaism.'

Sikhism, Zoroastrianism, the Bahai faith

The Sikh faith has double the adherents in Britain than Judaism but attracts far fewer converts than the estimated 350 per annum who become Jewish. This is partly because it is still seen as an 'immigrant religion', exclusive to those from the Indian sub-continent, while it lacks the biblical background that Judaism offers or the confident self-proclamation of Islam. The conversions that do take place are often as the result of marriage with those from other immigrant comunities. In some cases it is for positive reasons, as in the case of Gitta: 'He didn't encourage me to become a Sikh. But when you marry a person, you marry the family. I wanted to fit in, and to bring our children up as Sikhs. My little boy wears a turban; my daughter will grow her hair.' In other instances, it is for more negative reasons, especially where the convert comes from another minority faith in which there are ethnic or religious tensions with Sikhs. When Janhavi became engaged to a Sikh, her Hindu parents were livid, accused her of betraying them and disowned her. 'I was suddenly cut off from my family, while I felt it was impossible to carry on going to the temple under those circumstances. I had not intended becoming a Sikh, but having my religion pulled away from me left me in a void. My future husband's family were very welcoming, and it made sense to join his faith too.' As Sikhs become more integrated into British life, knowledge of their faith will increase and inter-marriage will rise, and conversion to the faith might also become more commonplace.

The same cannot be said for Zoroastrianism, for it is impossible to become Zoroastrian by conversion and one has to be born into the faith. In complete contrast is the Bahai faith, which, despite having its roots in mid-nineteenth century Iran, has managed to appeal far beyond any ethnic or geographical limitations and in Britain primarily consists of converts to the faith. Many are attracted by its willingness to accept religious truths from many different sources – including Jesus, Muhammad, Zoroaster and Buddha. The fact that it is also free of sacraments and clergy appeals to those who find other faiths burdened down with religous hierachies or ceremonies that tax their credulity. As Karina explained: 'After being brought up a high church Anglican and being put off by all its top-heavy structures and the supposed mystery of the eucharist, and then dabbling in Judaism and getting engulfed in its rituals, I found the Bahai faith to be a breath of fresh air. Ethical living is the main thrust, and although we gather together for special events and feast days, the emphasis is on how you live your life rather than prayer or ceremonies. Obviously the other faiths belive in ethics too, but somehow it feels that they can sometimes get lost in all the ritual paraphernalia that surrounds them.'

Internal conversions

Conversion need not always be to a different faith; it can also be within a faith. In some cases, it can affect someone who only had a nominal attachment to the religion in which they were brought up, but then came to see it afresh and take it much more seriously than before. In Britain, this applies to the Church of England in particular. As Mark, a vicar, laments: 'Being the established church means that the majority assume they belong to it without having either a firm belief or adequate knowledge. When people tell you they are "lapsed C of E" they imagine they still have a Christian connection, but frankly they don't, and they would be far better off calling themselves secularists or atheists.' William Abraham agrees, although he extends the lack of Christian commitment even to those who do attend services, and comments that 'One of the truly astonishing features of modern church life is that so many church members need to be evangelized'.[15] The launch of the Decade of Evangelism by the Archbishop of Canterbury was public confirmation by the ecclesiastical leadership of this need for internal mission. The result has been a proliferation of attempts to re-Christianize Britain: evangelical Alpha Courses have mush-roomed in local churches throughout the country, offering a chance to study Christian teachings and reflect on personal spirituality. In 1993 there were ten courses and by 1996 they had grown to 4,000. At the same time, American-style preachers hold mass rallies in major centres to whip up enthusiasm and re-invigorate faith. Meanwhile, entertainment-crusaders try to capture the attention of those interested in other matters and draw them to the church, such as Christian martial arts experts who break hard objects and tear up telephone directories, and then preach a message of 'muscular Christianity'.

This form of mission certainly appealed to Maria who had been taken to see 'The Power Team' perform in Hackney, East London, by her boyfriend as part of an ordinary date. 'He had heard that one of the men specialized in smashing concrete walls with his bare hands, and thought it would make a good evening out together. He never told me it was a Christian group, otherwise I'd never have gone, as I'd had enough of Jesus by the time I was ten. The evening was amazing. I wasn't interested in the tough-guy stuff, but was really impressed by how the performer then spoke about how he had experimented with drugs and alcohol, and then decided to give his life to Christ. That was real strength. When he asked people who wanted to do likewise to come forward, I found myself on stage! My boyfriend was amazed, in fact pretty cross, and we didn't see each other again. It didn't worry me, as I reckoned I'd found much more than I'd lost.' Maria's particular route back to Christianity may have been unusual, but she represents a large group of people who were baptized at birth but whose contact with the church either ended immediately afterwards or tapered off after a few years whilst they were still in childhood. Their Christian education, therefore, largely consists of memories of children's stories and totally lacks any theological awareness or personal spirituality. Christian in name, but in reality lacking both faith and knowledge, they hover on the borderline of Christianity and secularism, and need to be re-evangelized if the church is to claim their affiliation. The 'born-again Christian' is primarily a phenomenon of the latter half of the twentieth century and carries a double-edged significance, reflecting both the success of the church in regaining nominal adherents and its failure in letting such a large number of its flock lapse in the first place, many of whom never return. Indeed, in reaction to the massive drop-out rate, some ministers are calling for a major paradigm shift: from seeing the church as being for the churched to being as much for the unchurched, a situation that previous generations would not have thought worth considering.[16]

Whilst some previously lapsed Christians rediscover their faith, there are also committed Christians who change their denominational affiliation and there is a constant flow of individuals between the different groupings within the church. Moreover, some types of denominations lose their members at a faster rate than others do. A study of membership transfers shows that 84% of Anglicans who change churches do so within the same denomination, and only 16% go to churches of a different ilk; however, only 27% of Pentecostals who change churches do so within the same denomination (such as Assemblies of God or Elim or Apostolic Church), and 73% go to churches of a different type. This is partly because there are more Anglican churches in Britain from which to choose, but it also reflects the fact that not everyone finds the high intensity levels of the Pentecostals sustainable for a long period of time.[17] As Jasmine explained, 'I didn't have much of a religious upbringing, so when some friends persuaded me to come to the

Assembly of God church they worshipped at, I wasn't sure what to expect. But I was absolutely bowled over by what I experienced: the fervour, the warmth, the deep prayer, the handclapping, even dancing in the aisles. I started attending regularly, and in fact I carried on going even after those two stopped. I can't put my finger on what made me give up . . . but after a while it just became too much of an emotional commitment – especially with the prayer groups and Bible study midweek you were expected to go to. Maybe I'd just had what I needed and was ready to move on. I now go on a more occasional basis to the local church – it's C of E – which isn't nearly as exciting, but where I can pop in one week, disappear, and then come back two weeks later without feeling I've let the side down or consorted with Satan inbetween.'

The transfer of individuals between different churches operates in all directions, but two inter-denominational routes are particularly common. One, already referred to briefly in a previous chapter, is members of the Church of England who become Catholic. This is associated especially with the decision of the Anglican Synod in 1992 to accept women into the priesthood. For some the decision came as a fatal blow. The vicar of All Saints, Notting Hill, in London, Prebendary John Brownsell, gave a sermon to his congregation on the Sunday following the vote and told them 'last Wednesday evening at five o'clock, the Church of England died'. He went on to explain why he was leaving the Church of England and effectively summed up the position of those who resigned as a result of the issue: 'What are the options open to us? They are like the options open to everyone who suffers a bereavement. It is no option to pretend that it doesn't make any difference, that life will go on the same. We cannot sit in the room with the corpse propped up in the chair opposite the fire and pretend that it's not dead. We cannot live in our own home, which is devastated and ruined . . . we cannot go on as if nothing had changed. We must, all of us, make a new life'.[18] Some 422 full-time clergy left the Church of England, of whom 240 became Roman Catholic and, at the time of writing, over half have been ordained as Catholic priests.

A far larger number of parishoners joined them, some following their minister as a group into the Catholic fold, others doing so on an individual basis because they no longer felt in communion with the church they had hitherto attended. One lay member, Elizabeth Mills, described both the hurt and the new relationship to which it led: it was like being 'given the boot by someone you have loved for years . . . and then you suddenly realize that the boy next door has always looked rather attractive.' However, although the women priests vote led to a mass transference of membership, it should not be allowed to disguise the continuous trickle of Church of England converts to Rome. Indeed, this was high on the agenda of the Catholic hierachy itself, as Cardinal Basil Hume admitted three months after Synod's vote 'This could be a big moment of grace, it could be the conversion of England for which we prayed all these years.'[19] For many of them, the attraction was that in an age where individual freedom was the rampant dogma, the Catholic Church dared to set limitations. For Jack, 'Yes, of course, I like doing my own thing, but there comes a point where you need standards and to be told "this is definitely right and that is definitely wrong". I wasn't getting that in the Church of England any more. Anything and everything seemed to be okay. Not that I always reach those standards, but you need to know what to aim at and what to measure yourself by.' It is a theme echoed by many others who felt that the established church had confused accommodating sinners and accommodating sin itself. The strong moral tone offered by the Catholic Church appeals to those seeking 'good old-fashioned religion which leaves you in no doubt as to what you should and shouldn't be doing'. In addition, many have been impressed by two of the leading Catholic figures in the 1990s: Pope John Paul II epitomized moral firmness, while Cardinal Hume showed the compassionate face of the church. The lack of an Anglican figure who carried such stature or influence has meant that, for many, Christian leadership has emanated from the Catholics and they have quietly decided to join them.

Another inter-denominational trend is members of the Church of England who become Orthodox. Both the Greek and the Russian Orthodox churches in Britain were formed by members of the faith who had come here as immigrants and wished to pray in

the style to which they were accustomed. There was no proselytizing campaign, while the Greek and Slavonic prayers meant that
there was a built-in barrier to most English-speakers who walked
into church out of sheer curiosity. However, despite these factors,
a growing number of Anglicans have been attracted to Orthodoxy.
The point of contact was often chance or through friends, but
having been introduced to the services, they were captivated by
what they experienced. For Graham, it was 'the sheer beauty of
the music – something that is enormously important to me as a
means of religious expression. I have been a member of the local
church choir – C of E – for as long as I can remember, but when I
heard the Greek Orthodox service, my soul soared in a way it had
never before.' Aileen – also a regular churchgoer prior to her
change – found her first Greek Orthodox service equally over-
whelming: 'I was bowled over by the language, the drama. I
suppose it had to do with the beautiful liturgy, the candles, the
incense, but prayer seemed easier.' Unlike those who convert to
Catholicism for intellectual reasons, those turning to Orthodoxy
seem to do so more for emotional reasons and because of the
service itself. Richard, a convert to the Russian Orthodox Church,
quoted the description given in *The Russian Chronicle* by two men
on their first visit to a service as exactly matching his reaction: 'We
did not know whether we were in heaven or on earth. We cannot
describe it to you; of this only are we sure, that God dwells there
among men. For we cannot forget that beauty.' For Richard and
others, it is the sense of mystery that is so appealing, and it empha-
sizes the fact that while churches are rightly engaged in social
action and many other good causes, it is the ability to achieve a
sense of God that attracts adherents, while the lack of it deprives
the church of a key factor when competing with other activities for
people's leisure time involvement.

Other faiths are also witnessing internal changes. In Judaism,
the Progressive movements, which encapsulate Reform and
Liberal synagogues, have been growing as an increasing number of
previously Orthodox Jews switch allegiance to them. Unlike
denominational transfers in Christianity, the Jewish ones are
largely motivated by attitudes towards observances. Thus Harry

typifies many when he claims: 'For me, Judaism has to move with the times. What was right for previous generations living in the Middle Ages is not right for us. So it seems nonsense that you are not allowed to drive to synagogue on the Sabbath, because it counts as "working" and breaks the Ten Commandments. The result is that 95% of Jews do drive but then park the car round the corner so that the rabbi won't see you. I used to do that myself, until one day I thought "This is ridiculous – and not only is it totally unnecessary, but what sort of example does it set the children – breaking the law and then going to pray." So we joined the Reform instead, where driving is not an issue and where they're just pleased that you come in the first place.' As part of the attempt to marry the best of the traditions of the past with the realities of modernity, the Progressives have also transformed the role of women, both in ending the separate seating of the sexes, and in permitting women to particpate actively in the services. This, in itself, has been a major attraction, either because husbands prefer to go to a synagogue where they can sit with their wife and daughter, or for the women themselves, as Ruth emphatically explains: 'For years I sat upstairs in the women's gallery, looking down at the men praying below and felt totally divorced from the service. As a religious turn-off, it was great. Now I can sit in the main body of the synagogue, and I feel really involved. It's also wonderful to have the opportunity to be called up to open the Ark or read from the Scroll. I feel that for a long time I was a second-class citizen, whereas now I am as much a Jew as anyone else and have the same rights. And just as important, my daughter is given the same Jewish education as the boys – something I did not get growing up in an Orthodox synagogue, because "girls don't need to study Judaism, just know how to keep a kosher home". With attitudes like that, frankly, it was a miracle that I kept on going to synagogue for as long as I did.'

Nevertheless, it is not all one-way traffic, for there are also Jews from Reform and Liberal backgrounds who yearn for greater tradition and become Orthodox. Like Anglicans returning to the Catholic fold, they want a greater sense of 'the real thing' in which religious authority and personal obligations are much more in evidence than is found in liberal theology. For Sammy, 'religion isn't something I make up to suit myself; it's either God's word or it isn't. If it isn't, then why bother with anything at all – just throw in the towel and go off to the nearest pub. But if it is the word of God, which I believe Judaism is, then I have to take it seriously and I have to follow whatever is laid down in the Hebrew Bible. And if sometimes that is inconvenient, then the answer is not to change Judaism but to change the way I live.' Whereas his was a personal journey back to Orthodoxy, others are actively encouraged to change. Lubavitch is an ultra-Orthodox movement that is dedicated to missionary activity, although only within Judaism. They are not interested in converting non-Jews but in bringing back secular Jews. They consider that non-Jews would find it very difficult to 'acquire a Jewish soul' and be able to live up to the demands of Judaism – an attitude that borders on racism but is more guided by concern that those joining the faith maintain its code of practice to the fullest degree. For the same reason, Lubavitch are passionate that those who are born Jewish should keep up its traditions. Unlike many other ultra-Orthodox groups who are not interested in those less observant than themselves, Lubavitch have launched a series of 'outreach campaigns' targeted at lapsed Jews and designed to re-invigorate their faith. At the festival of Hanukkah, for instance, which is normally a domestic festival, they hold public candle-lighting ceremonies in shopping centres in Jewish areas. With similar inventiveness, at Sukkot, the Feast of Tabernacles, they drive a 'Sukkah-mobile' – a truck with a tabernacle erected on it – around Jewish streets and encourage Jews to step inside and say the appropriate blessing for the occasion. They have also excelled at using the latest advances in modern technology to communicate their message, with satellite conferences and Internet websites. As part of their philosophy of 'starting where people are at, and then bringing them to where we want them to be', they will use contemporary jargon to gain the attention of those who normally regard religion as old-fashioned nonsense. Thus a campaign aimed at Jewish students included posters urging them to get involved in POT and LSD – which the next line declared stood for Put On Tefillin (prayer boxes used at morning services) and Let's Start Dovening (praying).

It is often the case that converts are the most zealous advocates of their new faith. This is partly a way of persuading other members of the adopted faith that they are committed to it, and partly a way of justifying their defection to members of the faith they have abandoned. It also serves to dampen any doubts they may have at their decision to change if others follow the path they have taken. This applies particularly to a missionary organization that straddles both the Christian and Jewish world – often to the discomfort of both: Jews for Jesus. It arose in the 1970s and consists of Jews who claim to believe in Jesus whilst still retaining their Jewish identity. They observe many Jewish practices, such as lighting candles to welcome the Sabbath on Friday evening and reciting Jewish prayers, yet accept Jesus as the Messiah as well as Christian doctrines concerning Original Sin and the Resurrection. They harmonize this apparent inconsistency between practice and belief by describing themselves as 'fulfilled Jews' or 'completed Jews'. According to most Jews they are merely renegades who have left the faith but keep up certain Jewish rituals to assuage their guilt at adopting Christianity. For Christianity they are a puzzle as they hold their own separate services and sometimes act as if they are afraid to integrate fully in church life. Perhaps as a result of this indeterminate position, Jews for Jesus is actively engaged in persuading other Jews to accept Jesus. Its campaign headquarters is located in Finchley Road in London, an area of high Jewish population, and its members often attend Jewish events or Zionist rallies distributing missionary literature and wearing t-shirts proclaiming Jesus as the Jewish saviour. They are very skilled at presenting themselves in a way that is more acceptable to Jews than other missionaries, using familiar Jewish imagery and avoiding obviously Christian terms that might alienate listeners. Thus they refer to Jesus rather than Christ, and wear the Star of David rather than a cross.

The actual success rate of Jews for Jesus has been minimal, but its psychological impact on the Jewish establishment has been great. In the past, Christian conversionist activity came from out-

side the Jewish community and could be spotted from afar and
resisted as an external challenge. However, Jews for Jesus are seen
as posing an internal threat, inferring that you can be both Jewish
and Christian, and using Jewish symbols and Hebrew terms to
tempt gullible Jews into adopting Christianity. By way of response,
an organization entitled Operation Judaism has been launched to
alert the community to the supposed dangers posed by Jews for
Jesus, and it is especially active on university campuses where
Jewish students away from home are considered most vulnerable
to conversionist propaganda. It produces literature refuting
Christian claims and rebutting their interpretation of the Hebrew
scriptures. Its speakers warn parents of the possible danger their
children are facing, whilst counsellors meet with young Jews
who feel confused by missionary approaches they have received.
Operation Judaism also tries to reclaim the allegiance of Jews
who have been persuaded to convert to Christianity. Somewhat
ironically, this counter-campaign has been established not by the
mainstream synagogue bodies, but by Lubavitch, which is itself a
missionary movement. On the principle that 'it takes one to know
one', it may be felt that they are well placed to know what techniques to counter and how best to do so.

There are no equivalent anti-missionary organizations amongst
the other major faiths in Britain, as they do not feel threatened in
the same way. This is partly because they are much larger and are
less affected by missionary inroads, and partly because they are not
specifically targeted as are Jews. The special relationship between
Judaism and Christianity, with the latter emerging directly from
the former, meant that Christianity was always particularly keen to
convert Jews. As far as Christianity was concerned, Jesus was the
fulfilment of the Hebrew prophecies and so whereas members of
other faiths had to be educated afresh about such matters, Jews
simply had to be persuaded to accept the obvious. Moreover, the
conversion of the Jews was imperative if Christianity's claim to be
'the new Israel' was to be sustained. The fact that most Jews did
not convert was a major theological problem, posing a challenge to
the validity of Christianity's claims. Ultimately, it was solved by
blaming the Jews for being stubborn and for rejecting God.

Indeed, such was the importance of their conversion that it became one of the conditions for the Second Coming, and thus the conversion of the Jews became not just a desirable goal but a religious necessity. According to Rabbi Shmuel Arkush, Director of Operation Judaism, Christian missionaries who 'work the High Streets' or knock on house-doors handing out literature always have a pouch with special material for any Jews they come across. Whilst missionary activity to other faiths is encouraged too, it does not occupy such a pivotal role in the messianic process as does that to the Jews.

If the major faiths have different attitudes to conversion and hold different points of attraction to those in search of God, they also each have characteristics that deter would-be newcomers. In the case of Christianity, it can suffer from its identification with the imperialism of past centuries. This applies particularly to those from immigrant backgrounds who associate Christianity with colonial days. As for its theology, the emphasis on sinfulness – which does resonate with many – can turn away those seeking what they consider to be a more life-affirming faith. As Shirley commented, 'Coming from no religious background at all, I was keen to see what was on offer. But being told how sinful I was and that I could only obtain salvation through Christ was not for me. I wanted a faith that celebrates who I am and gives me a framework for living my life decently and purposefully. Christianity could offer the guidance, but I didn't want to be swirling in sin all the time.' The main obstacle for many in Judaism is its ritual demands. The insistence on circumcision as an entry rite for males can be a major stumbling block, while others find the laws on permitted and forbidden foods too fastidious. As Karen put it, 'How can having a ham sandwich have any bearing on my relationship with God? I admire many Jewish teachings, but the concern for minutiae is in danger of obscuring the larger message about loving God. When I was on my religious search, I went to Jewish books and got bogged down in details. I went to Christian ones and felt uplifted.' Islam often suffers from an image problem, being regarded as militant and oppressive. This largely stems from stories in the news about Hamas suicide-bombers in Lebanon, beheadings in Saudi Arabia, *fatwas* in Iran calling for the death of the British author Salman Rushdie, thieves in Pakistan having their hands cut off, and Taleban laws restricting women's rights in Afghanistan. In vain do British Muslim leaders protest that such activities are not representative of Islam, and certainly do not correspond to its Westernized version. It will probably take another generation for the label 'foreign and fundamentalist' to disappear.

Religious belief has never been an objective matter, despite constant attempts by various religions to find incontrovertible proof of their claims; instead, it is very much in the heart and mind of the practitioner. Even the very same aspects of a religion can be viewed positively or negatively at will. Thus Buddhism can seem ideal to those who want to concentrate on their personal fulfilment, but appear self-indulgent to those who believe in a Higher Power. The concept of the Son of God who took on human form through Jesus Christ can be enormously powerful to some, but akin to paganism to others. Islam's strong sense of discipline can attract those who yearn for moral parameters, but repel those who value total freedom of conscience. Judaism's close-knit community feel can appeal to those seeking a sense of cameraderie, but put off those who regard it as far too exclusive. One person's faith is another person's folly.

4

Taking the Plunge

The interview stage

'The object of the conversion course is not to turn you into a saint or scholar – because most Jews aren't either of those – but to give you the basic background knowledge of what it means to be Jewish.' These are the reassuring words with which Rabbi Joseph explains what applicants are about to experience. Most greet his words with a sigh of relief, delighted that their assumption that the process would be a nightmarish mixture of a MA exam course and a SAS endurance test had turned out to be mistaken. Father Thomas is at pains to overcome similar fears among those who approach him: 'I am constantly amazed at how many think they have to be, as they put it, holier than the Pope. You can see their face muscles relax when I say that I want to teach them the "abc" of the faith – to a level sufficient for them to feel at home in church and also to be able to pass it on to any children they may have. Naturally I am pleased if they wish to pursue matters further through extra study and home reading, but they have the rest of their life for that and don't have to cram it into a few weeks.' Not all are so welcoming and Brian recalls being told at the start of the conversion course he and others attended: 'A third of you will probably disappear in two weeks, a third of you will drop out half-way and a third will make it to the end. It's up to you which group you fit into.' When Sheila went to her first lesson, she received an even more negative response: 'The rabbi told me that the course was designed not just to educate candidates about Judaism but to ensure that only those who were truly sincere were able to proceed. Instead of being welcomed, I felt that I was going through a weeding-out process – a bit like taking an accountancy exam when you know in advance that 40% will fail. It made me very nervous; to tell the truth, I also felt a little bit angry – I didn't expect to be greeted with a red carpet rolled out, but I wasn't anticipating such a gruff reception either. After all, shouldn't he have been pleased that I'd decided to throw in my lot with his faith? I thought he'd have regarded it as a compliment rather than a nuisance.'

The less-than-helpful reaction of some ministers reflects not only their ambivalence as to the value of converts, but also a lack of understanding as to the enormous range of emotional challenges faced by converts. For some it is confusing; they are not entirely sure if this is the right path for them and caught in a situation in which they are unable to tell whether to go ahead unless they first take a step in that direction. The future is a great unknown. For some it is painful, knowing that they are upsetting parents by taking on a new faith and perhaps alienating irrevocably family members who feel betrayed by their decision. The stakes are high. For some it is demanding, necessitating an investment of energy and time when they are facing many other pressures, be it with work or young children. The physical strain can be enormous. For some it is worrying, feeling that they are embarking on a process that will then mean them losing control and being pushed along by other forces. There is a certain panic over where it will all end up. For some it is complicated, as the conversion is bound up with marriage plans, and failure to complete the course might jeopardize the relationship. Religion and emotions are jumbled up, and can make it hard to be honest or objective. For some it is puzzling, being expected to observe all the practices of the faith yet knowing that many born-members fail to keep them. It begs the question of why bother in the first place. For some it is daunting, as conversion means not only holding various beliefs, but also fitting in with actual members of the faith-community. Getting on with strangers can be much harder than talking to God. For some, it is nerve-wracking, consciously making oneself different from the majority of the population by joining a minority faith, with possibly detrimental effects on oneself or one's children. Changing religion can make one a hostage to fortune and social prejudices.

For some it can be hurtful, feeling that joining the new faith entails sacrificing parts of one's heritage and previous way of life. One can genuinely wish to convert yet still have a sense of personal loss. The combination of all these factors means that prospective converts are particularly vulnerable at the critical stage of step-ping into their first lesson. Very often their difficulties are not appreciated, and they are not always met with the sensitivity they deserve.

It can also be the converts themselves who fail to respond adequately at the initial interview with the minister. Very often this results from sheer nervousness, so that when they are asked if they have any questions about the procedure, they are afraid of appearing to express any hesitancy and so remain silent. Joanna remembers being asked by the iman she had approached if she had any queries and recalls 'Yes, hundreds – why do some Muslims seems to turn the idealism of the Koran into such hateful mili-tancy? And how does an all-powerful Allah allow wicked things to happen to good people? And will I meet up with Catholic members of my family in the world-to-come? But I couldn't get them from my head on to my tongue and just said "Which services can I attend?".' Father Thomas is well aware of the problem and is at pains to encourage converts to be more open: 'I always tell my class that the whole point of the lessons is to establish a relationship with church teachings and to feel at home with them. The class is precisely the point to raise questions and express problems, so that we can look at them together and sort them out. My role is that of teacher, not Inquisitor General.'

The conversion course

The teacher of the conversion course is usually a minister of the particular faith, although not necessarily so and it may instead be a knowledgeable lay person. This is especially the case in the Hindu, Muslim and Sikh faiths where many of the clergy are foreign-born and do not have sufficient command of English to lead classses in English and the task is deputized to a native-born member of the faith. But whatever the identity of the teacher, his or her role is crucial, as it is through that person that the faith is represented, and it is subject to their interpretation, personal foibles, sense of humour or lack of it. A different teacher might have turned away those who were enthused by the person guiding them, and equally might have inspired those who were so put off by the person who taught them that they dropped out. The relationship with the teacher is crucial, as is his/her ability. What is extraordinary is how haphazard is the selection of the teachers, resulting in some who are highly competent and others who lack the requisite skills. Sometimes it is left to the minister because 'he is the professional and it's his job' even though he may be wonderful at pastoral work but hopeless at adult education; other times it is given to a lay person who is known to be far from ideal, but 'he is the only one who volunteered or has the time'. However, goodwill and personal religiosity by themselves are not adequate if the teacher lacks the ability to communicate his knowledge or the sensitivity to the special needs of converts.

Sophie's experience highlights the situation and indicates how an applicant can 'get lucky or be in for a rough ride depending on which teacher they get'. When she decided to convert to Judaism, she felt she ought to 'shop around' first before deciding which synagogue to attend: 'I knew I wanted to be Jewish, but I realized that each rabbi would have a slightly different approach and that it would be worth the effort to sample various styles before getting deeply involved. I suppose it's a bit like buying a new car – you want to see what the range is and test a few out before making your choice. Why should religion be any different?' In her case it was a wise decision, as she found the classes of the first rabbi she met exceedingly dry and dull, and the second rabbi she approached made it clear that he was not keen on spending time with converts. The third rabbi turned out to be both interesting and interested, but she wonders whether someone with less perseverance would have given up by then. She was also lucky in having different synagogues near enough from which to choose. Applicants to whatever faith who live in areas in which there is but one option have to take what is available and make the best of it. Within some faiths, there can also be wide variations in the theological position of the minister/teacher to contend with. Thus the local Church of England minister might happen to be on the evangelical wing and a 'happy-clappy', but could equally be an Anglo-Catholic and much more traditional. Luck – or the will of God – can mean that the conversion course can vary enormously. Across the religious board, the minister/teacher acts as the gate to the faith, with some proving to be barriers that are impossible to pass, some serving as hurdles to be overcome and some beings doorways through which to enter.

Moreover, besides the problem of the lack of training for teachers, there is no obligatory core syllabus in most of the faiths. The major Christian and Jewish denominations have rough guidelines in the shape of subject headings, but they are so general as to effectively leave the content entirely to the local teacher. There are also booklists of recommended reading, although these are often the personal choice of a particular minister which has then been circulated to other colleagues and copied. There could be many disadvantages in having a highly centralized system – perhaps too rigorous, or too academic and divorced from the realities of ordinary parish life – but there can be equal problems with a free-for-all in which every minister does what he/she pleases and standards are not monitored. The only major faith in which such centralization does exist is Judaism, as converts are trained locally but appear before a national rabbinic court, or *Beth Din*, which examines applicants that are sent to it by local synagogues. Each denomination – Orthodox, Reform, Liberal and Masorti – has its own court, which operates according to different principles, but within each grouping they serve to harmonize procedures and ensure that the knowledge and practice of candidates reach a required level. Even here, however, much discretion is left to individual teachers, with courses ranging considerably in length and frequency, while some tutors demand much home reading, others expect short essays, and others simply require attendance at the classes.

The length of the course can vary enormously. In Islam there is simply no need for any pre-requisites, and to convert a person merely has to utter the *Shahada* either in its original Arabic form, *La Ilaha illa 'Llah Muhammadan rasulu 'Llah*, or in its English translation, 'There is no God apart from Allah, and Muhammad is the Messenger of Allah.' The learning process can then take place afterwards. Conversion in Judaism was originally very simple too. When a person presented himself for conversion, he was asked, 'What motivates you? Do you not know that, in these days, Jews are subject to persecution and discrimination, that they are hounded and troubled?' If he replied, 'I know this and yet I regard myself as unworthy of being joined to them' he was accepted immediately. Instruction in the principles of Judaism only took place after conversion.[1] Nowadays, however, rabbis demand attendance at a course prior to conversion, partly so as to ensure that the candidates fully understand that to which they are committing themselves and are genuine in their desire to adopt Judaism; and partly to guarantee that the learning process does happen, as it might be difficult to enforce it once conversion had officially taken place. Underlying the latter concern is the assumption that some candidates might take short-cuts, either out of laziness or because they feel they know enough already. For the rabbis, though, it is important both that the individual concerned has an adequate knowledge of Judaism, and that he/she can represent it properly to the wider world. It is always the case that each person is an ambassador for their own faith to those outside it, but a convert is under more scrutiny as they have made a conscious act of transition, while they also have much deeper links with that world. The actual length of the course can vary from a year amongst Progressive synagogues to up to five years in Orthodox ones, although in other countries, especially the United States, the period can be much shorter. As a generalization, the more Orthodox the synagogue, the more demanding is the course, although the Progressives would resist any implication that their standards were lower. Moreover, the two groups often concentrate on different aspects, with Jewish history and theology forming important elements of the Progressive course, whereas ritual observances have greater emphasis amongst the Orthodox. Similar variations in length of instruction are to be found in Christian circles, with some courses lasting six weeks and others three months.

The Jewish conversion procedure does stand out in one respect, in that in all denominations, payment is required. This is not because of any attempt to profit from converts, but simply to maintain the centralized structure of a rabbinic court before which candidates appear at the culmination of their course, a system that does not exist in the other faiths. They are usually obliged also to pay for the time given by their teacher. However, the fact that Judaism effectively charges for entry is perhaps also indicative of a deeper attitude towards conversion itself, and reflects its reluctance to engage in missionary activity and only accept those who make strenuous efforts of their own accord to join its ranks. Christianity, by contrast, has invested a considerable amount of money in supporting missionary organizations and providing material help to those who wish to convert. Much of the money comes direct from central church funds, while appeals are regularly made to congregations to make donations to help mission work in Britain or abroad. Although individual rabbis will reduce conversion fees for those in financial difficulty, the mere fact that charges exist speaks volumes and indicates that conversion is regarded as a benefit to the person concerned rather than to the synagogue itself.

In some instances – whatever the faith – the conversion class is conducted as a group activity, whilst at other times it is on an individual basis. Although the latter has the advantage of being tailored to the needs of the person concerned and at a time that is more convenient for them, these are probably outweighed by the benefits of a larger class. First, there is the sheer cameraderie that can be gained by approaching a new faith in the company of others. Indeed, the class can often act as a support group, helping those involved to discuss any problems they may be experiencing, as well as providing a social network as they enter a community that is very new to them. This was Jack's experience, who found that 'Even though I was just transferring from one Christian denomination to another – C of E to Catholic – it was still an entirely new world – with different practices and certainly a group of worshippers who were new to me. Knowing three or four others from the conversion course meant I wasn't a total stranger at

services or other events, and helped ease my path in.' The same
applies even more strongly to those joining a completely different
faith, having to face not only theological differences and a new
social set, but also cultural distinctions. Georgina found that her
Sikh instructor informed her very competently of the religious
principles of the faith, but 'I felt I lacked anyone to talk to about
practical things such as what to wear and how to greet people. I
wish now there had been a group of us converting so that we could
have discussed those sort of things together.'

Whether the classes are conducted as a group or on a one-to-one
basis, a common verdict from a wide range of converts to different
faiths is that the most useful courses were those that also prepared
them for the reality of communal life rather than just the theology
of the faith. Priests, rabbis and imams may extol the rituals of their
tradition, but there is a big difference between the way teachers
describe a faith and the way it is actually practised. Thea, for
instance, was enormously moved by the concept of tithing, of
giving a tenth of one's income to the church, both by way of thanks
to God and to help those in need. She was stunned, therefore,
when the person next to her thought she was mad putting a wodge
of £5 notes into the weekly collection plate, and told her to stop
showing off and give a pound or two like everyone else. For Jill,
learning to master the intricate laws of kosher food and altering
both her diet and her method of cooking to accommodate them
had been a struggle, but one she felt was necessary if she was to
convert. She was greatly taken aback, therefore, when she and her
fiancé went to dinner with various members of his family and
found that not only did they not bother with such details, but
actually served some of the foods that were specifically forbidden.
'It wasn't so much that I resented having to keep kosher myself –
because if other people want to break the rules then that's up to
them – but more that I felt lost at sea, not knowing what sort of
people did what when. It was very confusing and left me feeling
like a silly schoolgirl at a posh dinner and not knowing which set
of cutlery went with which course.' Similar shocks can greet
those who come to a faith through reading books on it rather than
through contact with members of that faith, and then find a great

gulf between the lines on the page and real lives. 'This is the reason', says Rabbi Joseph, 'that I always prefer someone who wants to convert who already has a Jewish partner, as it means they are familiar with how Jewish life is actually lived, warts and all, half-baked compromises and all, and whether or not I personally approve, at least they have a much clearer picture of what they are taking on.'

Once on the conversion course, and also attending services and other events, the person has to negotiate a minefield of mini-embarrassments that face newcomers. Shelley realized she had made a faux-pas by the look on the face of her future Jewish in-laws when she arrived at their house for tea clutching some home-made hot-cross buns. 'I realize now that it was religiously inappropriate – although frankly I looked upon them simply as being a tasty gift rather than a theological statement.' She also slipped up at their house one Friday evening when she asked if she could watch the news, forgetting that that the use of electricity on the Sabbath is forbidden. As she complained to her fiancé on the way home, 'Electricity didn't exist in biblical times, so how should I know it's banned?' Born members of a faith often fail to appreciate that what is obvious to them is not at all clear to outsiders. Derek felt equally embarrassed when he took a bottle of wine round to some Muslim friends for a party they were holding: 'It was just something I did automatically, whereas if I'd stopped for a moment to think I knew that everyone abstained from alcohol!' Martin caught himself congratulating someone at the Buddhist centre he had started attending on their kindheartedness and telling them 'that was very Christian of you'. Perhaps the classic misunderstanding is that recorded of Marilyn Monroe who converted to Judaism in order to marry Arthur Miller. On one occasion she was at his parents' for supper and she was served matza-ball soup – soup with ball-shaped dumplings made from unleavened bread (*matza*). When asked if she wanted a second helping, she declined saying 'Oh, I love it, but isn't there any other part of a matza you can eat?' Charles made a much more fundamental error. Having come to Judaism through reading the Old Testament, he was unacquainted with its ways in the twentieth century.

Thinking that modern Jews spoke Yiddish, he assiduously set about learning a language that is actually used only by those who are ultra-Orthodox and was somewhat taken aback when he went to synagogue and found people praying in Hebrew and speaking in English.

Even those who study the correct language for their new faith can find the linguistic differences problematic. Learning Arabic, Cyrillic, Hebrew, Sanskrit or other sacred tongues can present enormous difficulties to those who may be sincerely committed to the faith but hopeless at languages. It also means that it can take a considerable time before a convert feels at home in services, because much, if not all of it, is incomprehensible to them. Margaret remembers the sense of panic she felt on attending a mosque for the first time. 'I didn't understand a word. Before that moment I thought I knew quite a bit about Islam through reading books, and felt comfortable identifying with it – but when I suddenly hit the real thing I realized what an uphill battle it would be to actually fit in'. Corinne found herself equally tongue-tied at the Hindu temple she started attending with her fiancé. Although she mastered the prayers quickly through practising at home, she was still wary of reading them aloud for fear of the embarrassment if someone heard her mispronounce them. One of the attractions of Reform Judaism for Anne was that 50% of the services was in English, but it still felt strange. 'At first I could only catch the English bits – can you imagine how odd it would be to go to the theatre and watch a play in which you only understood every other paragraph? Gradually my Hebrew improved, so that I could at least follow the Hebrew prayers others were reading – although there was no way I could read at their pace; then I was able to join in the occasional word that I recognized; then I managed half a dozen words in a row before getting lost; and eventually I could read along with everyone else. But it really was a long and painful process, and there were plenty of times that I thought I would never get there.'

The customs associated with the place of worship can also present pitfalls the first time they are encountered. Vanessa discovered her belief in Christianity through the pages of the New

Testament but was shocked when she went to church for the first time and found the collection plate being passed along the pew towards her: 'I was flabbergasted. The one thing you never take to synagogue is money. So I had nothing on me. I must have looked so mean just passing it on to the next person. I can't tell you how embarrassed I was.' Jill had a similar experience, except in synagogue, when after an hour someone gently pointed out that she was holding the prayer book upside down. Rashid had long admired the pacifist traditions of the Society of Friends and was very excited when he attended his first Quaker meeting, but felt utterly perplexed as to when to speak and what was the etiquette about who was able to say what. Even simple movements that are second-nature to regular worshippers – such as at which prayers to sit, kneel or stand – can be a cause for concern to converts unfamiliar with set patterns. For many, the easiest way is to adopt Gavin's strategy. 'For the first few weeks I always made sure I was towards the back of the mosque – partly so that I could see what others did and imitate them, and partly so that there wouldn't be too many people behind me watching my mistakes. Even now, having been a Muslim for ten years, I still do that when I'm away somewhere and visit the local mosque, because each one has its own little customs and I don't want to be caught out by them.'

Sometimes, the problem lies with a partner's lack of foresight. 'It's amazing,' says Rabbi Joseph, 'when Jews have a partner who wants to convert, how many will take them to their first service on Yom Kippur, the day of Atonement, which is extremely long, very sombre, with massive crowds attending and very impersonal. It usually turns half of them off. Much better to bring a person along on an ordinary Friday evening service, which is short, tuneful, smaller and much friendlier.' Jill also adds a practical point: 'When my beloved fiancé told me he would take me to my first service, he never warned me that it involved standing for hours and not to wear high heels. The result was that I emerged with horrendous backache and no religious inspiration at all!' There can also be difficulties that relate to the clash between new rituals and the traditions in which a person had previously been brought up. Thus Pandith is fully committed to Buddhist teachings and philosophy of life. However, as a Jew he grew up learning that one should not worship idols and was weaned on stories of Jews preferring to die for their faith rather than bow down to statues. 'Intellectually I know that bowing before the Buddha is not worshipping idols but acknowledging the highest ideal for which I can strive, yet emotionally it just sticks in my gut. It's just so alien to my Jewish psyche. It was only after practising Buddhism for something like four years that I could actually bring myself to bow, and my Buddhist principles took control of my Jewish angst.'

It can also can take a long time to adapt to changes in domestic arrangements. With many faiths this can particularly affect the kitchen area. Judaism has a long list of foods that are forbidden, some of which can be hard to give up if they have been personal favourites. Brian had no problem in turning his back on pork, but found saying goodbye to prawns a great sadness. Jill's main difficulty was altering a lifetime's cooking habits: 'I had no objection to the ban of mixing milk and meat in the same meal until I realized that all the white sauces I used were milk-based and I was going to have to find a new way of cooking my meat dishes. Remembering not to plan a meat meal with anything afterwards involving custard or cream was also a nightmare to begin with. Eventually I got used to it – a bit like remembering to drive on the right hand side of the road when we are travelling in Europe!' Similar culinary issues face anyone converting to Hinduism, with a complete ban on meat meaning not just avoiding meat itself but also not cooking soups with stock cubes that are meat based. A ban on alcohol seemed perfectly easy to Catherine until she realized she had just ended a successful dinner party with brandy snaps. Of course, for many converts, it is precisely this concern for the details of everyday life that is so attractive and they approach the various regulations with enthusiasm. Nevertheless, it may still cause problems for those around them who are not of the faith. Friends can sometimes become highly nervous as to what to serve when entertaining them, whilst others can be completely oblivious to their new dietary habits. Jason found this when a friend invited him for dinner and proudly unveiled a rabbit pie he had personally made, totally unaware that rabbit is as unacceptable to Jews as pork. It is even harder with relatives who tend to be much more set in their ways and assumptions. Carla's parents had always enjoyed bacon and eggs for breakfast and so had she whenever she had returned home and spent a weekend with them. They knew about her conversion to Islam and, despite finding it odd, had no objections to it in principle. However, it took many months to register that they could not give her bacon anymore: 'What's a warm breakfast got to do with religion?' her mother had asked in genuine surprise when Carla first refused to tuck in, and they found the disruption to this routine much harder to come to terms with than any theological difference of opinion between them and their daughter. Reactions can vary considerably, and other converts find that their parents make every effort to accommodate their requirements. When Sheila returned home for a visit, she found that her mother had bought a kosher cookbook and took great pleasure in learning new recipes. Either way, converts quickly learn to warn family and friends in advance of any offers of hospitality, both to minimize any embarrassment and to ensure they are not left hungry, watching the others eat.

The bedroom can also involve a learning curve, particularly when one partner converts to a different faith from that of the other partner. When Bernard's wife became Jewish, she told him that use of a condom was forbidden according to Jewish law and she would feel more comfortable if they used a different type of contraceptive, such as the diaphragm or the pill. As it happens he was happy to see the change, unlike Helen's husband who was most put out that her conversion to Islam meant that any lovemaking during daylight hours was forbidden during the month of Ramadan. In their case a long talk together was needed both to calm him down and to explain that her change of faith would not just affect her but carried consequences for him too. However, problems over sexual mores can apply also to couples in which one partner joins the faith of the other but takes it more seriously. Rebecca's husband was delighted that she converted to Judaism a few years after they had married, but was horrified to discover she now wished to put into practice laws concerning times of sexual intercourse that he had happily ignored. It meant that instead of abstaining from sexual relations for five or six days during her menstruation, depending on how she felt, they would now abstain for twelve days a month as Jewish law demands. 'At first I was pretty cross,' he said. 'After all, I'm the born-Jew round here, so if I don't consider it's a law that is necessary to observe, what right has she got to come along and start insisting on it?'

Their case highlights a common problem of the discrepancy in religious standards between a convert and their partner, leading to disappointment on the part of the former and resentment by the latter. On learning the details of the faith they are entering, many converts are surprised to find how little their partner observes. In some cases, this can spill over into anger, as happened with Shelley who felt, 'Here was I learning all about his faith – and to be honest, I would never have dreamt of converting had it not been for him – and he knows this jolly well – but he doesn't actually seem to know much about it himself, let alone keep half the laws. After a while, I got fed up and said, "Look, if you want me to continue, you have to play your part too and take an interest." To give him credit, he did at the time while I was converting, but it's still me who's the religious driving force and makes things happen.' Sometimes the gap is because those born into a faith tend to have a more relaxed attitude to it than those who elect to join it. At other times it is because of bad childhood memories – being dragged to synagogue or forced to go to church Sunday school – which have survived into adulthood and influenced their perception of the faith. There is also often a major difference in religious knowledge, with most people of whatever faith gaining their religious education as children, be it at home or at special classes, and permanently having a child's view of the faith. The convert, by contrast, approaches it as a mature sophisticated adult, with much greater appreciation of its beliefs and practices. The gulf between the two perceptions can lead to much misunderstanding. This is one of the reasons why some ministers insist that if a convert has a partner, he/she should attend the classes too, both to educate them in their own right and to minimize any friction between them.

For their part, those born into the faith can be taken aback at the demands of the convert. Shelley's husband felt that he had made a major sacrifice in marrying someone not born within the faith and so he had played his part already and had nothing more to do. It took him a long time to appreciate that Shelley had also made a sacrifice in choosing to convert, and that his on-going support was important to her. Jill's husband typifies a deeper problem. He had been attracted to her because she was tall and blond, and had different attitudes from the Jewish girls he had been dating previously. He had wanted her to convert, partly to please his family and partly because he wanted his children to be Jewish, but not for any strong religious feelings that he might have. Expecting a nominal conversion, he was annoyed to find her refusing to cook pork chops – once his favourite meal – and generally acting like a Jewish wife. It was precisely because she was not Jewish that she had appealed so much to him and now he resented the fact that she was undermining the attraction. Sometimes the clash of expectations can prove too forceful to reconcile. One of Britain's leading Muslim clerics, Zaki Badawi, acknowledges that there are a number of cases in which women have converted to Islam to marry Muslim husbands but found their husbands to be less religious than themselves and have filed for divorce as a result. According to a recent study of converts to Islam, no fewer than 56% of them feel that they know more about the faith than do those raised in it.[2] Of course, it should also be noted that many spouses are only too delighted that their partner has joined them in their faith and practise it fully.

Those who join a new faith of their own accord and without a partner can also encounter certain difficulties. Most obvious is the lack of someone to act as a guide, but this is less necessary for those adopting Christianity or Buddhism which both, in their different ways, are much more individual-centred than other faiths. Those who come to Christian services or Buddhist meetings are welcomed in their own right, and the two faiths are geared towards them as individuals, be it guaranteeing their personal salvation or helping them reach personal self-fulfilment. Judaism, Hinduism, Islam, and Sikhism are – as a generalization – much more family-oriented faiths, which assume a person is but one part of a family unit and where many of the rituals are domestic ones or communal ones. Perhaps this is most pronounced in Judaism, with the welcoming of the Sabbath every Friday night being a family ritual, with the prayer book assuming that there is a husband, wife and children present and allocating roles for them. Whilst there are many benefits to such an approach, it can leave a convert who is single feeling very isolated, lighting candles by themselves. As Charles put it: 'It's a bit like going to the cinema and being the only person present in the entire auditorium. However good the film, you still feel very odd being there by yourself and it's certainly lonely.' In theory, it is incumbent on Jewish families to invite those who are by themselves for whatever reason to join them at the Sabbath and other festivities, but such invitations are not always forthcoming and even when they are, they cannot hide the fact that, in certain faiths, single converts are often dependent on the kindness of others in order to fully participate in religious life.

The festivals of the new faith can be hugely enjoyable but also personally challenging. Having been accustomed all his life to regard 1 January as the new year and to mentally gear himself to stock-taking then, Jeff found it immensely difficult to shift his thoughts to September/October, when the Jewish new year occurs. It was not any objection in principle, but simply that it took a long time for it to feel real. Also coming from a Christian background Seema was used to festivals being on set dates according to the secular calendar: 'Christmas was 25 December, year in, year out, and what's more it's always in the winter. I still find it hard to get used to Ramadan being a revolving date that changes every year, and sometimes being baking hot and sometimes freezing cold.' Moreover, it is only when a person converts to one of the minority faiths that they realize how much Christian influence pervades society. Evelyn felt that her attempts to bring her daughter up as a Muslim were constantly being thwarted by the surrounding culture, ranging from television programes such as Postman Pat which featured Reverend Timms as a central character, to her local nursery putting on a nativity play in mid-December. Indeed the 'December dilemma' can be a major headache for converts who are keen to avoid associations with their former faith yet find it hard to escape from office parties, high street carols, or neighbours' invitations to Christmas drinks. For Mary it was an important part of her conversion to Sikhism to turn her back on such festivities and show others that they were no longer part of her life. Nevertheless, she also admits to a tinge of regret, as Christmas holds many warm associations from her childhood. She also wonders whether she has deprived her children in some way by not celebrating it, although she tells herself that the many Sikh festivals they enjoy are more than adequate compensation. Jeff's problem is that he would mortally offend his parents if he did not take his family to them for Christmas lunch. 'It makes me feel very hypocritical – telling my children that we're Jewish and don't celebrate Christmas, yet taking them off to Mum and Dad for the turkey and tree. My wife and I give the children Hanukkah presents, but how can I tell my parents not to give them Christmas presents? It's their tradition as much as Judaism is mine. I suppose it's just part of the problem of living in two worlds, and although I have chosen to be Jewish I can't cut myself off from life around me.'

Amid all these pressures, it is little wonder that many people experience moments of acute doubt as they are preparing for their conversion. For some, it is a fear of sacrificing too much of one's upbringing. 'So much of Christian ethics and values is part of who I am,' said Derek, 'that I wonder if adopting Islam will be a step too far and simply rebound on me.' Others, too, voice the concern that 'the essential me will be swallowed up' in the new culture. By contrast, there are those who, like Yusuf, worry that 'I am not worthy enough to call myself a Christian.' They feel that they will find it hard to live up to the idealized picture they have created in their own minds. Others feel a sense of guilt at letting down a faith that previous generations had upheld, sometimes even in times of adversity, while there is also the guilt at the hurt a conversion can inflict on family. Very often these are temporary doubts – natural hesitations before embarking on a major change of identity in the same way that many a prospective bride or groom question whether they are pursuing the right course. As Charles put it, 'Yes, of course I had times when I needed to check with myself that it was sensible carrying on, but deep down I knew I'd be much happier once I'd taken the plunge and changed my status from being a tourist to a resident.'

Whilst many do overcome their nervousness and proceed with their conversion, there are others who feel that it is not appropriate for them and drop out for any one of a variety of reasons. Tracy had intended to convert to Islam, having studied the faith at school and kept up her interest for many years before deciding to adopt it, but 'when I started going to the mosque for lessons and prayers, it felt too alien for me. I still respect the faith enormously and will try to live by its principles, but somehow I knew it wasn't right for me. Strange, really, I was so sure that I wanted to be a Muslim, but somehow it's probably better to admire it from afar than immerse myself in it.' Claire's problem was not so much the new faith but the attitude of her husband: 'I'm not a particularly religious person but I was happy to convert to Judaism for his sake and to unite the family. The classes were fine, but we were supposed to go together and he kept on finding reasons for being unable to come too and it became pretty obvious that he wasn't prepared to put any effort in. After a while I said "Look, if you don't take an interest, why should I?" He just shrugged his shoulders, so I stopped going and that was that.' For others, particularly couples not yet married, the conversion can bring to the fore latent strains in the relationship. Michael and his fiancée had been engaged for three years, and although he had decided to become a Roman Catholic and had attended an introductory course, he kept on postponing the date for his baptism with the result that the plans for the wedding kept on being shelved. The priest he had been seeing asked whether it was attachment to his Jewish roots that prevented him from committing himself to the church, but Michael always denied that had any bearing on the matter and that it was simply that he was very busy at work. Eventually the priest met with both of them, at which it transpired that there were considerable difficulties between the two of them, totally unconnected with matters of faith, but which neither of them wanted to admit. Holding back on the conversion was a subconscious way of expressing doubts about the relationship and putting the brakes on the impending marriage. Shortly afterwards the couple split up.

For those who do stay the course, there are often special issues within each faith that have to be tackled. As Jeff put it, 'I was happy to sign up to most of the Jewish beliefs – justice, charity, kindness and so forth – but I couldn't see why all these important ideas had to be so connected with a tiny piece of land the other side of the Mediterranean. For me, being Jewish meant following certain values in life, not identifying with the State of Israel.' By contrast, born-Jews are used to regarding Israel as special, not just in a religious sense as the place where many of the events in the Hebrew Bible took place, but also as the land in which a high percentage of world Jewry is concentrated. In addition, those with memories of the Holocaust, or aware of its impact, view Israel as living proof of the Jewish will to survive, as well as being a place of sanctuary if ever such murderous antisemitism should occur again. It is the both spiritual home of Jews and the phoenix that has risen out of the ashes of the six million victims of the Holocaust. British Jews may not wish to live there, and may not agree with the political government in power at any one time, but still have a deep commitment to the land and the people. For most non-Jews, however, it is just another foreign country, with no greater emotional pull than Uruguay or Korea. Whilst some of those converting to Judaism do feel a special attachment and are keen to visit Israel whenever possible, many others cannot raise the same enthusiasm. Moreover, it can also present real dilemmas, as Jeff points out. 'At times it can be very uncomfortable when I'm in the presence of Jews and want to say something critical about what's going on in Israel, but feel obliged not to – partly because I know how much offence it will cause and also because it's in danger of undermining my Jewishness in their eyes, as if they might say, "Oh well, with views like that, it's clear your commitment to Judaism isn't 100%" – which is nonsense, as I am 100% committed to Judaism but not to Israel. It's even worse when I'm with non-Jews as they expect me, being Jewish, to be an ambassador for Israel and so if I do say anything critical, then even if they agree they look at me as if I'm some kind of traitor. I still haven't resolved it, and tend to take the easy way out and keep quiet whenever the subject comes up.'

Similar disquiet can face those joining the Roman Catholic Church. As someone brought up in the Protestant tradition, Gaye was used to the idea of the importance of personal conscience, as well as regarding the Queen as the head of the church. Although she was attracted by Catholic teachings on the sanctity of marriage and its strong stand against abortion, she felt uncomfortable with having to give allegiance to Rome and supporting the doctrine of Papal Infallibility. 'I like the sense of authority within the Catholic Church – something that ultimately stems from the words of Jesus himself – and I know that has to be interpreted through a human channel such as the Papacy, but I still can't accept that a man in Rome – conservative one moment and liberal the next, depending on who is elected – has absolute authority over what I have to believe is the will of God. Maybe it would be easier for me if I'd grown up with it like born-Catholics, but I find it a real stumbling-block.'

An issue that can trouble those joining any of the monotheistic faiths is how a loving God can permit evil to exist. Shirley did not come from a religious background and was attracted to Judaism because of what seemed to her to be its positive and sensible attitude to life. 'The one thing that really puzzled me, though, was how a Jewish God could allow the Holocaust to happen. If he could intervene in Egypt and hurl plagues at Pharaoh, why couldn't he have done the same in 1939?' Judy found that her new faith in Jesus helped her answer most questions in life, except the same one of why innocent people suffered because of the faults of others: 'It's not just major events such as the Holocaust, but even individual tragedies, such as a baby in a pram killed by a drunk driver: things that go wrong every day and without any reason. Sometimes atheist friends throw things like that at me when discussing religion and I simply can't answer them. And although it doesn't affect my faith – because I feel I know the reality of God in my own life – it does bother me awfully.' Some do find solutions – such as that it is part of God's plan which is beyond our comprehension, or that injustices will be rectified in the next world, or that it is the result of humanity having free will. Others are obliged to leave the question unanswered and, like Judy, take the attitude that 'being Christian means filling in the gaps and that I have to do God's work here on earth to bring peace and harmony wherever I can'. Of course, the question of why bad things happen to good people also concerns those born within a faith, but there is a big psychological difference between not understanding everything that is yours by birth, and being puzzled by aspects of a faith you are consciously electing to join. The former might lead to a nonchalant shrugging of shoulders, whereas the latter can cause a crisis of conscience and doubts as to whether one should be joining a faith in which such religious black holes exist.

As the course progresses and a person becomes more involved in the faith, many find themselves unconsciously imitating certain characteristics. Sally did not realize that she often punctuated her conversation with the phrase '*inshallah*' (God willing) until she heard a recording of herself at a skills training session. 'I suppose I just picked it up from hearing it around me in the new circle I was mixing in.' Similarly, Jason found himself using expressions influenced by Yiddish and its preference for interrogative statements. 'Once I would have said to someone I disagreed with at work: "I don't think that's quite right." Nowadays it tends to come out as "Are you kidding me or just pulling my leg?" I also throw in Jewish terms in a way I never did before, like "what chutzpah" or "that's not a kosher way to do business". It's cultural rather than religious, but I suppose it's a sign that I feel very much at home in an environment that was once totally strange to me.' Sartorial changes can also occur, with women who convert to Islam donning the *hijab*, new Catholics wearing a crucifix, and male Jews covering their heads. Seema did not wish to adopt the robes traditional for many Muslim women from abroad, but she did start wearing different clothing: 'Out went mini-skirts and low-cut dresses and in came much more modest items. It was partly because I felt that as a Muslim woman I shouldn't be flaunting myself in the "cor-look-at-my-bust" way that I had beforehand. I also felt that I would be seen by many non-Muslim friends as a representative of the faith and so had to behave even more decorously as they would judge Islam by my behaviour.' Her words apply equally to women who convert to other faiths in which personal modesty is valued.

Tell-tale signs of the new faith also start appearing at home, such
as a crucifix on the wall, a statue of Buddha in the corner of the
room, a *mezuzah* (small container with a quotation from the
Hebrew Bible) on the front door, or literature about religious
teachings and revered sages. For many people, conversion is not
just a cerebral exercise, but one which envelops their whole
lifestyle. Changes in their diet or clothing are physical ways in
which they both deepen their new sense of spirituality and express
their change of allegiance.

By the time they are ready to convert formally, many feel that
they have undergone a profound change. Sometimes this is
evident in general character. 'I was always fairly morose, the sort of
person who expected a disaster round every corner, but now I'm
a thousand times more outgoing and optimistic,' claimed Carole.
Other times, it is more of an inner change, outwardly the same
as before, but with a new sense of direction and personal confidence. For those for whom the path has been a long one, this self-
recognition is the culmination of several years' worth of searching
and testing, a long and sometimes convoluted route that has finally
arrived at its destination. For those fortunate enough to have gone
in a short straight line, the process is much quicker but can be
equally fulfilling. The point of arrival was summed up for many
when Evelyn said of her conversion, 'Becoming a Muslim allowed
my "outside" to match my "inside". In many ways it wasn't so
much arriving at a new place, but a deep sense of coming home and
being true to myself.' For Greg, the magic moment came when
instead of telling friends he could not come to a football-training
session as he had promised to go to a meeting at *the* synagogue, he
told them that the meeting was at *my* synagogue. 'It was just a
preposition's difference – but it stood for a lot. It meant owner-
ship: that the synagogue wasn't just someone else's place that I
went to on sufferance, but my place where I felt I belonged.' It took
an anti-Catholic joke in bad taste at work to bring Jack's change of
religious affiliation to the fore. 'I'd heard a few before, but just let
them pass me by as I was still new to the faith and a little nervous of
parading it in public. This time, though, I intervened without
hesitation. "I'm a Catholic," I said, "and I can tell you that we

Catholics don't act like that at all, and it's time you got your facts sorted out." He was stunned and muttered an apology, but not nearly as stunned as I was. I wasn't just a Catholic in name, but I really *felt* like a Catholic. I was also rather proud that I'd stood up to be counted.' It is this sense of inner identity that is the litmus test of when a person has not just formally converted but fully adopted a new faith. As Rabbi Lionel Blue wrote in comments that can apply equally to ministers of other faiths: 'Really every convert converts him or herself. Rabbis are only needed to certify it or administrate it'.[3]

Initiation

The actual initiation ceremony can vary from being very emotionally-charged to an anti-climax, depending on the way it is conducted and the expectation of it. Much also rests on whether it is seen as a moment of transformation, or merely the external recognition of an internal change undergone long ago. There are many who experience exultation, but for Evelyn, the latter applied, and she simply felt a quiet sense of satisfaction that what had been desired for so long was now achieved. 'Afterwards I went for a long walk – not leaping over fences, just breathing deep and taking measured paces.' The type of faith to which one has converted can also have a bearing on reactions; the more charismatic or evangelical it is, the more exuberant the feeling. When Sara became a Jehovah's Witness, 'it was like electricity was racing through my body and I felt as if I was dancing with the angels'. Another common reaction is that of being born anew. This is particularly so when total immersion of the body in water takes place, such as in charismatic churches or within Judaism. When Yasmin took part in a baptism in the sea, she emerged 'feeling like a new born babe'. On becoming Jewish, Sophie went to a *mikveh*, a small indoor pool for waters of immersion, and compared it to a second birth: 'It's an incredibly primeval experience – going underwater and feeling that you are in the waters of the womb again, and then bursting forth into air and light and gasping for breath and knowing that things will never be the same again. I

don't think anything so powerful has ever happened in my life.'
This experience can mean not only taking on a new identity, but
also letting go of aspects of one's past. Donna's conversion to
Christianity was typical of those who felt that 'by committing
myself to Jesus I was very consciously saying goodbye to parts of
my life that I was ashamed of and wanted to bury in the past. The
conversion was enormously cathartic, and I felt as if a great load
of weight was sliding off my shoulders. I could not have done it
by myself; I needed Jesus' help and the walls came tumbling
down.'

   In some faiths, there are different stages within the conversion
process. Thus Dharmishari Vishvanpana describes becoming a
Buddhist as a 'porous process', gradually assimilating the teachings and deepening one's knowledge. The first step is the
Novitiate stage, in which a person becomes a *mitra* or friend. It
marks a transition from being generally interested in Buddhism to
making a definite commitment. A higher level is Ordination – a
step open both to lay members as well as to those becoming priests.
It is achieved by reciting the traditional formula, the Going for
Refuge, in front of a monk. It signifies acceptance of the Buddha,
both as an historical person and an ideal of enlightenment. It also
commits the person to the teachings and practices of the Buddha
along with subsequent enlightened teachers and the Buddhist
spiritual community. Practices vary within different branches of
Buddhism, but those joining the Western Order are also expected
to recite the Five Principles, promising to abstain from taking life,
theft, sexual misconduct, false speech and substances that cloud
the mind. Within Christianity, too, there is a graded approach,
with baptism later being followed by one's first communion.
Through the act of drinking the wine and eating the wafer, the
convert symbolically drinks the blood of Jesus and eats his flesh. In
some Christian traditions, it is not a symbolic act but an actual one,
with the wine and wafer being transformed into real blood and
flesh. In either interpretation, the act of physically consuming the
wine and wafer for the first time can make a deep impression,
bonding the convert to his/her new Saviour. For Iqbal it was both
a terrifying and exhilarating moment: 'to physically feel the wafer

on my tongue and to actually swallow the wine was awesome. I was eating God! I was bringing Jesus into my body, consuming him and letting him enter my heart and bones and lungs. My everywhere. It was almost semi-erotic. Uniting oneself with God in a physical way, like a man and woman joining their bodies together.' Those who are baptized at birth, and therefore who are brought within the Christian community without being capable of knowingly committing themselves to it, will have a confirmation service in church at a later age when they are deemed able to make an informed decision.

The conversion procedure in Islam is both simple and unregulated. It occurs by saying the *Shahada* in Arabic or English, privately or publicly, and in any place. It is considered better, however, if it is performed in the presence of an imam, whilst if done privately it should be followed by a public act such as praying in a mosque. Some imams choose to ask the person a few questions before witnessing the declaration, although this is largely to determine that it is a free-will decision and not done under duress. Some mosques have a policy of issuing a certificate acknowledging the conversion, but this is neither uniform nor obligatory. However, some British converts to Islam find this informality unsatisfactory, being culturally attuned to ceremonies to mark life-cycle events, from christenings to eighteenth birthday parties to knighthoods. In response, some more ornate ways of conversion have begun to develop, with the individual concerned bathing, dressing in clean clothes and gathering Muslim witnesses to hear the *Shahada*.

Use of water is common to many faiths. Within Christianity, baptism is much more than a physical marker but a deep religous act of washing away the sins of the past and entering a new relationship with the Almighty. According to St Paul it also emulates the life and death of Jesus, so that by being baptized the convert encounters death and is then raised from the dead into new life.[4] For this reason, some Anglican clergy refuse to perform infant baptisms unless the parents are regular churchgoers who will ensure that the child grows up in a religious environment. The fear is that many parents who have no real attachment to the church devalue the baptism by using it as a social occasion or as a way of making the children eligible for a place at local Church of England schools. Within the Baptist tradition, baptisms generally occur after children have reached their teens, so as to ensure that the act remains spiritually meaningful. Immersion in water also takes place for converts to Judaism, although it is not necessary for born-Jews and so is a highly distinctive rite marking a person's acceptance into the faith. It usually takes place in private, albeit discreetly witnessed by two adult Jews, and has to be in flowing natural water, such as the sea, a river or a specially designed chamber (*mikveh*) which has water flowing in and out of it. The convert immerses him/herself completely and recites a blessing upon reaching that moment. Waters of immortality – *amrit* – are also used in the Sikh baptism ceremony, in which sweetened water is sprinkled on the person's face and then drunk, signifying the new future that has been gained.

Physical changes accompany the conversion in some faiths. Thus devotees of Hare Krishna shave their heads and don orange robes, the former symbolizing that they renounce vanity and egotism, and the latter symbolizing energy and creativity. On becoming a Sikh, males adopt the 'five K's': *kech* (uncut hair), *kanya* (wooden comb), *kachera* (special breeches), *kirpan* (sword), *karru* (iron bracelet), which signify respectively: strength, cleanliness, chastity, courage to uphold justice and truth, discipline. Male converts to Judaism are required to be circumcised, in keeping with a tradition incumbent on all males since the time of the founding father, Abraham. In the case of born-Jews, this usually takes place when they are eight days old and with no knowledge of what is happening and no recollection of it afterwards. For adult males, the rite can be very daunting, even though it is performed under anaesthetic, either local or general. In the Progressive tradition, those who are already circumcised are exempt from anything further, but in the Orthodox tradition they are obliged to have a token incision made. Fears as to possible pain, physical appearance afterwards and effects on one's sex life combine together to make it a major stumbling-block that prevents some candidates from going ahead with their conversion. Indeed, some Jewish authorities no longer insist on circumcision if it will be a cause of mental anguish or pose a danger to physical health. For them, sincerity alone is the important factor; others, however, regard circumcision as a test of sincerity and consider any hesitation as a sign of lack of commitment. Once the circumcision has taken place, there is often a sense of achievement that the convert is now 'exactly the same as any born-Jew', as well as relief at having overcome a personal challenge. To outsiders, it is a step that is by far the most demanding of all conversion rites. Within Islam, born-Muslims are circumcised, but converts do not face the same obligation and it is purely optional. Nevertheless, some authorities recommend it and there is a perception that it is a sign of sincerity if it is performed. Another step facing Jewish converts is that Judaism also demands that they appear before a court made up of three rabbis, which has two purposes. The first is to publicly register and certify the conversion, as matters of status are much more regulated in Judaism than in other faiths where self-identity is often the determinant factor. For Judaism, it is not enough to declare oneself to be Jewish, but a person must be able to prove it through documentation, otherwise membership of a community, marriage in synagogue, and burial in a Jewish cemetery may be denied. The second purpose is to ensure that converts have attained a minimum standard of knowledge of Jewish beliefs and practices. For this reason, a woman who is heavily pregnant is usually discouraged from appearing before the rabbinic court, lest her condition influence the members to be unduly sympathetic to her and allow her to pass even if she falls below the required standard. Sincerity by itself is insufficient, as a Jew is expected to keep a variety of ethical and ritual commandments, and without adequate knowledge of them, the convert will neither practise Judaism properly nor fit into the existing Jewish community. The fact that converts to Judaism have to reach far higher standards of knowledge than is often possessed by many born-Jews is irksome to some, who regard it as unfair. For the rabbinate, however, it is the price of entry which those who do not wish to pay need not undertake. It is perhaps also the one group of people over whom they are able to exercise the sort of control that they would like to impose on most lapsed Jews but have no power to do. As one person complained, 'Rabbis can't control their own flock, but they throw their weight around with us.'

When an adult converts who has young children, they will often accompany their parent into the new faith. This is particularly the case when a person converts after marriage in order to unify the family. In some faiths, much depends on which partner is the one that converts as the children's status is predetermined according to internal status definitions. Thus the children of a Muslim male are considered Muslim, so there is no need for them to convert if their non-Muslim mother decides to adopt Islam. Conversely, the children of a Jewish female are considered Jewish, so there is no need for them to convert if their non-Jewish father adopts Judaism. Rebecca already had a two-year-old son when she decided to join her husband's faith and convert to Judaism. 'Obviously he couldn't decide for himself at that age, but at the same time it would have been daft not to convert him and to leave him as the odd one out in the family.' Within Judaism, minors do not need to face the rigorous test that adults have to undertake to convert. Providing they have a Jewish education at home and, if old, enough, go to Religion School, they convert automatically with their mother. They do, however, have to undergo the same ritual requirements, with boys being circumcised and both sexes being immersed in the *mikveh* at the same time as their mother. In Christianity there is less emphasis on family status and more on personal salvation. One's own baptism, not a parent's gender, is the critical factor in religious identity, so if one parent converts, the children may or may not join them in the faith, depending on their personal views and those of the other parent. As a lifelong atheist, Trevor did not object when his wife became a Christian, but insisted that the children should not be brought up Christian but be left to make their own choice in adulthood. Although her conversion resulted in splitting the family religiously, it is an increasingly common scenario now that faith is often seen as a personal matter rather than a family identity. With a rise in the number of married people who convert to a different faith from that of their spouse, there is an accompanying rise in the number of children who convert with them. However, a goodly number are left in their existing identity so as not to disturb the marital relationship.

In virtually all faiths, a change of religious identity is symbolically reinforced by a change of name too, the variation in outer nomenclature being a sign of inner transformation. In similar fashion, Saul the persecutor of early Christianity became Paul the promoter of Christianity. In most instances, though, it is an additional middle name, with converts adding after their given forename the first name of a biblical character or saint. Moreover, as the new name is a symbol of the religious values the convert is emphasizing, it could be one belonging to the opposite sex. Thus Anne Widdecombe took the name Hugh after St Hugh of Lincoln and in remembrance of Bishop Latimer who died in flames for his faith some four hundred years earlier with the words 'We shall this day light such a candle by God's grace in England as shall never be put out.' In Judaism, too, an additional name is adopted by converts for worship purposes. Sometimes it is a Hebrew name of their choice or a Hebrew version of their name, so that 'Mary' becomes 'Miriam' and 'Simon' becomes 'Shimon'; alternatively, males often take 'Abraham', who was the first Jew, and females take 'Sarah', the first Jewess, or 'Ruth', the famous convert. Generally the name is only used for being called upon for ritual purposes in synagogue, but some individuals decide to employ the name in everyday life too, thus using it to make a public declaration of their change of faith. In Islam, it is not obligatory to either add or change one's name, although some converts do alter theirs to an Arabic one as an expression of personal piety. The only time those joining Islam or Judaism are told that it might be more appropriate if they changed their forename is if it is identified with another faith, such as Christopher, Christine or the Hindu god Shiva. In Hinduism, however, a change of name is not just an adjunct of the conversion but is the very means by which an individual entrance into the faith is recognized. The ceremony is called *namakarana* or 'naming rite', which entails the abandonment of a person's former name and the adoption of a Hindu name, usually that of a god or goddess. The complete switch of name serves to stress the rejection of the convert's past life as much as the acceptance of a new path.

The type of reception after the conversion can also vary. Brian and Charles both converted to Judaism, but the former just received a gruff handshake afterwards in the rabbi's study, whereas the latter was given a joyous public ceremony of welcome as part of the synagogue service the following week. Brian felt he had been 'grudgingly let in by the back door', while Charles felt 'that the whole community was rooting for me and saying that it was important not just for me but also for them'. The discrepancies reflect not only the sensitivity of the ministers involved, but also reveal underlying attitudes to conversion. For one rabbi, allowing the occasional convert is seen as a major concession to a largely exclusive club; for the other, it is the natural right of those who wish to become Jewish and a wonderful compliment to the community at large which is cause for celebration. Here, as in other faiths, the more public the welcome, the more indicative it is of a positive attitude to conversion. That in turn can be helpful to the convert, as Yusuf found when, to his surprise, the handful of people he had expected at his confirmation was swelled by well-wishers whom he had come to know from attendance at the church: 'As I entered the church, all the niggling thoughts I'd had in the car journey there – about turning my back on Islam or being worthy enough to call myself a Christian – were swept away by the warmth and care of everyone there. They didn't have to come and the fact that they did moved me enormously and made me realize how lucky I was to be part of that community.'

5

Reactions – Expected and Unexpected

Family reactions

In principle, conversion is a joyous event, with a person discovering something very precious and meaningful that enriches their life. In theory, therefore, everyone should be pleased for that individual and glad that such a positive event has occurred. In many cases this is exactly what happens and there is a real sense of pleasure for them, as will be seen below. However, this is not universal response, for it can also lead to hostile reactions. These can be especially acute amongst those who have known the individual the longest – such as members of the immediate family – who tend to be the most emotionally involved with them and whose personal feelings take precedence over any other judgments.

For parents there can be an explosive mix of different emotions when they first discover that their child is about to convert – however old that 'child' might be. Some feel anger. Not only do they do not approve of the decision, but they challenge the right of the person to take that decision in the first place. 'It's wrong, it can't be done, it's not right,' can be the spluttering reaction, which does not articulate a particular reason for it being wrong but just expresses a deep sense of hurt and confusion. Some feel rejected. They see the conversion as a personal slap in the face and a criticism of the upbringing they provided. Sometimes this is indeed true, for the religious home life might have been so oppressively strict that the child was determined to throw it off and look elsewhere as soon as they were independent enough; alternatively, it might have been so lukewarm that it left a spiritual vacuum that they sought to fill in adulthood in their own way. It may also have been open to the charge of hypocrisy, with parents demanding standards of the child that they themselves did not keep, or showing a public religiosity to the outside world that was totally at variance with their private life. In such instances, the person's decision to seek out a new faith untainted by the negative associations from childhood is a direct reflection on their parents.

However, in a large number of cases, the conversion does not carry any implied condemnation. As Sally explained, 'I came from a warm loving home. My parents took their Methodism very seriously and educated me in it in a way I can't fault. They did all the right things. It's just that although I respected it, I knew it wasn't for me.' In these instances, adopting a new faith is part of the maturation process and a person developing their own identity. It is more a matter of their attraction to the new path than a rejection of the old one. Just as they will choose a different career from that of their parents, or a different area to live, not to spite them but because of different interests, needs and circumstances, so too with their religion. Moreover, it does not imply, as some parents assume, that the child loves them any the less. The conversion is a religious decision, not a personal attack, and does not necessarily imply any withdrawal of affection for them now, or lack of appreciation for the upbringing that they received. In a curious way, the conversion could even be said to be a compliment to that education. As Gemma pointed out, 'It's not because my parents brought me up wrongly – on the contrary they brought me up well – to question, to think for myself, to search for the truth and to avoid easy options or other people's answers. It may be that I now differ from the answers that my parents found, but that's only because I followed what they taught me exactly!' Nevertheless, there are parents who profess that they wish to give their children complete freedom of choice, but are horrified when the children exercise it in a way that they deem unsuitable.

For some parents the key feeling is a sense of disloyalty. They regard the conversion not so much as a personal affront but as a fault-line in family unity. Family and faith are seen as one, even if they are not a particularly practising family. Nevertheless, the faith is part of their identity, whether a once-a-year observance or a daily backdrop. Leaving the faith is seen as breaking the family bond in some way. Personal spirituality is irrelevant; all that matters is 'the way the family is'. For other parents, there is an inability to even conceive of conversion. Comments abound such as 'Once a Catholic, always a Catholic,' or 'A leopard can't change its spots,' or 'You were born a Jew and you will die a Jew.' It is not that change is considered undesirable – it is considered impossible. There are tribal boundaries that cannot be crossed. Others do recognize the religious transformation that has taken place, but feel desperately guilty about it. They blame themselves and ask 'Where did we go wrong? . . . why didn't we do things differently?' Rather than castigate their son or daughter, they assume the fault is their own. As was seen before, in some cases there may be a justification for their guilt, but it is just as likely to have been beyond their control and one of many areas in which parents have to watch children establish their own life. For others, the reaction is more one of embarrassment. Their difficulty is how to tell other people and what the wider reaction will be. As one father put it, 'How can I possibly face the vicar again, when the girl he confirmed is now a Muslim.' There can be equal concern over informing relatives who are perceived as being head of the family, or of nervous disposition: 'What on earth will your grandmother say? She will be horrified.' This particular reaction can be sub-divided into at least three different categories. First, when there are genuine reasons to fear the explosive reaction of those 'whom we'd better tell before they hear about it from someone else'. Second, when the expression of embarrassment is merely a projection of their own disquiet, which they feel unable to voice directly and prefer to allocate to a third party. Thirdly, when the assumed reaction of others is actually misjudged, as exemplified by a Jewish parent who took several weeks to summon up the courage to tell her rabbi that her son had become a Buddhist only to find that instead of being outraged, the rabbi said it was a fascinating religion which contained valuable insights.

Other reactions are on religious grounds. Carla's parents felt that by adopting Islam she was turning her back on God and putting her soul in jeopardy. For them, salvation was through Christianity alone, and however moral other faiths might be, there was only one sure way of obtaining God's grace. This view was confirmed in their eyes when, shortly afterwards, Carla was taken ill and had to spend several weeks in hospital. It was seen as a sign from God and they used it to beg her to return to the family faith. The fact that Carla eventually recovered without changing her mind failed to dent their belief that God had intervened to try to show Carla the error of her ways. Rachel's parents objected more on historical grounds, feeling that she had betrayed the sacrifices of past generations: 'They gave me this long sob story about how Jews in the past had suffered to keep the faith alive and now I was abandoning it. They even threw in the Six Million and accused me of doing Hitler's work and murdering them all over again. It was horrendous and I didn't speak to them for a week afterwards.' In other families, reactions are more a matter of prejudice, concerned not so much for the faith that is being left, but objecting to the faith that is being joined. Jackie's parents were not particularly religious but were aghast at her conversion to Islam. 'They associated it', she said, 'with being foreign, coloured, fundamentalist, backward and violent.' This is especially the case with offspring who convert to faith-groups who are largely seen as ethnic minorities. Gaura's parents knew nothing about Hindu practices and theology, but severely condemned his decison to convert to it. 'It was sheer racism on their part. For me Hinduism meant a spiritual path; for them Hinduism meant mixing with brown people.' Racism can also be found amongst those who are minorities themselves, as Kewel discovered when he became a Muslim, to the disgust of his Hindu parents. They were not interested in his religious explanations and just repeated how appalled they were that he had joined 'such people'. Other objections are more connected with the lifestyle that the offspring will lead because of the cultural traditions of the new faith. Thus the father of a woman who became a Muslim lamented that she would not be able 'to wear fashionable clothes or have the occasional drink any more, but be dressed in a tent and be the odd one out at family parties'. Ignorance can also fans the flames of parental ire. One father demanded to know 'who's this Harry Krishna guy that you keep on singing about? I'd like to meet up with him and see what's so special about him.'

There are a range of other negative reactions that are based more on practical matters than principle or prejudice. One is a worry that the conversion will lead to a breakdown in family relations, with the person becoming more and more immersed in their new circle and having less and less in common with their parents. It is based partly on a fear of the unknown and partly on the nervousness of all parents when children take a different direction from themselves. 'That's such nonsense,' Anne claimed. 'Judaism is all about family togetherness. And every synagogue has an emblem of the Ten Commandments blazing forth "Honour your father and your mother". My parents really don't have to worry about me turning my back on them, otherwise I would be undermining the very Jewish values to which I was attracted in the first place.' There may also be worry that, even if lines of communication are kept going with the son or daughter, the parents will find it very difficult having a relationship with any grandchildren if they are brought up in a different culture. Concerns range from 'Will we be able to give them Christmas presents?' to worries about everyday contact 'if they won't come to our house and eat with us'. The latter fear applies especially to those converting to Judaism and Islam whose dietary regulations mean that many previous family favourites, from bacon and eggs at breakfast to steak and kidney pie for Sunday lunch, will no longer be deemed acceptable. Here, too, many of these concerns are more linked with the new culture that the person is adopting rather than the new theology itself.

It is certainly true that conversion to some faiths can involve a radically different lifestyle – such as a Jew not travelling on the Sabbath, or a Hindu being vegetarian, or a Muslim observing a totally different festival calendar. However, some fears are irrational, such as one couple's concern that their Muslim grand-child would only speak Arabic and so be unable to talk to them, whereas in fact he would be be as fluent in English as they are, but also know enough Arabic to read the Koran. Another worry is that

even though the parents are genuinely not prejudiced, they fear
that others will be and that their offspring will suffer from it. As
Jeff's father said, 'I still remember the Second World War and I
know what Hitler did to the Jews, and I don't want my son being
next in line if anything like that happens again.' Much more
immediate worries bothered Hadijah's father, for he was highly
concerned about the effect of his daughter donning the *hajib*:
'I know it's only a bit of cloth but in some areas it's a walking
provocation, and she's had insults shouted at her and even someone spitting. I get really scared someone's going to throw a brick
one day.' Mary's parents were thinking ahead to the next generation. They had no objections to her becoming Sikh, but were
extremely agitated that any grandchildren might be called names
in the playground at school. 'Children can be so cruel,' her mother
said, 'and I hate to think of some of the things that might happen to
them.' Sometimes the parents themselves are recipients of negative reactions, as those of Jacqueline Du Pré discovered when it
became public that she intended to become Jewish. They received
letters from both complete strangers and close friends declaring
that 'Jackie will be eternally damned because she will have to
renounce Jesus Christ,' and 'If you don't stop it, you will have to
answer to God.' They found such letters highly upsetting and her
father described their situation as 'a hundred bowlers bowling
simultaneously while you, as the only batsman, try to defend a
one-hundred-yard-wide wicket. If you missed even one ball, you
would be out'.[1]

Equally common are worries as to whether the decision to
convert is right for the person concerned. Some parents fear that
they are being unduly influenced by friends or a partner. This can
be both true and irrelevant, for although the person might not have
thought about converting but for a relationship, the conversion
may still be very appropriate for them. As Gitta freely admitted,
'As a Hindu I would not have considered becoming a Sikh, or even
changing my faith in the first place, were it not for meeting my
future husband. But I did meet him, and I feel comfortable in his
faith, and so converting was a natural process.' However, some
parental fears are justified and various types of coercion are to be

found. Jill referred earlier to the pressure she felt she was put under by her Jewish fiancé to become Jewish, although in her case it was unspoken and left hanging in the air. Others, though, are given a straight alternative: convert or call off the relationship. Gurjeet was faced with this dilemma when, after a three year courtship, she was suddenly told that if they were to get married she would have to become a Muslim. 'As it happened I had no objection to converting, but I did resent the way in which it was done and the lack of option I was given. In fact, at first I refused, out of principle; but I knew I wanted to marry him and might have converted voluntarily if he had not held a gun to my head, so eventually I relented. In fact, it was my parents who were much more upset and they still keep asking me whether I made the right decision, even though it happened five years ago. For me, it's not an issue any more, whereas they can't let go of it.'

In other instances, it is not the partner who makes demands about conversion but other members of the family. This might be the parents, who feel much more strongly about religious traditions or family identity than does their son or daughter; alternatively, it could be the grandparents, particularly when they occupy a position of influence in the family. Sushil was not bothered whether his bride-to-be became a Hindu or not. He was non-practising and she had a nominal Church of England background. Religion was neither a major issue in his life, nor had it ever caused any problem between them. Yet his grandfather, as head of the family, demanded that she did become a Hindu before he sanctioned the marriage and made it clear that failure to do so would result in a major family rift. Sushil was torn between not wishing to cause such disruption and not wishing to impose on her in this way. However, family roots proved the stronger and with great embarrassment he did tell her that 'life would be much easier if she did convert, and once that was out of the way, everything would go back to normal'. To his immense relief, she consented and she is now as much a nominal Hindu as she was a nominal Christian. Her parents realize why she felt it was worth going through with the conversion, but still feel that it was degrading for her to do so. 'She's a wonderful person, bright, cheerful, very caring, and full of warmth. We feel they are jolly lucky to have her as a daughter-in-law and she didn't need "improving" in any way.' Other scenarios can be even more difficult. Patricia also agreed to convert to her husband's faith under family pressure, but has resented it ever since: 'I am doubly angry. Angry with them for asking me to do something I didn't want and angry with him for not standing up to them. I suppose I'm also angry with myself for not being strong enough at the time to tell them to mind their own religious business. Still, they have lost out in the long run, because although I'm officially Sikh it doesn't mean a thing and we've sent the children to a C of E school. And as we don't live near them – nor ever will, I can assure you of that – they don't actually have much influence on our family life.'

Those partners who do refuse to comply with the pressure to convert have mixed results, with some finding that the relationship comes to an abrupt halt, and others discovering that, after a difficult period, the partner's family eventually comes to terms with the decision and accept them as they are. Very often, the parents can only look on in horror at what they regard as religious intransigence causing their son/daughter such heartache. Of course, some might be accused of the very same thing themselves, as in the case of one set of Jewish parents who threatened to cut off all contact with their daughter if she converted to Christianity. Those who are in the midst of this parental blackmail – whether it be to convert or not to convert – inevitably feel highly resentful, and such actions leave a trail of bitterness whose effects are often more detrimental than the actual conversion that was so feared or desired. It can also lead to angry complaints about inconsistency. When Tara's Anglican parents objected to her conversion to Catholicism, she remembers rounding on them with righteous indignation. 'I was so cross. They had brought me up to be tolerant and open-minded, and for me to have the freedom to make informed choices – all of which I really appreciated – but then when I chose something of which they didn't approve, suddenly choices were a bad idea. In the end, they had to concede, but it left a bad taste in my mouth for some time.'

Parents of the person converting may also be concerned about pressure of a different sort, namely that stemming from the faith itself. 'My son went along to this group's meeting and has never been the same since. He was subject to all sorts of emotional pressures, made to feel he was so special to the group and had such a lot to offer, and has become totally sucked into it. We're devastated. I mean, it's one thing to have a strong belief, but another to turn your life upside down and completely abandon family and friends and just restrict yourself to a tiny sect.' Other parents speak of 'brainwashing' and 'religious kidnapping'. Sometimes this is merely an emotive explanation for what to them is an otherwise totally incomprehesible decision. For one father the question 'Why on earth would he wish to do such a thing – shave his head and dress up in yellow robes' could only be answered by way of brainwashing, and he was unable to understand that the new faith could offer his son a way of life that he found fulfilling. They also fail to appeciate that most of the major world-wide religions today started off as breakaway groups or cults based on the teachings of a charismatic religious personality. Nevertheless, there are parents who have sound reasons for their fears, particularly those whose offspring have joined one of the New Religious Movements and have been systematically indoctrinated. 'I wouldn't mind all the crazy beliefs she now has,' said one mother, 'if at least she looked happy with it. But she's withdrawn and subdued, with none of the sparkle she once had, and she seems to be just wasting her life at the feet of some guru. At first we tried to talk her out of it, but she took the criticism of the cult personally and it just alienated her. So now we try not to say anything that will give offence and keep the channels of communication open, in the hope that one day she will see sense.' Other parents are more pro-active, and try to 'rescue' the child from the religious group in which they are immersed, either through their own efforts or with the help of anti-cult organizations. As Joan put it, 'I am very well aware that one person's truth is another person's nonsense, and that in principle I have to let my daughter make her own choices in life. But I am equally sure that if she makes choices that are unhealthy for her, or even dangerous, then it is my responsibility as a parent to try and help her. I know that there are all sorts of whacky religious beliefs that are perfectly harmless and they don't bother me, but most of the major faiths regard respecting parents as an important religious value. So when I found out that her leader tries to separate new converts from their family life so as to prevent them reverting, then all sorts of warning bells began to go off, and I realized that I had to act quickly before she was totally submerged in it all.'

This wide range of negative reactions can be forthcoming from other members of the family too. Grandparents and siblings might be slightly less emotionally involved than the parents of someone who converts, but they can still feel the same sense of anger, fear, embarrassment, concern and disappointment. When Vanessa gave up Judaism and became a Christian, her sister understood her motives and had no doubt that 'it was probably right for her at the time, but I still felt hurt. Objectively I knew she had merely converted and it was purely a religious issue, but subjectively it felt like she had converted *away* from us and that one of our bonds had just been broken.' When Gai Eaton converted to Islam, his cousin was horrified at what he thought was Gai's descent into a faith of narrow bigotry and tried to give examples of irrational behaviour that might convince him. He told the story of a woman dying painfully in hospital who had summoned the strength to get on her feet and move her iron bedstead so that she could die facing Mecca. 'My cousin was sickened at the thought that she had added to her own suffering for the sake of a "stupid superstition". To me, on the contrary, this seemed a wonderful story. I marvelled at this woman's faith, distant as it was from any state of mind that I could imagine.'[2] For their part, grandparents can be more concerned with the continuity of the family tradition. Perhaps more aware of their mortality than others in the family, they are keen to ensure that religious allegiance is maintained, and even if it is a nominal attachment, there is still a desire to pass on their sense of roots to subsequent generations. Consciously or not, it is seen as an affirmation of their existence and part of their contribution to the family saga. This is especially true if they themselves had made sacrifices or experienced hardships because of their faith, whether it be Hindus who had been persecuted in their former country, Jews who survived the Holocaust, Muslims who suffered discrimination, or Catholics who were bullied at school. Against this background, conversion can be regarded as a betrayal of that endurance, and even 'going over to the enemy' depending on which faith the grandchild adopts.

Another factor in family reactions is the physical environment in which they live. If the family is living close together, with grandparents and parents nearby, then the impact of the person's conversion can be more keenly felt. Parents, for instance, may be equally upset at their son's conversion if he lives a hundred miles away, but it can more painful if they have daily reminders when they see him in the street with a turban or walk by the synagogue which they know he now frequents. This also applies to the size of the area in which they live. In a village or small town where local gossip can encompass the whole population, there is less ability to 'keep our shame to ourselves' than in a more impersonal city. Much depends also on the degree of unfamiliarity with the faith to which the person has converted, and the more exotic it is, the more difficult it can be for the family. A Baptist who becomes a Catholic undergoes little overt change and merely prays in a different building. Someone from the Church of England who adopts Hare Krishna might be seen with shaved head and saffron robes, dancing in the street shaking a tambourine and chanting mantras. For a conservative family this can prove the ultimate nightmare. Nick's parents lived in a relatively small Welsh mining village and were so distraught at the implications of his decision to adopt Sufism that, even though he was living elsewhere, they tried to have him declared insane. They were unable to persuade the local doctor to take such claims seriously, but did tell their neighbours that he had been 'acting funny' for a while and they were still hoping that they could section him and bring him home for treatment. Such rumours helped them explain matters when he did occasionally visit home looking markedly different and certainly earned them expressions of sympathy rather than the disgusted tuts they had so feared.

The reaction of friends and clergy

Friends, too, can react unfavourably, albeit from a different perspective. When Derek became a Muslim, he received congratulations from some friends, but a variety of responses from others. One of them remarked how strange it felt as 'I don't know any Muslims.' When Derek replied 'Well you do now,' his friend said, 'To be honest, I don't think I want to know you any more' and abruptly ended the conversation. It later transpired that the friend felt that Derek had compromised him by becoming a Muslim, and although Derek dismissed it as sheer prejudice and said, 'Frankly I'm better off without friends like that,' the episode was still hurtful. He also found that a certain couple stopped asking him round for dinner. At first he thought it was a social slight but he subsequently discovered that it was simply because they were ignorant of Muslim dietary customs and assumed that he could no longer eat in a non-Muslim household. Other friends took his conversion personally in a different sense. They were very critical at first, but later admitted that it was a defensive reaction because they felt challenged by it. 'They told me that me converting made them think about whether they were fulfilled in their faith or whether they should convert, be it to Islam or anything else. It's something they would not have thought about normally, but my action threw it in their face and made them ask uncomfortable questions they would have preferred not to have bothered about'. He was equally upset when another friend inadvertently made an antagonistic reference to Muslims and when Derek objected and said 'Hold on – I'm Muslim and I'm not like that,' he was told 'Oh, but you don't count.' The inference, as far as Derek was concerned, was that he was not a real Muslim and the great religious journey he felt he had undergone was considered window-dressing by others.

In many of the instances cited above, the initial parental shock was assuaged by a combination of passage of time and patient explanation. Many come to realize that their child's conversion is not a rejection of them personally but a matter of their own development. They also discover that fears of what they thought would be a radical and alienating change of lifestyle are often unfounded. Despite some surface knowledge of other faiths, most people are ignorant of both their theology and their practices. There is also a tendency to equate a minority faith with extremist cults. Thus the father of a woman who became a Muslim fully expected her to have to jettison her promising career in corporate management and was delighted to find that the two were compatible. Similarly, when Martin became a Buddhist, his mother was terrified that he would have to go to Tibet and study for several years, and was greatly relieved to find he would still be living in his bungalow in Reading. Nevertheless, not all parents are accommodating and temporary rifts can harden into permanent fault-lines. Indarjit's father objected vehemently to his son's conversion to Christianity and has refused to speak to him since. On one occasion they passed in the street and the father deliberately crossed the road so as to avoid eye contact. Ten years after her conversion to Islam, Hadijah's parents still find it highly distasteful and dislike any reminder of it. As a result, she feels obliged to remove her *hajib* whenever she visits her parents, even though she finds this hypocritical and knows it would upset her husband if he found out. Georgina's mother knows that her grandchildren are being raised as Sikhs but insists on reading them Bible stories and teaching them Christmas carols whenever she comes to stay. When challenged by Georgina she replies that it should be part of their general education, but Georgina is convinced that it is really a rearguard action to instil in them the love of Christianity that her mother thinks they ought to have.

If parents, siblings and friends can be shocked at a person's conversion, the effect on a spouse can be even more devastating. Fazal's wife was horrified on religious grounds. When he converted to Christianity, she considered that he had not only publicly demeaned her but that he had betrayed Allah, and she sought a divorce immediately. Cynthia – a strong Christian believer – was also hurt by her husband's decision to become a Buddhist, but felt it was her duty to honour her marriage vows. 'The worst part was still going to church, but this time going alone. Sunday worship together was important for me as a person.

Some friends suggested I try to reconvert Chris, but I knew that would just result in endless arguments and make life even more difficult. I do find the situation painful, but I have resolved to live with it and try to be loyal to both my own beliefs and my duties as a wife.' Bernard, by contrast, was more concerned about the personal consequences of his wife's conversion to Judaism: 'It wasn't so much anything against Judaism itself – I like to think of myself as pretty open-minded – but more about what it might do to our marriage. If one partner starts getting involved in a new social group, going off to services and meetings, then it's bound to lead to tension at home, isn't it?' He had no doubt that their marriage was in danger of breaking up and insisted that Katie limited the number of times she 'went off by herself to Jewish things'. That in turn caused her to resent his attitude. 'I would never dream of saying he could not go to a football match or have an evening at the pub with his mates. So when something comes along that is important to me, I feel he should respect my wish to pursue it. I also resent the implication behind it all; that taking up a new faith means I will be unfaithful to him. That's what is really bothering him, and it's both insulting to me as a person and to our marriage, as if the last fifteen years counted for nothing.' However justified she may be logically, there are many partners who react emotionally and fear that such a substantial new element in the marriage could upset the domestic applecart. Their situation highlights the need for all those who convert to explain to family and friends both why they have taken this step and what practical changes it will involve. At the same time they need to invest con-siderable time reassuring family and friends that embracing a new faith does not mean rejecting previous relationships. In particular they need to address the various fears, spoken out loud or unex-pressed, that their act can provoke in those closest to them.

The reactions of the clergy of the faith which the person is leaving can also be very negative. Vicars, priest, rabbis and imams alike generally feel a sense of failure when a member of their flock chooses to join another faith. When a person becomes a lapsed member of the church or synagogue, this can be blamed on the prevailing influence of secularism or the distractions of work or the leisure industry. However, conversion to another faith carries the clear message that the person did have strong spiritual inclinations, but failed to find fulfilment in the faith of their birth. Some ministers might ascribe their defection to 'the work of the devil', or blame the parents for not providing a more religious upbringing, but many will be disappointed that they themselves could not fill the spiritual vacuum. A number will make attempts to 'talk the person out of it', but very often the person concerned has no desire to even enter such a conversation. As Pandith said, somewhat exasperated 'Look, I was a Jew for thirty-four years – they had me for three and a half decades – and throughout that time I never felt spiritually charged, so what use would a five-minute chat with the rabbi be?' Margaret was even more dismissive: 'The vicar's phone call made me really resentful. He'd never shown the slightest interest in me before, and then just as I'm leaving he gets all concerned. Well, I told him it was too late.'

For some clergy, the issue is saving the soul of the person concerned and preventing them from falling into the hands of those they consider ungodly. For others, it is the reputation of the faith itself that is at stake. When Yusuf first announced his intention to convert, the imam sent a delegation of elders round to try to dissuade him. 'Their main argument was the dishonour I would bring upon the faith. They could not understand that what I was interested in was my own spirituality. That was irrelevant for them. In the end it got quite acrimonious and I asked them to leave. No one shook my hand and one of them said that I would come to regret this, which I took as a threat, although nothing actually transpired.' Gerald was not so fortunate. Although he came from a middle-of-the-road Jewish family, his brother had become highly religious and joined an ultra-Orthodox community. When he heard of Gerald's impending conversion, he organized a group of young men to follow him in the street, harassing him either through verbal insults or physical intimidation. After several days of such treatment, he took out a court injunction against them. 'At the time I was both scared and angry. Now, when I look back, part of me feels sorry for them. What sort of faith do they have that makes them try and force people to believe in something they don't believe. I know all Jews aren't like that, but it certainly confirmed for me that it was the wrong religion to be in.'

The effect of persistent criticism can lead some to reassess their conversion. In Raymond's case, the opposition of both his parents and his wider family was so strong and persistent that he eventually began to question whether his adoption of Christianity was the right decision. 'I had come to the church through the fellowship of a number of Christian friends – although I want to emphasize that it really was my choice and there was no pressure by them – they were just the people who introduced me to it, and I came to value it enormously. But my family has always been important to me and frankly to see them so upset was dreadful. I'd always been close to my Dad and I was taken aback by how let down he felt, while my sister found it difficult speaking to me without her voice breaking. This went on for months. It began to sour the joy I had from the church and instead of praying as a Christian I kept on praying for God's help as to whether I should be a Christian in the first place. Eventually it just got too much for me and I decided that I had to put my family first and so I told them it was all over. I didn't formally renounce my baptism, but just stopped going to church and moving in those circles. I certainly didn't become Jewish again – just got on with everyday life and watched more TV. Part of me was very sad at what I'd given up, but I just couldn't carry on with all that tension.' In many other cases, though, criticism leads not to giving up the new faith but breaking with the family. Reza's two brothers could not accept his conversion to Islam even though they themselves were lapsed Christians. Their constant attempts to persuade him to give up the faith led to regular rows, and he decided to cut off relationship with them entirely. 'It's very sad, losing two brothers, but frankly matters had deteriorated to such an extent that seeing them was no fun either. We occasionally meet at some family gathering and give a nod to each other, and when that happens it hurts. I'm sorry, too, that my children are missing out on contact with their uncles and cousins, but there came a point when they had to accept who I was or not have any contact, and it turned out that it couldn't be the former, so it had to be the latter. The irony is that

Islam values family life and so in a sense they are stopping me from being a fulfilled Muslim, but I doubt if that worries them.'

Conversion can also force a change of domicile when state authorities take a hostile stance against those who change their faith. Tariq came to Britain because he feared that his conversion to Christianity in Pakistan would endanger his life. Under Law number 295c in the Pakistan Penal Code, insulting the Prophet Muhammad carries a mandatory death penalty. Conversion comes under this category, and although all cases so far have been commuted under appeal, Tariq was keen not to become an exception to the rule. 'But it wasn't just the law that I was afraid of. My family disowned me and local people would spit when I passed by. My home was no longer home, and even though I moved to a different town, being a Christian from an obviously Muslim background made life very hard. Too hard. I knew I had to leave and go to a Christian country where I could practise my faith undisturbed.' Oswald Rufeisen had the opposite problem, being refused admission to a country because of his conversion. Born a Jew, he had later become a Christian and entered the Carmelite Order where he was known as Brother Daniel. Many years later he provoked a national debate in Israel when he applied to settle there under the Law of Return, which guarantees automatic citizenship of Israel to all Jews living abroad. He claimed that even though he was a member of the Catholic faith he still belonged to the Jewish people and had always been proud of his Jewish roots. His case went to the High Court in Israel, at which it was decided to refuse him citizenship because although technically he was right in claiming to be a Jew by virtue of his birth, according to national-historical consciousness of what it meant to be Jewish, he had left Judaism. It was ruled that through his 'apostasy' – his conversion to Christianity – he had removed himself from the general understanding of Jewish nationality and did not have automatic rights of citizenship.

Conversion can also result in fiscal penalties, such as when Muslims convert to a different faith. Islamic law of inheritance stipulates that a non-Muslim may not inherit from the estate of a Muslim. This has been challenged by some Muslim scholars who hold that once a Muslim has made adequate provision for near-relatives, they may leave money to non-Muslims, especially if they are family members. However, this is not universally accepted, while in Britain the original law still holds much influence even if it lacks legal enforcement. Yasmin's father was sufficiently horrified at her conversion to Christianity to cut her out of his will. She has been assured by a solicitor that as she is the only child, and as her mother has already died, she should have a good chance of being able to overturn the will if her father does not amend it before his death. However, it will involve considerable time and expense, and with no guarantee of success. She is equally upset by the inference that 'my father will die childless, whereas I'm still his daughter and still love him dearly'. The result is that her conversion may prove very costly, both emotionally and financially.

Much attention has been given to hostile reactions from members of the faith from which a person has converted. This is partly because they stem from a variety of different causes which need to be distinguished from each other, and partly because they are so common. However, there are also many instances of neutral reactions. For family or friends who have no particular faith, a person's conversion can be totally irrelevant. Some might still object on racial grounds, prejudiced against the group to which the person has allied him/herself, whilst others may fear a loss of contact if the person throws him/herself into an entirely new life-style and becomes divorced from former associates. For many, though, religion has become such a personalized subject – a matter of free choice and for the individual concerned – that it is simply not an issue for others. Despite being thirty-one years old and living away from home for more than a decade, Daphne was slightly apprehensive at telling her parents she was converting. 'They aren't religious in the slightest, but I suppose I was worried that they might see it as some kind of slap in the face. I needn't have worried. My mother said "That's interesting", chatted for a bit about it and then got bored with the subject, while my father just wanted to know whether he had to do or not do anything special when he came to visit me at my house.' There are also parents who are religious but do not automatically object to a child's conversion, for they know the value of faith and can recognize the need to pursue it in whatever form, even if it is different from their own way. Surinder was concerned at the reaction he would receive when he told his father, a practising Sikh, that he was becoming a Hindu. 'Dad was saddened that I wouldn't be keeping up the family tradition, but he told me that the whole point of giving me a good education was so that I could make informed choices in life, and if that applied to religion too, then so be it.'

Ben's father took a similar stance on hearing his son was changing from Judaism to Christianity 'He was disappointed – no doubt about that – but he also said that he'd far prefer me to have a different faith to him than have no faith at all. I really admired him for that, and hope I can take the same attitude with my children.' Other parents had no qualms and reacted with delight. 'Obviously Buddhism does not mean anything to me, 'said Robert's mother, 'but I am pleased he has found something that means a lot to him. I have no problems with it and hope it lasts.' This can apply to partners too. Kerry's husband was somewhat bemused when she went to a Billy Graham rally as an interested observer and came back a committed Christian. 'I wasn't sure how long she would keep it up, but either way I was happy for her to have a faith or not. It's completely up to her. As it happens she's stuck with it, and although it means she goes to church without me, there are plenty of things I do without her, and we talk about the things we each do, and that's fine.' Donna's family were overjoyed for another reason. For years they had despaired at her involvement in drugs and had failed to find any way of weaning her away from them. Her conversion to Christianity had achieved that object and had led her to mix in a totally different social circle. As her brother put it, 'Frankly, the rest of us are not very religious at all, but we can see how much it's improved the quality of her life. For the first time in a long time we can actually think of her having a future worth talking about, and that's got to be good news.'

Reactions from members of the new faith

If reactions to converts from members of their former faith can be expected to be mixed, it is much more surprising that the same applies to members of the faith they are joining. Naturally there are many who are delighted at the conversion. Ten years on, Rachel still recalls the joy with which she was greeted by members of the church she attended when her baptism was announced. 'People I hardly knew came up to me and hugged me and I felt enveloped in a sea of love. It was a wonderful experience and I can feel it even now.' The motives behind the welcome can be due to a number of different factors. One is because those already within the faith believe it will benefit the person concerned, and that it will have a positive impact on their life. Alternatively, it can be because they feel it validates the faith they themselves profess. A new addition to the religion is seen as affirmation of its truth and what it has to offer. Every conversion helps to reinforce existing members in their beliefs. This is particularly the case when those members feel under attack from surrounding mores. Thus many belonging to the Church of England today regard themselves as a minority faith despite being the established church. Other Christian groups are painfully aware of the attractions of secular culture and the inroads it has made into their own membership. Those faiths that have a high percentage of immigrants often feel doubly challenged, being both a religious and ethnic minority. When someone chooses to join any of these religious groups, it can be a powerful fillip to their aspirations. As one Muslim leader put it: 'Every convert means we have got the message right; but a white convert is even better than a black one, because that shows that Western culture is not as superior as it thinks and we have got something to offer too.' In addition, for those faiths who are committed to missionary activity, a conversion represents one more step along what they perceive to be the divine task allotted to them. Thus each individual conversion has much greater ramifications on a cosmic scale, leading ultimately to the redemption of the world. For others, though, it is simply the delight at welcoming a new soul, especially if the person comes from a background that they themselves respect. Sara's mother-in-law is a deeply religious Christian, and as she put it: 'I am lucky enough to have a daughter-in-law who used to be Jewish.'

The acclamation that greets many converts is not the only reaction. When Anne told a Jewish friend that she had converted to Judaism, she was informed: 'I am not sure whether to offer you congratulations or condolences.' Although she was taken aback at the time, she came to view it as a wise remark, preparing her for the enormous variety of responses she would receive, including many negative ones which in turn stem from a wide range of motives. Some view conversion as simply impossible and they see it as a flawed attempt to be something that cannot be. Anne quotes a letter she received which stated: 'A true Jewish heart is not created. It is born in one, irrespective of the depth of religious knowledge or observance, and cannot be acquired through a well intentioned course of study and instruction. I hope you will understand that although I have every respect for you personally, I cannot accept you as Jewish.' She remembers exploding with fury after reading it: 'Why should Jews have a monopoly on Judaism? Especially those that don't take it seriously. It's like a child who doesn't want to play with his toys any more, but then won't let anyone else have a go with them.' As Judaism itself accepts conversion, the writer of that letter is at odds with his own faith, yet there is often to be found a discrepancy between what a faith advocates and what its members practise. Whilst this may be of little relevance in other areas, it is particularly important for proselytes, because although the clergy may convert a person, the way in which they are received by the membership will determine how much they feel at home in the faith, or even if they drop out of it. For some, the objections are based on tribalism. If the religious group has a deep sense of identity based on being different from others, it can then find it very hard to lower a drawbridge to the outside world and let someone else in. This applies even more so if members of the faith have experienced persecution at the hands of others, and have maintained their faith at some personal cost.

This was one of the reasons why a number of Catholics were horrified at thought of countless former adherents of the Church of England joining their ranks in the wake of the women's ordination controversy. There was also a suspicion that 'single-issue converts' lacked true sincerity and it was stated that there should be no welcome for 'those people'.[3] They were even publicly warned by the then Cardinal of Westminster, Basil Hume, that they had to accept the entire range of Catholic doctrines and that it was 'Table d'hôte, not à la carte', although his remarks may have been more to reassure nervous born-Catholics. In vain did many of the newcomers protest that they were helping to reinforce the Catholic Church, yet they were still treated as intruders and seen as a threat.[4] In a similar way, a ghetto mentality has survived amongst Jews long after the physical ghettos have been destroyed and they are often suspicious of non-Jews who wish to convert. For some Jews it is an inability to abandon previously held stereotypes of the outside world, for others it is more a desire to cling on to the sense of being separate and special, with the fear that changing the former will also change the latter. In many instances, this opposition verges on prejudice and inverted racism. It is as if Jews are so used to fortifying themselves to withstand antisemitism than they find prosemitism hard to accept. In Islam, too, there are many who feel that, despite the universal tenets of the faith which recognizes no racial barriers, those who are white are less authentic. One study showed that 51% of new Muslims felt isolated because of the prevailing attitude that to be a good Muslim one had to be Arab or Pakistani, and anything else was suspect.[5] Despite injunctions in the Koran for Muslims to 'Help one another in what is good and pious' (5:2), many sense a 'them and us' divide between born-Muslims and converts. It is certainly noticeable in Britain that despite the large number of converts, few white converts have been allowed to achieve positions of responsibility within the faith or are allowed to make pronouncements on religious matters.[6]

In some cases the objections to converts are articulated aloud and given concrete reasons, such as fears that their new-found faith might prove to be very shallow and they might lapse. In this case, it would not only be a dishonour to the new faith, but prove hurtful to those who had invested time and energy in teaching the person or welcoming them into communal life. Amos was astonished to find a Muslim friend who was staying with him for the weekend hunting through his clothes drawers. When challenged, the friend said that he had been told to check that Amos had not secretly kept any crucifixes or copies of the New Testament, despite his conversion to Islam. Another fear is that if the convert marries someone within the faith, they might influence them to drop out or even convert them to the person's original faith. Sometimes such concerns are projected onto the potential influence that the convert's family might wield, for even if the convert is sincere, his/her parents will retain their own faith and may one day secretly initiate any grandchildren into their religion. Other worries are that converts might dilute the faith and 'water down' the beliefs and practices that they are supposed to be upholding. When Georgina became a Sikh she was told by one member of the gurdwara, 'I will be watching you to make sure you don't start trying to change anything. Our faith has been unchanged for centuries and that has been our strength. Don't think you can come along and undo it all in five minutes.' The fact that such a remark is completely unhistorical – virtually all faiths have changed in some way as a result of both contact with outside influences and natural development – is irrelevant compared to the assumption that converts cannot be trusted to maintain the purity of the faith. Little wonder that Georgina felt that 'I was constantly on trial – even after I'd been converted for several years,' a sentiment echoed by many in other religions too. Conversely, there are those who are concerned that converts are becoming too involved and 'taking over', which is usually untrue and just reflects the participation of one or two individuals. What is more significant is the sub-text behind such a concern, namely that it would be bad for the faith if converts were to be in the ascendant because they cannot be relied upon to uphold it. People can be equally prejudiced if a person comes to convert because of the faith of their partner, in which case it is often dubbed 'the marriage motive' and seen as an automatic indication of insincerity. This is even though only a small percentage of mixed-faith relationships actually lead to conversion and only those partners who feel an affinity with the faith opt to convert, while the vast majority remain in the faith, or lack of faith, in which they started the relationship.

The reservations about proselytes can be held as much by those who do not take the religion seriously as those that do. Sometimes, it is the former who are the most antagonistic as they feel most threatened by the proselyte's superior knowledge or deeper commitment. The one claim they have over converts is the blood-line and the fact that they stem from several generations of the faithful, and thus, in their eyes, have a superior relationship with the faith that no amount of enthusiasm by converts can ever dislodge. Not surprisingly this can lead to anger among converts who feel that their faith, though recent, is just as valid as that of others. It can be especially galling to be treated as inferior by those whose own religious involvement is questionable. Sometimes, the acceptance or rejection of a convert can depend on nothing more substantial than their looks. Jill is acutely aware that she is always treated more coolly by Jews than is her sister-in-law, who also converted to Judaism. 'The difference is that I am blonde and don't look Jewish, whereas she is dark-haired and can play the part better. I remember my father-in-law saying when he first met me that I would always stand out as different. At the time I thought he meant it as a compliment, but now I realize it was an expression of regret.' Sometimes this latent antipathy is apparent in terms in which converts are addressed, as when Sheila's father-in-law refers to her as my 'shiksa daughter-in-law'. 'Shiksa' is semi-derogatory Yiddish slang for non-Jew. Technically it is totally inappropriate for Sheila, who converted to Judaism some years earlier, but it obviously reflects the way in which her in-laws still regard her. When Sheila once challenged him on his use of the term, her father-in-law laughed it off as a harmless phrase 'that didn't mean a thing', but despite this denial the message it gives declares unequivocally his perception of her. Equally telling was when she and a Jewish friend were shopping together in a supermarket. When Sheila took care to examine the ingredients of some biscuits she was buying so as to check they were free of animal fats and corresponded to Jewish dietary laws, her friend asked 'Why are you so fussy about that?' The clear implication was that her

Jewishness was only surface level and there was no need to pretend that she was taking it seriously. Sheila remembers biting her tongue at that point, 'but I wished I had answered back and said something like: "Look I'm as Jewish as you now, and I wouldn't have bothered becoming Jewish if it didn't mean a lot to me." '

The problem of acceptance applies to all faiths, but has a particular twist within Judaism because a person who converts is often given a special label at the time. Part of the conversion procedure is for the convert to be given a Hebrew name – which born-Jews receive at birth – which is occasionally used for certain rituals during services. The name involves a first name and a patronymic, the Hebrew name of one's father. However, as converts do not have a father with a Hebrew name, the tradition has been to call them the 'son/daugher of Abraham our father'. The intention is to root them in Jewish tradition, relating them directly to the spiritual father of all Jews, Abraham. However, the result is that whenever a name in synagogue is called out in this way, it immediately tells everyone else that the person is a convert and remind others not so much of their current Jewish status but their previous non-Jewish origins. In view of the negative effect this custom has had, changes are beginning to take place and some rabbis advise the convert not to take the traditional patronymic but to select any other name and thereby avoid publicly drawing attention to themselves. As Rabbi Joseph explained, 'It's not that I advise them to hide the fact that they are proselytes – on the contrary I regard their conversion as a great compliment to their dedication – but to remember that that name goes with them for the rest of their life, and twenty-five years on it's simply not appropriate to flag them in that way. Once they've become Jewish, that's that, and no distinctions should be made as to what sort of Jew they are or what route they travelled to get there.'

In some cases, negative attitudes to converts can take highly offensive forms. One Muslim groom-to-be was taken aside by two uncles on the day before his wedding to a convert and he was offered a handsome amount of money if he called off the marriage. 'I turned it down with a laugh but actually I was shocked by what it meant they thought of her. I saw a lovely woman, but they saw an infidel. When I pointed out that she was now a Muslim too, they said that it was still a dishonour to the family to marry someone without proper Muslim credentials. Needless to say they didn't come to the ceremony the next day, but I never told my wife why.' Greg received no such protection, for at his wedding reception a distant relative, who did not realize that he was a convert, confidentially informed him that 'converts are the AIDS of Judaism'. Greg decided not to make a fuss and spoil the atmosphere. 'I rationalized it to myself afterwards that he must be pretty insecure in his beliefs to come out with such vile nonsense, and I practised in my head all sorts of stunning put-downs in case he ever said it again.' Others are less insulting in their opinions about converts, but will admit to feeling constrained in their presence and ill at ease as to what they can and cannot say. In many cases this infers that they would make derogatory remarks not so much about converts but about those outside the faith, and are worried that the converts might object or take it personally.

This nervousness reflects the insularity and 'them and us' mentality that can develop amongst many faiths or denominations despite the generally accepted principle to love all human beings as fellow creatures of God. This can affect particularly those who already have a convert in their immediate family. In some instances, it can make them more appreciative of the contribution of those born outside the faith and happy to welcome others into the fold. However, it can also have the opposite effect, with families being very sensitive about the reputation of 'their convert' and not wishing to encourage the acceptance of others whom they perceive as being of a lower standard which might then, in their eyes, cast aspersion on all converts, including theirs. Being hostile to new converts is a way of 'protecting' the uniqueness of the existing one, as if to say that he/she is of such exceptional quality that they alone merited the privilege of entry. Once again, it is a reaction that implies that converts are fundamentally different from those born into the faith, with the clear implication that they are less authentic. This was made clear in no uncertain terms to Derek who had converted to Islam for its own sake and who later fell in love with a Muslim girl. He was told by the girl's brother, 'If you love my sister, leave her.' He might be Muslim in faith, but was not Muslim enough.

Indifference can sometimes feel as hurtful as hostility. Joanna never experienced any negative reactions when she became a Muslim, but neither did she receive anything positive. 'I was rather taken aback that I was so ignored. People were never unpleasant, but nobody at the mosque went out of their way to talk to me or involve me in anything. I am sure that they were pleased that I had converted, but it ended there and they didn't feel obliged to help integrate me in any way.' Her story is remarkably similar to comments of others: 'I am interesting and something to be shown off . . . but always a novice whose opinion never counts. They would be upset if I returned to Christianity or became a Hindu, yet they make no real effort to assimilate me into the community.' As another convert to Islam put it, 'Ultimately you're just a feather in the cap against this horrible, awful Western society'.[7] The remarks emphasize the cultural and racial divide that converts often have to overcome, especially if it is a white person from the majority Christian culture joining the ranks of a minority faith largely consisting of first or second generation immigrants. A high percentage of white converts to Islam, for instance, are middle class, well educated and professional. They have to integrate into a community that is often lower class, poorer, and less educated. The convert may feel totally at home reading the Koran, but can feel ill at ease in a mosque that, to them, can more resemble a Third World bazaar than a place of worship. It can be especially difficult when elements within the Muslim community automatically identify white people with outsiders. Thus graffiti on a wall near a mosque in Bradford declares 'Islamic Jihad against whites', while the term 'kafir', meaning 'non-believer', is commonly used by some regarding white people. There is also an inherent racism in the way in which converts are spoken of. Although the more respectable way of referring to them is 'New Muslims', they are also often called 'White Muslims'. The former term denotes that they are recent additions to the faith, whereas the latter highlights the fact that they are different from most born-Muslims.

It often seems that converts are in a series of 'no-win' situations. If they convert because of their marriage, they are dubbed insincere, whereas if they come of their own accord, they are regarded as interlopers. Similarly, if, after conversion, they do not participate greatly in religious life, they are accused of lacking faith, whereas if they become very active, they are labelled as pushy. Moreover, if their knowledge is poor, they are ridiculed as unworthy, whereas if they are learned in the faith they are resented as arrogant. Some converts accept this as an inevitable part of the conversion process, even regarding it as a test of their convictions. Seema realized that 'as a white woman entering a mosque largely of people from the Indian sub-continent, I was bound to be different. I knew that they weren't objecting to me personally – how could they? Most of them didn't even know my name – so I didn't get hung up on personal angst but got on with trying to become a good Muslim and eventually people came to accept me.' Others are not so generous and Sheila freely admits that 'there were times when if it wasn't for my husband I would have told some of them to get stuffed and keep their holier-than-thou attitudes to themselves. I know those sort of people don't represent the faith as a whole, which is much more positive, but as they are the people who you come into contact with regularly it does begin to rankle and make you wonder.'

The attitude of those whose partner has converted to their faith typifies the general ambivalence that has already been seen. Many are delighted, either because they see it as an affirmation of their own beliefs, or because it unites the family in one faith and means that they are 'heading in the same direction'. It certainly makes the religious upbringing of children much easier, avoiding potential conflicts over their education and confusions as to their identity. A conversion can also help ease family tensions if one set of parents objected to the fact that it was a mixed-faith marriage and caused difficulties for the couple. In some cases, the partner had been actively encouraging such step by inviting the person to their place of worship or providing books for them to read. In other instances, they had taken no action but secretly hoped that the person would take the initiative of their own accord. Jeff's wife had never put any pressure on her husband to convert to Judaism. 'I told him I loved him as he was – and that was true – and neither before or after our marriage did I ever suggest he do anything to change. It's a very good relationship and he was as happy for me to be Jewish as I was for him not to be. But deep down I always felt it would be even better if he did become Jewish, and I can't tell you how overjoyed I was when one day he turned round and said he was thinking of converting.'

The conversion can also have a positive effect for the partner's own religious involvement. When Hussein's wife became interested in Islam she bombarded him with questions about his beliefs and practices. 'I often found I didn't have a good enough knowledge to answer. Being brought up as a Muslim I take a lot of it for granted and never stop to ask why we do this or what are the origins of that. I had to start doing some background reading myself and found it fascinating. I also went to lectures on Islamic history and culture with her – something I'd never have done by myself. I'm probably a much better Muslim now, and certainly more informed.' Many others can tell a similar story, of how their partner's interest stimulated their own awareness and deepened their faith. However, there are also those who can be worried by their partner's interest in converting. For those who are not especially religious they can be fearful about what sort of demands might be made on them. Jackie's husband was a non-practising Muslim and was slightly apprehensive that her enthusiasm for Islam might lead her to insist he go to the mosque more often or be stricter about abstinence from alcohol. 'I know I don't keep all the rules, but I'm comfortable with the way I am.' Jonathan's concern was more for his wife and that she did not feel she was under any pressure to convert. 'Part of me was delighted when she announced her decision, but I also spent the next six months asking her if she was sure it was right for her. The one thing I didn't want her to do was to convert for my sake. It had to be because she wanted it and I would have felt an enormous burden if it was just to please me.'

Strange as it may seem, there are also those who strenuously object when a partner decides to convert to their faith. Roopa sensed that her husband felt threatened by it: 'He would never say why he was so against my converting, but just said that it wasn't necessary. Personally, I think it was because it meant he was no longer the expert in the family, the one who said what we had to do when and why. Now I would have equal knowledge and be able to pre-empt him or contradict him. It's all to do with power, not religion.' For others, the conversion brought unwelcome changes into the household. Jill's husband came to resent the fact that her new attachment to Judaism meant he was no longer allowed to have bacon and eggs for breakfast. He feels that her conversion has changed the mutual understanding that they had upon getting married: 'Look, it's a strong relationship, so we're not heading for divorce, but I am equally aware that Jill now is not the Jill that I married. I realize that this happens in all marriages, and it just so happens that in our case the change has been on a religious level, but I also reckon that if I'd wanted to marry a wife who kept kosher, then I'd have married someone Jewish in the first place. So, yes, she has changed the goalposts and every morning I resent it for five minutes or so.' As Esther Rantzen famously commented after her husband of many years decided to become Jewish: 'What? After I've gone to all this trouble to marry out?' In turn, such reactions can be demoralizing for the person converting. As Jill commented: 'On one level I understand his point of view, but it also makes me sad that he doesn't value the religious heritage he was born with. There are also times when I get angry that he makes such a fuss about something that I value. I try to make room for what's important to him – be it freshly ironed shirts or Manchester United – so why can't he do the same for me?' Once again, converts can be placed in a no-win situation. If the convert does not succeed in making the partner adopt a new lifestyle, the convert can feel let down; but if they do force changes upon the partner, it can lead to friction. Either way, the conversion can result in an emotional minefield, and they will look with envy at those converts who do receive the support and approval of their partners. This lack of welcome can be even more difficult for those who were the subject of hostility from members of the faith which they left. The result is that, as Jill found out, 'you can feel as if you are in a religious no-man's-land, rejected by the family whose faith you once shared, and kept at arm's length by those whose faith you are joining. It's a double isolation and can leave you feeling very alone.'

It is little wonder that a variety of support groups for converts have sprung up in different faiths. The Association of British Muslims was established in 1973 to help converts adjust to the Muslim community. Nominally open to all Muslims, it consists primarily of proselytes, and is seen as forum for white middle-class British born and educated Muslims to find those with a common social and cultural background. An older group is the Circle, which is largely for converts to Islam who are professionals, which meets regularly for both social and learning purposes. A group of female converts to Judaism met in the 1980s called the Ruth Group, named after the famous biblical proselyte. Their aim was to share their experiences together – including the slights and prejudice they sometimes received – but also to try to educate others within the Jewish community both as to how converts felt and ways of integrating them better. As one member put it: 'After fifteen years as a Jew, I am at last being accepted as fully Jewish. That's a ridiculously long probation period, and I don't want others to have to go through the same hushed embarrassment I had to face for so long.' The Ruth Group would set its meetings to coincide with potentially difficult periods, such as just before Christmas or Passover, which can lead to various domestic tensions. Members of the group also had the possibility to call meetings if ever they felt they needed special support. Useful as such groups are, they can also present certain problems. Those who choose to mix primarily with fellow converts thereby delay the process of integration and can reinforce their sense of marginalization from the majority of the members of the faith. The groups can also lead to some resentment from those already within the faith, being seen as 'exclusive'. This applies especially to the Association of British Muslims, which is regarded in some quarters as a club for white Muslims who feel too superior to mix with born-Muslims. As with so many aspects of conversion, intentions and interpretations can often differ widely.

6

After Conversion

Everyday matters

Adopting a new faith can be compared to a couple who fall in love. After the excitement of the courtship and the wedding comes the marriage. So too with converts. After the joy of the first encounter and the initiation ceremony comes the mundane reality of everyday life. These can include a host of religious chores, personal dilemmas and difficult relationships. For many, it is only at this stage that the real religious work begins, along with the process of acclimatization into the new culture. According to Jewish tradition, a convert is like a newborn child, starting afresh, learning to breathe in a totally new environment. While this may not hold true for everyone – especially those who had identified with their new faith for several years before formally converting – it is an image that applies to many others. There are new customs to assimilate that are often not official parts of the faith and not mentioned in any textbooks, but are deeply embedded in the culture surrounding it. There is a new circle of people among whom one mixes and new forms of communal activity. There are new perspectives on the course of the week, while the cycle of the year can change even more radically. These, combined in some cases with different ways of dressing and eating, can mean that the rhythm of one's life can change dramatically. It can also entail hard work to achieve both integration into the new community and a personal sense of ease. As Margaret put it: 'I may have become *a* Muslim, but it still took a long time before I could honestly say "I am Muslim." ' It is the difference between official status and actual state of being. Rather like learner drivers who have passed the test but still drive afterwards exactly according to the rule book, they eventually come to drive by instinct, knowing which rules to keep, which to ignore, and how to react when unforeseen circumstances arise.

It is no coincidence that one of the most repetitive daily human activities – eating – is often invested with regulations and rituals by the various religions. It is part of sanctifying the ordinary and ensuring that the faith encompasses all aspects of one's existence. For those born into a faith, the dietary laws are natural and automatic, but for those new to it they can demand much attention and preparation. Anne had no problems with the principles of keeping kosher, but often got caught out with the practices. 'Old habits die hard, and many a time have I enjoyed a meat dish, and for dessert poured some cream over the pudding and then remembered we don't mix meat and milk products in the same meal. Whoops!' She also confesses to salivating whenever she passes by a Wimpy restaurant. 'They used to be my favourite, and although I don't eat them anymore that doesn't stop me remembering how good they tasted. Especially the cheeseburgers. That would be a double sin now – not only non-kosher meat, but mixing it with cheese.' When Derek converted to Islam, he was living in London and found it easy to obtain halal meat, but a move to Devon meant there was no local supplier and that forced him to make special arrangements. 'On one level it was a real nuisance, but on another I know got a sense of pride at having to put myself out for my faith. As a Christian, food didn't count as a religious rite at all. You could have anything anytime. Now I have certain limitations as to what I can consume, while at Ramadan it also affects when I eat. At first, I had to spend a lot of time consciously reminding myself not to eat before sunset during the festival, whereas now it has become second nature. I guess that shows I've got there at last.' For Kewel there was a different problem. Having been brought up a Hindu and lived in a vegetarian environment for twenty-eight years, he found it hard to adapt to a meat-eating culture when he became a Muslim. Although he was happy to remain a vegetarian and knew he was not transgressing any Islamic rules in so doing, some Muslims found his behaviour suspicious and questioned whether or not he had truly given up his Hindu faith. He found this mildly irritating and a symptom of the fact that, in certain circles, converts feel they constantly have to prove themselves: 'The truth is that, having uttered the *Shahada*, I am now a Muslim. It's not conditional on future behaviour, although of course I should not do anything to dishonour the faith. So I sort of resent having to be at a supreme level of piety all the time and it would be nice to feel I can be an ordinary Muslim without other people suddenly thinking I had lost my faith.'

A potentially much more serious food problem is when new dietary habits can act as a barrier between a convert and their family. When Anne went to her parents for a meal to celebrate her father's birthday shortly after converting and her mother served up 'Dad's favourite – roast pork – my heart sank. Now it's become automatic to warn them, and other hosts, in advance about what I do and don't eat. But it's not just a matter of pre-planning. I think my mother resents my dietary restrictions, because she feels it then restricts what she can cook.' Derek was surprised by his father's objections to him eating only halal meat. 'Dad never does the cooking at home, so it didn't really affect him, while Mum was quite happy doing fish or something whenever we came by . . . so I suspect it was something deeper . . '. his way of objecting to my conversion altogether, except he was reticent about saying that directly, so it all got channelled into criticizing the meat.' Margaret was hurt for another reason. Her mother was more than happy to obtain halal meat from a local halal butcher whenever she entertained Margaret and her husband. However, when he was away on a business trip and Margaret came round for dinner by herself, she found that her mother had bought ordinary meat. When Margaret queried her action, she replied that as her husband was not present, Margaret could eat what she liked. 'That upset me more than the wrong meat. It meant she thought I was only doing it for my husband and not for myself. Clearly she hadn't come to terms with the fact that it was my decision and for reasons of my own. Maybe she didn't want to accept that I really had changed and projecting it onto him was a way of not facing up to it.'

Far more difficult, though, was Jackie's experience. Her parents had already made known their objections to her conversion to Islam, but after lengthy discussions she thought they had reached an agreement to disagree civilly. She was therefore appalled when she came home for a weekend to discover that Sunday breakfast was bacon and eggs. 'It was quite deliberate. We never had cooked breakfasts on Sundays, and Dad hardly eats bacon much anyway. It was their way of making me feel uncomfortable. Mum mumbled something about how she'd forgotten I didn't eat pork any more and would I like a soft-boiled egg instead, but she hadn't forgotten, and I felt really hurt.' As it happened she had a similar experience a few weeks later with old friends of hers, 'but this time it was for a different reason. They simply didn't connect food with religion. It's so alien from the Christian experience. It made me realize that being Muslim demands a completely different mindset. It also means I not only have to think for myself but think ahead for others and help them take account of it.' The opposite scenario applied to Brian. After his conversion to Judaism, he gradually became more and more observant to the extent that he only ate in homes that kept high standards of Jewish dietary laws, not just in terms of the food but the cutlery and crockery that were used. 'Going to my parents became quite difficult from that point of view, and eventually the only way to resolve it was to take my own food and use a disposable paper plate that had not come into contact with any non-kosher produce. My mother understood to a certain extent and went along with it for my sake, but I suspect part of her felt upset that she couldn't provide food for her own child. Truth to tell, it made me feel a little odd too, as Judaism tells me to honour my parents and here I am inadvertently slighting them.' It can certainly be emotionally confusing for many converts when they find that new forms of daily behaviour separate them from those to whom they are close. The clash between the demands of their faith and their loyalty to family and friends can be a source of unexpected conflict. Moreover, previously inconsequential details can become highly significant, as with a slice of bacon being invested with much more importance than it ever once attracted.

Clothing is another daily routine that can take on particular significance for the new convert. Those brought up in the Christian tradition see little connection between faith and dress. A vicar may wear a Geneva band, a nun a wimple, and a monk a habit, but these are badges of religious orders, and the ordinary worshipper is not obliged to follow any sartorial rules. But when former Christians convert to another faith, they often face such obligations. Gerry converted because he was very much impressed by the teachings and lifestyle of the Sikh faith. However, he was less sure about the need to wear a turban. 'I suppose, to be honest, I was plain embarrassed. I was proud to be a Sikh but very embedded in the English tradition of not wearing your faith on your sleeve . . . and in my case, on your head. In fact, I put off conversion for while so that I didn't have to face the issue. In the end I told myself I just had to get through the first week's worth of stares and after that it would be okay. And it was.' Jason was equally committed to Judaism but felt that it would be inappropriate to wear a head-covering at work. He, too, was influenced by a Christian culture which tended to distinguish between daily life and church life, and limit displays of faith to the latter. 'I know Judaism holds that religion should permeate all aspects of life and has as many daily rituals as it does Sabbath ones, but I decided that I would simply feel too uncomfortable making overt public statements about my Judaism. I don't hide it, but I don't advertise it either. So I wear a head-covering on the Sabbath eve at home or at services in synagogue, but not during office hours.'

Yasmin has the opposite problem. Coming from a Pakistani Muslim family she was used to wearing a traditional woman's robe and shawl and continued to do so after her conversion to Christianity. In doing so, however, she has sowed much confusion, as her Christian friends object to what they consider to be her retention of vestiges of Islam, while Muslim friends object that she is masquerading as a Muslim. Yasmin finds both reactions puzzling, as she regards her clothes as reflecting her ethnic origins and devoid of any religious message. Seema, by contrast, was keen to maintain her individuality by not adopting the traditional robes when she became a Muslim. 'Yes, I had changed my faith, but I was still the same essential me and I felt it would be wrong to adopt a veil. I still wear a smart business suit and a reasonable amount of jewellery, although I am careful not to be indecorous or flashy. Islam affects how I dress, but not what I dress.' Those who do take on a totally new attire often become used to surprised expressions by those who jump to assumptions about them. Roopa wears a white sari and often sees a look of astonishment on people's faces when they first hear her strong Irish accent. 'Some people get very embarrassed and apologetically say that they didn't know there were any Irish Hindus, others realize their prejudices have been caught out and laugh at themselves.'

Whether or not to wear religious symbols is a similar decision that confronts new converts. When Anne converted to Judaism, she rushed out the next day and bought a Star of David neckchain to celebrate. 'It was a tangible symbol of the change I had made. I was very proud of being accepted as Jewish and I wanted everyone to know.' Vanessa felt just as happy at her baptism, but when a friend gave her a cross on chain as a present, she decided to wear it underneath her clothes. 'My conversion has caused quite a bit of upset in my family, and although it hasn't stopped me going ahead, I don't want to flaunt it in their face every time I see them. I know the cross is there, and that's all that matters.'

Standards of food and clothing are matters of conscious decision which converts can consider at leisure in advance. A more difficult aspect to control is everyday speech and mannerisms. Charles found that he kept on saying 'Jesus Christ' at odd moments, such as if he dropped a glass or tripped over something on the floor. 'It's fine saying that in a pub, but when you say it in synagogue there's a deathly hush. What's even worse, it makes people think how deep my conversion is or whether I'm still a Christian.' There are also various expressions that are not overtly religious but are embedded in Christian culture – such as saying 'touch wood' – which can be innocuous to most ears but raise eyebrows in certain circles who see them as alien religious influences. In this respect the position of converts is more sensitive than that of others. A born Jew, for instance, can say 'touch wood' without co-religionists thinking him a secret Christian, whereas a convert who says it is viewed with suspicion. 'It's very unfair,' said Charles, 'in that I have to watch myself in a way that others don't have to. I suppose there will come a time when I'm not on guard and can be myself, but I sometimes do get annoyed with the fact that although I converted three years ago I have to keep on proving it every day.' Others try to acclimatize into the new faith by actively adopting various expressions and mannerisms. Helga, for instance, consciously peppered her conversation with Yiddish expressions, while Brian's friends noticed he was increasingly talking with his hands or shrugging his shoulders. Public perceptions can be a motivating factor to other types of action. Ever since becoming a Muslim, Reza has taken the obligation to give to charity very seriously. 'I try to budget a monthly amount to give to good causes rather than wait for a disaster and appeals to come round. The trouble is that even if I have given my monthly allocation, if I pass a charity-collector in the High Street, I feel I have to give some extra because it will look bad if I as a Muslim walk past without bothering to help.'

Religious observances

It might be expected that in specifically religious matters, converts would be highly observant and put into practice the ritual obligations of the faith they had chosen to join. This is often the case, but not universally so and a varied picture emerges. Many do take ritual demands very seriously and the popular wisdom that a convert is more zealous than someone born into the faith is often true. Attendance at public services, prayers at home and personal rituals are often scrupulously observed. 'Of course I go regularly to church and read the Bible daily,' said Donna, 'that's precisely the reason why I converted, because it means a lot to me. Why on earth would I have bothered otherwise?' Brian records how a friend he made after becoming Jewish confided that he knew Brian must be a convert because he took it so much more seriously than anyone else he knew. 'It was as if my faith was a give-away sign. In one respect I felt rather pleased that it was noticeable that my Judaism was very important to me, but I also questioned what that said about everyone else and where their level of commitment was.

It would be much better if everyone was so keyed up that I didn't stand out.' It is an experience that crosses the faiths and Evelyn recalls that on one occasion in the mosque she was gently warned that she was giving converts a bad name by being so over-enthusiastic and putting off born-Muslims. 'I was astonished. I was prepared to accept criticism for not doing things right because I was a newcomer, but not for being too religious!' Converts will also be keen to involve themselves in wider communal life, such as cultural or educational activities. Faith and community are closely related, and for many their new faith is not just a matter of personal worship but of identifying with the community that shares that faith. Many are aware, moreover, that the conversion course covered only a small aspect of the religion and they still have much to learn through other courses. A number are also keen to share the joy of their new faith through teaching others. Most synagogues in Britain have a Religion School for two hours on a Sunday morning, and amongst Reform and Liberal congregations a disproportionately high number of teachers are converts. As Jill put it, 'It's quite noticeable – to me at least – that three out of the eight teachers are proselytes. I suppose we feel very strongly we want to play our part in the community and so are motivated enough to drag ourselves out of bed on a Sunday morning at a time when many born-Jews are still fast asleep!'

Not all are so scrupulous. Many clergy notice that once an applicant has been welcomed into the faith and achieved their new status, their attendance suddenly declines. This is particularly so in the case of those who convert for the sake of marriage or to unify the family and less for the own spiritual needs. For some ministers this is very upsetting. Mark, a vicar, says that 'when this happens I feel an acute sense of betrayal. Having invested a lot of time and energy into guiding someone into the church, it can be very hurt-ful when they suddenly disappear. Unfortunately it also makes me a little wary when I am next approached by someone else, and I have to struggle with myself not to say "Oh, here we go again," but to treat them as openly as they deserve.' Rabbi Joseph is more phlegmatic and reckons that 'when a person converts they are not becoming a saint or messiah, but an ordinary Jew; and although I want them to be as observant as possible, I also recognize that they have earned the right to be like everyone else and somewhat lapsed.' Other factors may be at work too. The conversion course may involve heavy demands in terms of class or reading at a time when those concerned are also busy with work or children. When the course ends, it is very easy for the time to be ploughed back into those other commitments, without any disrespect to the faith that has just been joined. There are also particular time pressures on those about to marry – often accompanied by a house move – that mean energies are employed elsewhere. Rabbi Joseph is content to wait for the 'boomerang effect': 'Very few born-Jews are 100% involved all the time, and they often go in cycles, such as disappearing after marriage, then coming back when they have children and want to involve them. It's the same with proselytes. They wouldn't have gone to all the trouble to convert if it didn't mean something to them, and so when the time is right they will return.'

Very little research has been done on the personal observances of proselytes after their conversion or at ten-year-intervals thereafter. However, some initial work has been begun on Muslim converts who largely converted without having a Muslim partner.[1] The study shows a considerable gap between ideal observance and what actually happens. 49% reported that they practise the five daily prayers, while the remaining 51% did not do so but felt that they should. There was a higher degree of observance concerning Ramadan – perhaps because it is a 'one-off' and they were prepared to make a special effort for it – with 73% maintaining the fast for the whole month. Only 32% of the men underwent circumcision after their conversion. It is noticeable that converts tended to practise the 'don'ts' rather than the 'do's' of Islam, with them being more likely to abstain from pork and alcohol, with 100% avoiding pork and 94% shunning alcohol.

Another factor that may contribute to the lack of observance of some converts is a nervousness about how to perform rituals properly. In theory, such matters should have been learnt during the conversion course, but that does not always happen. Thus Shirley felt unable to light the Sabbath candles on a Friday night until after she had converted to Judaism, but then was unsure what to do. 'It was silly really, but I wasn't sure what the exact way was, like which candles to light first, and whether to say the blessing while lighting them or before or after. I got so confused that I decided not to do it till someone showed me, but then found I was too embarrassed to ask people such basic questions. In the end I was lucky enough to be invited to someone's house on a Friday evening and saw the wife do it and then just copied what she had done.' Public ceremonies can prove even more difficult. Derek recalls attending a wedding at a mosque and being uncertain how to congratulate the bride 'I didn't know what the form was – could I give her a kiss, shake hands or just say something, and in which case was there a special form of greeting? I didn't want to ask because I felt I ought to know and didn't want to seem ignorant, so I mumbled something incoherent and went home to look up what I should have done.' This sense of insecurity can be fuelled by an acute awareness of a lack of a past. Unilke others in the church, mosque or synagogue, converts have no childhood memories to which to refer or older members of the family to fall back on for advice.

This can also prove embarrassing when engaged in social conversations with co-religionists who are enthusiastically trying to make connections, as Greg found. 'I was on holiday and visiting another synagogue when this person started chatting to me. "Where did I come from?" and all that. When I told her I was from South London, she said "Oh do you know Barry? He's your age from the same area? Which Religion School did you go to as a child?" It's not that I mind my past, but it leads to labels I'd prefer to avoid, but so many innocent conversations always seem to end up with the punchline "Oh, you're a convert are you?" and although it's usually in a friendly sort of voice, I wish I had an ordinary Jewish past that wasn't so afraid of questions.' Even compliments can be perceived as double-edged, as when Jeff was told by a friend 'you're a better Jew than me.' 'Part of me was very pleased that he thought highly of my level of knowledge, but the other part of me wondered whether he would ever use that turn of phrase to a born-Jew, and whether, in the nicest possible way, there was a sub-text that said "Even though you are a convert, you're a better Jew than me". Sometimes it's hard to know when to be pleased and when not'. People do not change religions in order to become a convert, but to become an ordinary member of that faith; yet often they find they are unable to make that transition as easily as they thought.

One aspect that sometimes catches converts by surprise is the denominational divide in the different faiths. Those who are fully accepted in one branch of the faith can be taken aback to find that they are not so welcome in another branch. Thea felt thoroughly at home in the Anglican church into which she was received, and enjoyed visiting other churches when away at weekends. On one occasion she was shocked when she was about to go up for communion and the friend whom she was visiting held her back and said that it would not be a good idea to go up as she was not a Catholic. 'It seemed so sad that I had come to Jesus late in life only to find that those already there were squabbling over him and shutting doors in each other's face. Of course I knew about the theological differences between Anglicans and Catholics – not to mention all the rivalries in Northern Ireland – but I never thought that meant I'd be physically stopped from taking communion on a Sunday.' Jason received a much worse rebuff when he was told by an Orthodox acquaintance that as he had converted through a Reform synagogue his conversion was invalid and he was not considered Jewish. 'I was devastated. I realized there were major differences in approach between Orthodox and Reform in their interpretation of the Bible and whether certain rules could change with the times or not, but I never thought belonging to one group would mean I was still non-Jewish in the eyes of the other. Actually I am quite angry. I pray in Hebrew, keep the Sabbath, observe the festivals, eat kosher food – how can they say that's not Jewish?' Converts caught up in such denominational rivalries, particularly amongst the non-Christian faiths, can feel doubly vulnerable: belonging to a minority faith within the country at large, and belonging to only one group within that faith. As Jason explained: 'It's quite an invidious position to be in. According to non-Jews, I'm Jewish, but according to many Jews, I'm non-

Jewish. So where do I belong? Obviously what's important is my faith itself, so I've no complaints, but it would be more comfortable not having to be a minority within a minority.'

The indices of integration can be three-fold. The first is recognition by others. Thus Jill was told by a new acquaintance, 'I had no idea you weren't always Jewish,' which made her feel that at last she was not 'standing out like a sore thumb' but blended in with the Jewish life around her. Others prefer to be accepted as someone who openly came to the faith of their own accord in adulthood but now is thoroughly immersed in it as much as anyone else. Joanna never tries to hide her Catholic roots and was delighted when the elders of her mosque suggested that she stood for the Muslim Parliament. 'It showed that they accepted my Muslim credentials without my past being an issue. I converted eight years ago and I want people to treat me as a forty-year-old with a past and not an eight-year-old with no prior existence.' A second index can be the convert's acceptance of co-religionists who are less observant. 'At first, I was so critical of born-Sikhs who did not take their faith seriously and broke all the rules that I was making such an effort to keep,' said Georgina. 'It was partly because I felt it undermined my efforts to keep the faith, and partly because I felt they were dishonouring their heritage. Then I started worrying about my children growing up and seeing fellow-Sikhs not keeping everything that I was teaching them Sikhs keep. But over the years I have come to terms with the fact that people break some rules but still feel passionately about others and not to be so judgemental. I've learnt that there are different ways of being a Sikh, something born-Sikhs take for granted, and I feel I've now arrived at the real starting point'.

A third index of integration is self-identity and the point at which one 'thinks Jewish' or 'acts Muslim' without any conscious effort. For many converts the early years are spent deliberately performing certain rituals or participating in communal events out of a desire to 'do what Jews/Muslims/Christians should do'. The identity is external and self-imposed, albeit willingly and through choice. At a certain point, such actions become second-nature and internalized. For Pauline the defining moment came when she met a friend in the High Street who invited her to stop off for a cup of coffee together. Pauline declined, not because, as she usually put it, she was 'going to the mosque', but because she was 'going to my mosque'. The difference in preposition signified that the relationship with the mosque had changed from 'me and it' – a formal relationship – to 'mine' – an intimate one – with a feeling of being thoroughly at home. Pauline also expressed the sense of privilege that many converts feel at their situation. 'Despite certain hiccups in becoming fully assimilated into Islam, I actually think I am luckier than most born-Muslims. They inherited Islam from birth and so never had the possibility of saying "I chose to be a Muslim"; whereas I did have that option and made that choice out of conviction. Not that my faith is in any way superior to theirs, but it is the result of a conscious and objective route that I am rather proud of.'

This sense of belonging can be important not only for the person's spiritual development but also as a help in combating any prejudice that they encounter after converting. The negative reactions of some family, friends and clergy has already been examined in the previous chapter, but problems can also arise with people with whom the convert had had no prior connection. Sometimes it can be from those at work, as when Liz decided to wear a Star of David chain around her neck and was subject to jibes by others in the factory. Reza chose to wear Muslim robes after his conversion and found he was spat on in the street during the Gulf War. Religion even cost Karina her job. As a lapsed Anglican she was acceptable as a Religious Education teacher at a Church of England girls' school, but when she became a Bahai she found she was treated as an outcast. 'It was as if I was okay so long as I was still theoretically within the fold – however disbelieving and however non-practising – but once I stepped outside that boundary, then I was unacceptable. It's ironic to think that they valued me more as a lapsed person than when I became religious. In the end I felt so uncomfortable I left.' Catherine's difficulties started some time after her conversion when she married a Muslim. 'As Catherine Peterson my religion was a purely personal matter and of no concern to anyone else. But the moment I became Catherine

Ur-Rehman, suddenly I was a Muslim and my faith was everybody else's business. It was quite noticeable how people's attitude changed when giving my name over the phone to companies and I often got told to wait or call back in a tone of voice I had never experienced before. It was a real eye-opener and quite shocking.' Equally upsetting was the response that Roopa encountered. 'Perhaps I was naïve, but when I became a Hindu I told everyone I knew – even acquaintances or people I met at work. I was not trying to convert anyone, but was really filled with it and thought others would be interested too. I quickly realized from the number of put-downs I received that they disapproved. No one said it out aloud, but I got the definite message that white girls shouldn't go in for that sort of thing. I was surprised most at those people who are churchgoers themselves – you'd have thought they would have known better, but there's definitely a sort of religious racism that says God is white and speaks English only.'

Prejudice of another kind can be encountered by Jews who convert to Christianity and find some sacred texts are highly negative towards their former faith. Ralph was shocked 'when I came across anti-Jewish passages in the New Testament that are not often read out in church but are still part of the Holy Scripture, including John 8. 43 where Jesus says of the Jews: "You are of your father the devil, and your will is to do your father's desires. He was a murderer from the beginning . . . He who is of God hears the words of God; the reason why you do not hear them is that you are not of God." I may not be Jewish any more, but my parents and brothers still are, and although we differ in matters of belief, I acknowledge them to be God-fearing, decent people. It is very painful when I read passages like that because it puts me in an awful position: do I say Jesus got it wrong, or do I condemn my parents? It's a clash between faith and family that doesn't happen very often, but it really hurts when it does.' Judaism itself can be considered guilty of discrimination against converts as Anne found out when she started dating someone only to be told that they could never marry as he was a *cohen* – a person descended from the priestly line within Judaism – and a *cohen* was not allowed to marry a proselyte. 'The implication is that a *cohen* is special and has to keep pure, whatever that means, and as a proselyte I was impure. As it turned out we weren't right for each other for all sorts of other reasons, but at the time I was pretty offended and still do find that law offensive and a slur on proselytes. It definitely makes me feel second class.' Many rabbis would agree with her and the Reform and Liberal synagogues have abolished that ban, but it still applies within Orthodox Judaism.

Life-cycle events

The various life-cycle events that everyone faces not only bring the usual mixture of joys and sorrows, but can present proselytes with special challenges. When Shelley converted she knew about boys being circumcised but gave it little thought until she herself became pregnant. 'At first I got very tearful at thought of having a boy and it facing a circumcision. Eventually I talked it through with a lot of other Jewish mothers and realized it was nothing to be worried about, but I was really aware of the contrast between myself and another Jewish lady in the maternity ward who gave birth to a baby boy at the same time as I did. She was really looking forward to the ceremony whereas I was very nervous about it.' However, Shelley also faced the problem of her parents' reactions. 'My Dad went ballistic and said that no grandson of his was going to be mutilated. Mum also gave me a hard time. It was something so alien to their experience. At least I was used to the idea even if I was nervous about it. In fact it was very difficult for me having to defend it to them while deep down I was scared stiff.' Yusuf's problem was his son's baptism. Ever since his own conversion to Christianity, relations with his family had been extremely difficult and he knew they would not come to church for the ceremony. 'Despite the joy of the occasion I felt very sad that my parents weren't there to share it with me, and even worse to know that they disapproved. There was also a real imbalance in that only one set of grandparents and aunts and uncles were present, and although I'm very fond of my wife's family, it pained me not to have mine there too.' Marriages can also prove daunting experiences if family members had expressed hostility to the person's conversion and

are then asked to come to an alien place of worship for the
wedding. Some show their continued displeasure by boycotting
the ceremony, while others, like Sara's mother, turn up in black.
'What was even worse, she cried throughout the whole ceremony,
and I knew it wasn't out of joy but because she was so upset it was
a church wedding rather than a synagogue one.'

Of course, in contrast, many relatives are delighted to attend
such a joyous event and are genuinely interested in the proceed-
ings, and find it colourful and enriching. Father Thomas advises
couples in such a situation to prepare a short guide to the wedding
service which is sent out with the invitations or distributed in
church. It usually contains a short description of the service and
the significance of the rituals involved, as well as a guide to the
architectural features of the church itself. 'It helps non-Christians
feel more relaxed if they understand what's going on and
appreciate the meaning of the ceremony.' He also advises sensitivity to mixed-faith needs in the planning: 'I remind the couple
that if they are going to give everyone champagne while they are
waiting around for the photographs to be taken and the bride or
groom is a former Muslim, then there will be a lot of people unable
to have alcohol and to provide for them too. After all, you don't
want to have a religious war over the drinks!' Conversely, those
who have converted can sometimes feel a tinge of regret when
attending weddings connected with their former faith. Sara was
taken aback by the 'wave of emotion that swept over me when I
went to synagogue for a friend's wedding. In fact it was the first
time I'd been back in synagogue for years. My own wedding was
wonderful and I have no complaints whatsoever, but something
inside me felt very wistful when I saw her under the wedding
canopy in front of the of the ark, and knew it was an experience I
would now never have.' It was not so for Gitta. She felt very
uncomfortable returning to the Hindu temple for a friend's
wedding. 'Members of my family had had marriages after I
became a Sikh, but they never invited me to their ceremonies, and
I was very unsure whether to go back even for this one. Although
the people there were civil to me, it was a not something I enjoyed
– it was a bit like having a divorce, moving away and then going

back to the house you and your husband had once shared, with bitter memories outweighing any good ones.'

Parenthood can also provide ambivalent moments, as Joanna found when bringing up her children. 'Islam has a wonderful sense of family roots and certainly provides a strong moral framework for children and all sorts of celebrations too. So I don't feel they are missing out, but I am sad that they don't have the excitement of waking up on Christmas morning and looking at their stocking, or hunting for Easter eggs in the garden. Still, they do other fun things instead, so maybe it's more a matter of me regretting that I won't have the pleasure of seeing them do the things I remember so fondly from my childhood.' To a certain extent this can be compensated by the convert's own excitement at enjoying for the first time through their children the traditions that they themselves never experienced as children. Anne recalls the delight at playing with a *dreidl* at the Jewish festival of Purim with her five-year-old son: 'It's such a lovely tradition I've introduced it to my sister's children. Just because they're not Jewish, why shouldn't they enjoy it?' It is at this point that many converts find themselves going through a considerable learning curve, as much of what they learnt applied to an adult understanding of the faith, whereas now they have to relay it to children. 'It's partly a matter of getting to know Sikh children's stories that I never heard in my own Hindu childhood, but also being much clearer about the faith as children ask piercing questions which demand straight answers,' said Janhavi. 'I found myself continually rushing to books I hadn't touched for years to check my facts or to find out obscure information that only a six-year-old could possibly want to know.'

At the same time a convert-parent faces sensitive issues in the light of their own background. One concern is how to introduce the subject of the conversion to children and present it in a positive way. Much depends on the attitude to conversion in the circles in which the couple mix. Those who have been welcomed with open arms find it easy to talk of their decision to join the faith and describe it as a joyous moment. Conversely, those greeted with wariness and a critical eye often feel they have to justify their conversion and apologize for their past. Some have even gone so far as not to tell the children, because of negative attitudes to converts, in the attempt to spare the children any sense of embarrassment at their origins. A second issue is how to explain their own past in a way that affirms the decision to change faiths without casting those members of one's own family, such as the child's grandparents, in a bad light for remaining in the old one. Joanna recalls stumbling over the fact that 'I was trying to say two things at the same time: that it's great to be a Muslim and that's the way our family is, yet it's also okay to be Christian like all my own family. I wanted my son to be proud of being Muslim, yet respect those who are related to him who are not.' It also means that those with a convert-parent are exposed to the different domestic rituals of grandparents, aunts, uncles and cousins to a much greater extent than other families. It can sometimes be an effort to prevent the children being confused if they go, for instance, from one set of grandparents celebrating Christmas to another set the next day celebrating the Jewish festival of Hanukkah. A third issue is whether to insist that the children's faith is theirs for life or whether to allow for the possibility that they too will one day change religion. As Anne put it: 'Having worked so hard to become Jewish and valuing it so much, I would feel devastated if my children then gave it up for another faith. Yet how can I deny them the right to change that I myself took? It's a real conflict of interests and something I hope I never have to face.'

A death in the family can also be the source of mixed reactions. When his father died, Martin felt very uncomfortable being in church again: 'It was the first time I'd been back since becoming a Buddhist and it was upsetting that at a time when I wanted religious comfort, instead I felt totally out of place and alienated. It was also mildly embarrassing to sit tight-lipped during the hymns and prayers. I didn't want to give offence by not joining in, but frankly it would have been totally hypocritical to mouth words that I don't believe in.' Mary experienced the opposite problem. She felt very much at home in the church service for her father's funeral and found herself singing the hymns with gusto. 'I felt a little guilty singing Christian sentiments, but it was all so familiar from my childhood and carried a warm feeling. Also I know Dad would have wanted me to mourn him in "his way", while it was important for Mum for me to be there for her and join in fully. More of a problem was my husband. As a born Sikh, it was very alien to him, and he was surprised that I was so enthusiastic. I think he feared that I was reverting to Christianity and I noticed him telling our five-year-old not to join in.' Her guilt was further compounded by the fact that although she observed some Sikh rituals for her father, she found them very unsatisfactory: 'I suppose it was because I was doing them for the first time, so I was learning what to do as I was going along, so it felt more like a course of instruction than anything else and wasn't particularly helpful emotionally.' It is a common problem for many converts at a time of bereavement when emotional reactions are at their most acute. Mourning rituals often have meaning because of long familiarity and warm associations. It can take a considerable period of time before the rituals belonging to the new faith take on the same resonance and depth as those learnt in childhood.

A death in the family can also lead to a religious crisis. When Shelley's first child was still-born her Catholic instincts rose to the fore and her first thought was to have it baptized. 'It was totally irrational, as I don't believe in the concept of original sin – and it certainly wouldn't have said much about my commitment to Judaism, would it – but it was a shock to realize how powerful my Catholics roots are even though I renounced them long before I became Jewish.' Even more upsetting for her was when a friend of her mother's suggested that it was punishment from God and maybe she should take the opportunity to repent. 'I was appalled – what sort of God would take an innocent child's life in order to teach the mother a lesson? I could never believe in a God who did that, and I also found it incredible that she could. Still, I have to admit, the thought had flashed through my mind of its own accord, and although I dismissed it immediately as nonsense, I was amazed at myself for even having the idea.'

The death of a convert's partner can bring not only the usual sense of loss but raise religious questions that other spouses do not have to face. Rebecca's husband died relatively young, leaving her as a thirty-six-year-old widow. After the funeral she was horrified when one of his relatives asked her whether she would now go back to her own roots. 'I was very upset by the assumption that my conversion had been just to please him and held nothing for me. I reminded the person in no uncertain terms that I had converted only after we got married and even after my son was born, and that I did it for me and that my roots were now Jewish ones. I think they were a bit taken aback by how ferocious I was – and they probably got some of the anger I felt at his death mixed in with it all – but frankly it disgusted me to think that they had been carrying round that assumption for so many years.' She also admitted that it made her especially scrupulous in observing the traditional mourning rituals as she did not want anyone to think that as a convert she did not know what to do or that she was personally slipping away. Nevertheless, the loss of a partner can lead to religious lapses. After her husband's death Margaret felt very lost religiously. 'Perhaps it's because Islam is such a male-dominated world, I felt that I no longer had a place. And although I count myself as quite knowledgeable, it was always my husband who was the expert on religious issues and practices. I feel very cut adrift now. It's almost a double bereavement – losing him and losing my umbilical cord to Islam.' Over the next two years she found herself attending the mosque less and less until eventually she stopped going altogether. 'I still call myself a Muslim if anyone asks, but there's no doubt the fire's gone out of it as far as I am concerned.'

Thoughts of one's own death can also have an unsettling effect on converts. Gerald is middle-aged, healthy and thoroughly committed to his local Anglican church. However, when his mind turns to the eventuality of his own demise, he regrets that no one will say for him the *kaddish*, the traditional prayer of mourning that has been said throughout the centuries by Jews. 'I know I won't be around to hear it or miss it, but somehow it seems a shame that a custom I remember so strongly from my upbringing won't apply to me.' For Frank, now in his early seventies, the issue is somewhat more pressing: 'I joked the other day that when the time came, I would like the imam to have a special mass for me. But perhaps it wasn't so much a joke after all, but me thinking that I'd like something at the end that reflected not just my Muslim life now but some of the Christian traditions that were important to me for many years earlier in my life.'

Festivals

The occurrence of festivals can bring a similar mix of new traditions and old memories. This applies particularly to Christmas which is so much part of national life and High Street culture that it is impossible to ignore. Joanna always feels wistful in December as the festival approaches. 'I have such wonderful associations from my childhood: carol singers, presents, family gathering, a long walk after Christmas lunch. My husband has no such associations, and just regards it as a horribly commercialized day and can't understand what I see in it. Jesus is recognized as a prophet within Islam, but I feel it would be wrong to celebrate Christmas as such, and so we do nothing. Still, for me it'll always be an annual regret.' Others keep a vicarious Christmas through their relatives. Thus Jill always goes to her parents on Christmas Day and joins the family celebrations there. 'I wouldn't dream of having a Christmas tree in the house – it's a Jewish home and I am happy for it to be so – but I can see no reason why I shouldn't join in with what my parents do. Enjoying a Christmas cracker doesn't mean I'm a Christian, but I'm not going to cut myself off from my past or the lifestyle of those that mean most to me.' Others do feel obliged to show that they do not observe their former faith in any way. Sheila was shocked to hear her rabbi say that he had sent Christmas cards to some Christian friends. 'I would never do that. I suppose I feel the need to show that I'm different now. Sending a Christmas card might give the wrong impression, and anyway people would reciprocate to me, and I certainly don't want to start receiving them. I might ring up a few close friends and wish them a happy new year, but I avoid anything Christmassy like the plague.'

It can also be difficult identifying thoroughly with the new set of festivals a convert acquires overnight. A child would gradually get familiar with them over several years, and come to learn about them through different mediums, starting through food, stories, games and evolving a more sophisticated appreciation through study and prayer commensurate with their age. Converts are suddenly presented with the final product without the process of long years of identifying with it. Corinne was very conscious of suddenly being expected to leap into Hindu festivities with which she felt little connection. 'To be honest, at the beginning I felt almost bereaved. It seemed that I had lost Christmas but without finding Diwali. It took some time before I felt properly at home in the various festivals and could actually feel the joy of them rather than just go through the motions.' When Brian became Jewish, it was the festival of Passover that gave him most difficulty. 'I could identify with the theme of freedom all right, but felt very self-conscious reading lines about "when we were slaves in Egypt" or "this is what our ancestors did in those days" when that patently didn't apply to me. I was so bothered by it that I asked my rabbi if I should omit those words but he said it could be taken as my spiritual ancestors; that made me feel better, but it was probably only after ten years or so that I really started looking forward to the festival and not worry about my relationship with it.'

The December dilemma and other conflicts highlight the fact that, although converts gain much through their new faith, there can also be a sense of loss. This might be apply to particular ceremonies they previously enjoyed and now miss, such as the festivals, or to traditions that carry deep echoes of their own past which they have now turned their back on, such as a baptism or barmitzvah. The image of a marriage, already compared to conversion at the beginning of this chapter, can be employed in another sense. Both marriage and conversion bring the enormous joy of a new and fulfilling relationship, but they also entail rejecting a previous lifestyle and rule out certain freedoms. They involve a self-imposed limitation, and however wonderful the advantages, there are major sacrifices too. Whether it be altered relationships with family and friends, or new dietary habits and forms of dress, the convert can go through major changes to familiar patterns of behaviour. Moreover, on many occasions there is not a straight swap of one lifestyle for another. There can be a limbo period between jettisoning old ways and coming to terms with new ones. As Fazal noted on his journey from Islam to Christianity, for several months there was 'an awkward period where I had given up being a Muslim and lost contact with many friends as a result, but had not yet been assimilated into the Christian community. It was a very lonely time, and my faith had to be very strong to sustain me during it. There was also the problem that when I converted it was a time of great emotion and excitement for me, and then daily life took over and it all fell away without a proper structure to maintain it. As far as Islam was concerned I was now an outsider, but I wasn't yet an insider in terms of Christianity. I felt I belonged nowhere, except by myself. My only comfort was that I felt I was suffering for my faith, like Jesus himself in a way, and by being able to identify with him in that respect it helped pull me through till I was more at home in church life.'

There were also those whose joy at conversion was marred by suffering pangs of guilt. In many cases it was at the hurt caused to relatives who took the conversion – wrongly – to be a rejection of family ties or a deliberate snub to them personally. In Pierre's case, though, it was religious guilt: 'I was certain that I wanted to leave Catholicism behind – it had done nothing for me and I felt no attachment to it – yet I was still wracked by enormous guilt for having forsaken Christ and turned my back on the Redeemer. It was as if I was crucifying him all over again and I had nightmares for two weeks after my conversion. It made my transition to Hinduism very difficult, and I think it's fair to say I was not a very good Hindu to begin with as I kept on feeling that the local priest who taught me as a child was looking over my shoulder and tut-tutting all the time.' Such feelings tend to be more common amongst those who move directly from one faith to another without an in-between period in which they lapse totally from the original faith. It might be described as the difference between remarrying after a period of being alone, as opposed to terminating one marriage and going straight into a second. With religion, as with relationships, it can be helpful having a period in which to let feelings of anger, resentment and guilt emerge and exhaust themselves, rather than embarking on a new venture and taking into it unresolved issues from the past.

Such difficulties indicate the importance of support for converts in the period immediately after they have joined the new faith. Up to that point they usually have the benefit of participation in a class with other converts and a close relationship with the minister or teacher. Once the conversion occurs, however, this structure evaporates and the support is removed. In theory they are then a full part of the community, but as has been seen above, integration into communal life can be a slow process, and the change from the intimacy of the small group to the wider congregation can be fraught with pitfalls. Anne remembers with fondness the cameraderie of her conversion class. 'There were five of us and during the year we got to know each other pretty well and discussed a lot of issues together. We also got very close to the rabbi who taught us himself. Now we just see him at services along with everyone else. He's always friendly and gives me a wave, but somehow the warm relationship has disappeared and I feel less special. I know it's compensated for by being a regular member of the community now, but it's sad that that aspect has been lost.' It is at this critical point of conversion that the response of the rest of the community is crucial in determining whether the convert makes an easy transition into greater involvement or feels marginalized and discouraged. Awareness of this has led some churches to set up a 'Care Ministry' which ensures that the new member is invited to study groups, given hospitality and made to feel part of the congregation. According to David Lamb, 'Unless someone finds seven friends in the first five months of being at a church, they leave'.[2] A few synagogues are now beginning to establish 'buddy groups' to help converts assimilate. In such instances, the rabbi will often ask someone who themselves had converted in earlier years to take the newcomer under their wing, the assumption being that they will best understand the needs and concerns of the new convert.

Converts can also feel vulnerable if they move to a new area because of a job-change or other reasons and have to begin anew the process of integrating within a different congregation.

Although they are technically in exactly the same position as any other member of the faith moving into the area and are no more or less strange to regular worshippers, they can often feel self-conscious because of their lack of roots within the faith. When Jason's company relocated to another part of the country 'my heart sank at the thought of having to go to a new synagogue where I did not know how I would be received. Not all rabbis are well-disposed to converts and so it was pretty daunting to think I might have to prove myself all over again.' For Sandra, however, it was a golden opportunity to cast off her past associations and 'to be accepted as a fellow Catholic who had just moved into the neighbourhood, rather than that person who converted last year'. Although she was determined not to deny her non-Catholic origins, she was relieved not to be burdened by the label she felt she had in other people's eyes. Sometimes the move can bring unexpected surprises. Tina was taken aback by the traditions she met in the mosque she attended when she and her husband moved to Leeds. 'Things were done very differently from the Regent's Park mosque in London. At first I thought I had strayed into a new sect, but I began to appreciate that there can be different interpretations within the faith depending on the personality of the imam and the traditions of the community. Looking back I realize I had mistaken Regent's Park Islam for the whole of Islam, whereas it's much more varied than that.'

One way in which converts are sometimes encouraged to play a part in the community is by being given the special role of ambassador to the wider world. This is particularly the case if the convert joins one of the minority religions that has a high ethnic component, in which case he/she may be considered to have better communications skills in certain situations. As Gai Eaton said of himself: 'In this respect the Western convert is a "frontiersman" linking East and West'.[3] This might apply, for instance, if a gurdwara or Hindu temple is being visited by local schoolchildren and it is felt that someone who comes from their socio-cultural environment would be a more suitable spokesperson. Some converts themselves volunteer for such tasks, especially in cases of inter-faith dialogue, where the person feels that he/she can be a bridge between the faiths. Seema recalls the time when the mosque was asked to send two delegates to an inter-faith conference being organized by the Borough council: 'My hand shot up. It seemed an ideal opportunity for me to be able to contribute, having a foot in both worlds and being able to represent the one to the other. There are so many areas in the communal life in which I feel a novice, but with this I reckoned I could do something useful for the faith and represent it in a positive light.' Not all are so keen, though, and some feel that the role is inappropriate. Shortly after converting, Carla was asked to act as guide to a group of visiting Christians to the mosque and decided afterwards never to do it again. 'For a start I felt as if I was on show, like some sort of trophy that Islam had won and Christianity had lost. But I also don't want to be singled out as different from any other Muslim; the whole point of converting was to be one of them, not stand out as an oddity.' It might also be said that some converts may be the least equipped to be ambassadors if they still have only a beginner's knowledge of the new faith and lack depth of experience. In addition, it can be a mistake to assume that someone who converted from a Christian background necessarily knows much about their former faith. When Rachel, herself formerly Jewish, showed a Synagogue Ladies Guild around her Catholic Church and remarked that, like Jews, Catholics considered abortion to be akin to murder, the cries of protest from her audience indicated that she had slipped on a religious banana-skin and got her facts wrong.

There are also those who find that once they are fully immersed in the faith, they actually identify more with a different denomination than that through which they entered. Very often it can be chance that dictates the particular church or synagogue to which a person had first been introduced, whether it be the invitation of a friend or an appealing poster on the noticeboard outside. Thus Helga had initally converted through a Liberal synagogue after reading an article by a Liberal rabbi which had stirred her. 'I was very grateful to the congregation for the warm welcome they gave me when I first appeared, but I felt that something was missing in the service. Initially I thought it was something to do with me, but when I went to a barmitzvah at a Reform synagogue I realized I preferred the greater use of Hebrew and traditionalism there. It was with some sadness that I left the Liberals and I still go back from time to time to keep in touch with friends I had made, but I feel much more at home in a Reform setting.' For her part, Vanessa had been baptized through the Anglican church to which her university friends had introduced her. 'I stayed with the Church of England when I moved and settled down, and was quite happy there till a change of vicar altered the character of the community. When I complained to a friend about the lack of atmosphere, she told me about a Greek Orthodox congregation that was nearby. I went and was overawed by the spirituality it exuded, and have never looked back.' It was years of study that persuaded Robert to change denominations within Buddhism: 'As I delved into the different teachings, I found that I was more in tune with the Tibetan school of thought than the Zen version I had initially become immersed in. At first I felt somewhat guilty at the change, but then I realized that was because I was still in the Jewish mindset of belonging to one particular group and not betraying it for another, whereas Buddhism teaches you to seek wisdom wherever it is to be found, and a true Buddhist master will teach his pupils eventually to leave him and seek their own destiny. Who knows, maybe in a few years time I will join another sect.'

Reversion

For some proselytes, the changes in their attitude to the faith after conversion can be even more dramatic and result in profound discontent. Eventually this leads to them formally rejecting their new faith and either reverting to their former one or lapsing into a state of nothingness. The reasons can vary enormously. As described in an earlier chapter, Raymond fell prey to parental pressure and found he could not continue attending church knowing how much it hurt his Jewish parents. 'I know it's my life, and spirituality above all is a personal matter. But family is an important part of my life too, and the problems it was causing negated any of the spiritual benefits I was receiving. In the end it just wasn't worth it, and although I still don't call myself a Jew, I don't describe myself as a Christian either.' Farah also felt unbearably pressurized, but in her case it was her own sense of guilt at having left Islam. 'I had certain reservations at the time I was baptized but I was carried along by the surge of faith I had then. I thought that once I had converted, those reservations would subside, but unfortunately they didn't. In fact they just grew stronger and nagged away inside. The words "traitor" and "betrayer" kept on running through my head. In the end I couldn't bear it, went back to the mosque and acted as if nothing had happened.' Gemma's guilt was triggered by an external event: 'It was the time of setting up a War Crimes Unit to catch former Nazis hiding in Britain and I was annoyed by reports of British Jews who opposed the idea on the grounds that it was stirring up the past and would only cause problems. I thought they were denying their own people's suffering. Suddenly I realized that I done exactly the same myself. Somehow what had once seemed so important to me – my own spiritual fulfilment – now seemed very petty compared to people-hood. And that was it. I knew I had to take up my Judaism again and just pursue my search inside it rather than outside it.'

Divorce can also lead to a radical re-evaluation of one's situation. Although many a convert will remain in the new faith after a divorce – especially if they had become integrated in the life of the new community – others find that the break-up of the marital relationship leads to a religious separation too. Mohinder had converted to Islam on marrying her husband, and although she felt at home in Islam she freely admits that if she had not married a Muslim she would not have considered converting. 'I admired the principles of the faith enough to feel comfortable in it while the marriage lasted. But unfortunately the marriage didn't work out and I didn't feel sufficiently attached to want to continue the Muslim traditions by myself.' Others can feel much more antagonistic to the faith that they had adopted for the sake of their partner, particularly if the divorce is a very bitter one. The offended party will view anything connected with the former partner as abhorrent, be it that person's favourite food, film or holiday resort, and including their religion. The faith becomes irrevocably tainted with their partner's faults, and both are rejected together. A religion that was adopted on marriage is often liable to be spurned on divorce.

For others, though, the problem is the new faith itself and the fact that 'the promised land' turns out to be less than what they had expected. Aman had converted to Islam at university after becoming part of a group of friends who were predominantly Muslim. The faith appealed to him and he decided to identify with it fully. However, after they graduated, their new jobs took them to different parts of the country and they generally lost contact with each other. 'I knew I was still part of the Muslim community at large and went along to the local mosque, but somehow it felt much less meaningful. I felt I was a wanderer in a strange country and, frankly, felt lost and alone. I decided that maybe it was wrong to separate myself from my roots, started making cautious contacts with the local Hindu community and found it surprisingly welcoming. It was like coming home, and so now I am back in the fold.' The pull of roots can also occur without any specific trigger, but often accompanies the ageing process. Sandy surprised his Buddhist friends when, after a period of absence, they saw him enter a church. He explained that he still admired Buddhist teachings and still used meditational techniques, but had simply become homesick. 'The old adage about once a Catholic always a Catholic is true – or at least it is in my case. Something deep inside me misses it. Over the years I often thought about going back and when I hit sixty, I thought I ought to do it before it's too late.' Others leave it almost until the last moment. Flora astonished her two adult sons by asking them to fetch a priest as she lay seriously ill in hospital. They knew she had adopted Islam before they were born, and she had never said or done anything to lead them to think that she did not identify with the faith. Apparently, though, once in hospital her mind had turned to her childhood memories and this had evoked a desire to end her days as she had begun them. For others, long-ingrained thoughts of salvation and damnation can unexpectedly surface as they approach death, which is what led Marianne to ask to be re-baptized and buried in consecrated ground despite her conversion to Judaism several years earlier.

The death of a partner can also lead a convert to reconsider their religious identity. May learnt how to cook Jewish-style food from her mother-in-law after she converted and boasted that she 'made the best gefilte fish in town'. However, her husband's death made her realize how much her involvement in Jewish life depended on him. 'Don't get me wrong. I wasn't insincere. I was quite happy being Jewish. But without him it was different, and every now and then I go back to church.' Barbara's problem was at the opposite end of the life cycle. She had converted to Islam in good conscience three years earlier, although primarily because she had come into contact with it through her husband and wanted to share his faith with him. However, when she became pregnant she suddenly developed an antipathy to the faith. 'It shocked my husband, but it shocked me even more. I didn't know where all these negative feelings were coming from. Eventually I realized what was going on. I simply couldn't hand over my future child to another faith. Even saying it like that – 'hand over' – indicates the depth of alienation I felt. I was extraordinarily fortunate in that my husband understood and agreed for me to revert to Christianity and bring up the child with knowledge of both faiths. But it could easily have led to divorce and I still lie awake at night thinking of all the awful traumas we could have had.' Not all will return to their original faith. Some find that they have journeyed too far away from it to be comfortable within it again. Daphne found that she was no longer enjoying Islam, but having been used to a strict monotheism in which God was indivisible and incorporeal, she could not return to belief in a God who became man or who could be subdivided into the Father, Son and Holy Ghost. 'Theologically speaking, I was out of the womb and couldn't get back inside. Beliefs that had once seemed natural to me now felt alien. So I gently lapsed into a nothing, keeping all the ethical principles of both Christianity and Islam, but giving up any rituals and doctrines.' Danny found himself in a similar situation when he decided that Buddhism was not the answer that he had originally thought it would be: 'But that didn't mean I raced back to my Jewish roots. Having experienced the freeing of the spirit from institutional religion, there was no way I was going to return to the legalism and tribalism that I'd fled from in the first place. Nor would I ever accept again the idea of an all-powerful male God with his own chosen people. Instead I read widely, keep an open mind and try to do useful things for others.'

A feature common to many of these individuals was that they were single. Those who convert and then marry within the faith find they become entwined into the social and cultural framework of the faith to such an extent that it is much harder then to break away. Even if their religious enthusiasm evaporates completely, their involvement with family and friends compensates for it and is reason enough to stay with the social structure of which they have become a part. A number of converts will admit to having lapsed completely in their beliefs but still be happy to remain in the faith for the wider benefits. Alternatively, their motive in staying within the faith may be to avoid any domestic unpleasantness. As Gurjeet put it: 'With Islam, frankly I can take it or leave it, and given the choice I'd probably leave it and go back to my own tradition, but I love my husband and I know it means a lot to him, so I keep the formal side up as much as is necessary. He pleases me in lots of ways, and this is one way of me pleasing him. I don't think of myself as hypocritical as I don't pretend to be a fervent believer, just a devoted wife.' When a convert who married within the faith does revert, it can have serious consequences for the marriage. In Barbara's case above, her partner was very accommodating, but for Fiona it caused major ructions with her husband when she decided she could no longer act as if she was a Muslim. He accused her of cheating him, and said he would not have married her if he knew she would eventually drop out of the faith. Up to then the marriage had varied in quality but had been largely acceptable, but thereafter it deteriorated sharply and ultimately led to divorce.

For those who do wish to resume their former faith, some simply return to their original place of worship and carry on as if they had simply been away on an extended stay abroad. As Farah had already noted above, she went back to the mosque and acted as if nothing had happened. She found that although a few people treated her coolly, most greeted her like a long-lost friend and she quickly assimilated back into the community. For his part, Aman was glad that when he decided to return to Hinduism, he was living in a different part of the country from where he had been brought up. 'My conversion to Christianity hurt a lot of people at the time, not just my family but communal elders and even some of my friends. I think it would have been too difficult to be re-accepted by them, whereas I was now living in London where nobody knew me, or my past, and I could take my place in the local Hindu community without any black looks or recriminations.' Some religious leaders demand that the revert undergoes a form of penance and reconversion. Thus Barbara was asked by her vicar to attend the course he led for those becoming Christian so that she could re-familiarize herself with church teachings, as well as be certain that the step back into the Christian fold was indeed what she wanted. She also underwent a second baptism to symbolize her formal return to the faith. In the Jewish tradition it is technically impossible to lose one's Jewish status, so that a Jew who converts to another faith is still considered a Jew, albeit a 'sinning Jew'. Those who wish to return to Judaism do not therefore need to undergo any formal ceremony of re-admittance. Nevertheless, for psychological reasons, they may be asked to say a prayer in synagogue in front of the Holy Ark renouncing their adopted faith and renewing their Jewish allegiance. It helps to draw a line under the past and enables the person to re-establish him/herself in the congregation with their head held high. In some cases, it is not so much the rabbi who suggests it but the revert who requests it. Russell had spent five years with Hare Krishna, but when he attended an inter-faith gathering, he suddenly found that he was identifying more with the Jewish delegates present than with members of his own order: 'It woke me up to a yearning to return, and when I did eventually approach a rabbi, I asked for a ceremony to signify my re-entry into the faith. It was important for me to mark the point of transition. I was very conscious of an enormous shift in my personal direction and I needed to separate the different sections of my life.' He made an appearance before a *Beth Din*, a rabbinic court, and was issued with a formal certificate confirming his Jewish status.

A related question is whether the process of rejection is two way? A convert can reject their new faith and revert to their original one. Can a faith community decide that a person who has converted no longer merits the right to be part of the faith because of his or her conduct? For most religions, there is no mechanism by which a conversion can be annulled. It is seen as an act of commitment to the deity by the individual concerned and it can only be broken if that person renounces his/her personal relationship with the deity. Those who converted might be castigated as errant in their theology or condemned for being lapsed in their observances. In extreme cases their membership of a particular community can be rescinded or they can be accused of heresy, but their initial act of conversion cannot be revoked. If the religious status of a person depended on maintaining the requisite level of observance, then every convert would remain in a state of limbo, because at some future date they may fail to observe all the laws. The only possibility of an annulment might be if the conditions under which a person converted were later found to be improper in some way. Thus if someone converted to Christianity but it then emerged that they did so under pressure and in reality did not subscribe to Christian beliefs at the time of conversion, then their conversion is deemed invalid. Alternatively there may be technical errors in the process, such as if someone became Jewish but appeared before an Orthodox rabbinic court that did not contain the minimum number of three rabbis, in which case their conversion would be regarded as flawed until the correct procedures had been observed.

Bearing in mind the host of everyday dilemmas, family issues, personal crises and potential hiccups that converts can face, it is clear that for many people the act of conversion is the easy part; much harder is maintaining the faith afterwards. The conversion experience itself can bring a sense of excitement and fulfilment, but this feeling inevitably declines once that moment has passed. Those who are best able to keep up their religious enthusiasm are those supported either by their own partner or by friends within their new community. They make the person feel valued and serve to reinforce the belief that the person had made the right decision. They can also help him/her deal with the unexpected problems that arise, either through practical advice or through emotional support. To use again the image of marriage: like a bride and groom's relationship with each other, the convert's relationship with the faith needs to be nurtured as much after the ceremony as beforehand if disillusion is to be avoided and ongoing joy is to be maintained.

7

Special Cases

Children

If converts face many issues, so do their children. Much depends on the way in which they are told about a parent's conversion, and whether it is presented positively, negatively or as a simple matter of fact. Some are not told, and the conversion is kept secret from them until a later date or until they find out from another source. Reactions can also vary depending on whether the parent converted before the children were born, or it happened after they were born and involved the children themselves taking on a new faith.

Much also depends on the climate towards conversion within the particular faith to which the family belong. For those faiths which encourage and value conversion, the fact that a parent has converted is seen as a positive aspect. Kevin recalls from an early age his mother telling him how Christ had come into her life and it was one of the most wonderful things that ever happened to her. 'I grew up with the sense that my mother was really lucky that she had had this experience. It also made me feel that she was a true Christian in that she didn't go to church because it was the done thing, but because she really wanted to and did so out of strong personal belief. Certainly in the early years it made me want to share as much of Christianity as I could, and that has largely stayed with me the rest of my life.' David – also known as Dawoud to some friends – knows his father converted to Islam and later met his mother through a friend at the mosque. As far as he is concerned it is not an issue. 'He has brown hair, he works in an office, he's a convert – it's not a big deal. There are lots of people who convert to Islam because it's a great religion.' But whereas he does not attach any value judgments, David was surprised when he met his father's brother and his family, and realized that he had cousins who were very different from him. 'It was strange to see one of them wearing a cross, or the Christmas tree they had up in December. It made me realize what a different childhood my father must have had from me.' He was also taken aback when his paternal grandfather died and they all went to the service in church. 'Seeing my Dad join in the hymns was odd. I didn't mind, but it made me think how I might have been brought up Christian if he hadn't have converted.'

Zoe's situation was very different as her mother became Jewish and married into a family that was very concerned that her origins should not be advertised. 'Of course I knew, because we saw her parents and family, but in the Jewish community we didn't mention it. When I was older I realized that conversion is a respectable route to Judaism, but at the time it felt rather like a dirty secret. I remember being highly embarrassed at the Sunday school when we were asked to do a family tree and show where everyone was born and what they did and so forth. I didn't want to put that my uncle and aunt were called Jones and lived in Canterbury – a real give-away sign that they probably weren't Jewish – so I left them off the tree altogether and pretended I didn't know about them.' Equally problematic are situations where children are subconsciously used to express their parent's own ambivalence about their conversion. Thus Linda, who had converted to Judaism purely for the sake of her husband, gave her six-year-old daughter a crucifix and a star of David on a chain to wear around her neck. She was genuinely taken aback when her husband pointed out the incongruity of the two emblems co-existing and told him, 'I don't see the problem – we share a home together quite happily.' It was clear that she still viewed herself as a Christian even though she had officially changed her religious passport.

Children brought up in a secretive climate can experience enormous conflict and confusion over their dual heritage. Some can become very ashamed of their 'other roots' and seek to hide them through exaggerated attachment to their official identity. They can even develop a form of religious xenophobia and display hostility towards other faiths as a way of supposedly proving their own credentials. It can turn into a neurotic process, because the more they assert their religious zeal, the more insecure they become about their secret being revealed. Others become interested in the other faith that their parent came from but feel guilty at betraying the family identity or going behind their backs. It can lead to furtive behaviour or inner turmoil, especially with teenagers seeking to establish their own persona. Manazir, previously known as Martin, was aware that his father had come from a Muslim family before he converted to Christianity, but it only became an issue for Manazir when he began to rebel against his parents around the age of fourteen. 'I despised their bourgeois values and loathed going to church with them. In fact I stopped going around that age, and when I was sixteen I decided to investigate my Muslim roots. My father was furious as it was something he felt he had left behind, but that only served to attract me. That was it and I never looked back. I became quite observant, changed my name and left home as soon as I could. I'm still in touch with my parents, but live in a very different world.' Roma had a much less extreme reaction, but one that still causes her dilemmas. Her mother converted from Islam to Hinduism on her marriage, and Roma and her brother and two sisters were brought up as Hindus. Roma feels at home within Hinduism, but is much closer to her maternal grandparents than her paternal ones. She often goes to their home, admires their beliefs and enjoys Muslim art and rituals. In recent months, she has taken to reading and discussing a section of the Koran with her grandfather whenever she visits. 'My problem is that I want to study more about Islam, not necesarily to convert, but just to know more about that side of my family, but I don't want to upset my parents. At the same time I know my grandfather feels guilty about teaching me about the Koran in case my mother gets upset about it. We all seem to be walking around on eggshells and it's quite uncomfortable.'

There are some parents who choose not to tell their children that one partner has converted. Their reasoning is lest the knowledge confuse the children, or lest it lead to a sense of insecurity. However well-intentioned their motive, in reality it can cause even greater anguish when the true facts seep out, as they inevitably do even in the most unlikely situations. Ricky's mother came from a Jewish family in Glasgow but moved to London for a new job and later converted to Christianity. When she met her husband they decided to settle in Cornwall, where they became involved in local village life, were active in church affairs and never mentionned her Jewish origins. Ricky was blithely unaware of being 'half-Jewish', as he put it, until someone else from Glasgow happened to move to the same area and sent their son to the same school as Ricky. They were not Jewish, but had known his mother's family and their son told Ricky about the special candelabra and other Jewish items he had seen at the home of Ricky's cousins. 'I remember being shocked at the time. I had never met any Jews and they were people I only heard about in readings from the Bible in church, often with unpleasant associations. They were certainly responsible for the death of the Saviour, and suddenly I found I was one of them. When I confronted my parents, my mother was deeply embarrassed that I had found out, while my father got angry about people "spreading rumours". A bit of me was very cross my parents hadn't been honest with me, but I was also very intrigued by my new-found roots. When I was older I started reading a lot about Judaism, and although I am still a churchgoer I am also very involved in inter-faith work and see my role as building bridges between the different communities.' Abigail only learnt of her origins when her mother died. As her father had already passed away and she was the eldest child, it fell upon her to make arrangements for the disposal of her estate. Whilst she was going through old family papers, she discovered a deed poll through which her mother had changed her forename from Christine to Sarah. It came as a bolt from the blue. 'We had always been an actively practising Jewish family, all very involved, and inter-marriage might have been rampant elsewhere in the Jewish community but not in our family. But Jewish girls aren't called Christine and it rang all sorts of alarm bells in my head. A couple of days later I came across the piece of paper that I had been dreading I'd find: her conversion

certificate. It was the worst possible way to find out, and also the
worst posible time, because how could I justify getting angry with
the mother I was mourning? But I was angry, not so much at the
hard fact, because why shouldn't she convert, but at the lifelong
deceit.'

In a very different category are children who are themselves part
of the conversion experience. This usually happens when one
parent converts and the children formally change faith at the same
time. In some instances this takes place within the existing family.
Thus Rebecca decided to convert to Judaism only after she and her
husband had been married for some time and she felt at home
within the faith and a genuine desire to become Jewish. Their son
was two at the time and so he converted automatically with her.
Older children who convert with their parents can sometimes be
puzzled by the need to change status, as they were usually being
brought up in the faith already and cannot understand why they
need to be baptized or appear before a rabbinic court to prove
what they take for granted. It is, of course, a matter of religious
bureaucracy, so as to match external status with internal perception, and sensitive explanations can ease any confusion. Conversely, insensitive explanations can leave hurt feelings, such as
the nine-year-old who had been brought up Christian but never
baptized and was then told he would become Christian next week
at a special ceremony. Instead of feeling pleased, as his parents
expected, he burst into tears at the thought that he had been a
non-Christian so far and that all his prayers and good deeds may
have been in vain. Nevertheless, providing such anguish can be
avoided, it is generally far better to harmonize actual status and
self-identity rather than leave discrepancies until adulthood when
they can be more time-consuming to solve or cause legal problems.

This happened to Roddy, who had been brought up Jewish even
though his mother had never formally converted and nor had
he. The consequences never occured to him or his parents until
he came to make his wedding arrangments and found that the synagogue marriage he and his fiancée were planning had to be
changed because he was technically not Jewish and under Act of
Parliament, rabbis are empowered to conduct only those

marriages in which both parties are Jewish. However, some child conversions involve taking on a different faith from that to which they were accustomed. This often applies to children involved in a divorce and when the parent who has custody of them later marries someone of a different faith, wishes to join it and enrols the child at the same time. Alice was in this situation when her parents split up. They had been a semi-religious Christian family with occasional church attendance and she had been going along to the Sunday school for two years. Church involvement waned after they moved to a new area, and four years later her mother met and married a Muslim, with she and Alice both adopting the faith. Alice recalls finding many of the home rituals strange, and sometimes getting her theology confused: 'I was told off at the mosque when I said that Muhammad was the Son of God. The end result was that I never felt truly at home in Islam, while I also lost contact with my Christian roots, so I dropped out of organized religion and I just try to keep the ethical elements common to both faiths.' In Alice's case, her mother had sole care and control of her, and was therefore legally entitled to make decisions about her religious identity without consulting her natural father.

In cases where the care and control is shared between the parents, any religious changes are subject to joint agreement. Sometimes they can become yet another battlefield in the ongoing acrimony between ex-partners. Fazal's conversion to Christianity from Islam had precipitated a divorce with his wife. Because of his wife's illness, their two-year-old son remained with him and experienced a Christian way of life. However, she took legal steps to prevent Fazal from having the child baptized. It meant that the boy often went to church with his father, but was unable to accompany him to the altar to receive the communion, something he found confusing and his father found upsetting. In other instances, the objections have nothing to do with religious principles and are simply a matter of malice. When Suellen and her husband divorced they were both highly lapsed members of the Church of England. Three years later she met someone Jewish and converted in order to marry him. She very much wanted her six-year-old daughter to become Jewish too 'so that everyone in the house would share the same faith, and also so that she shouldn't feel the odd one out or that I was abandoning her in some way. It made perfect sense. But my "ex" refused point blank to allow it. Not that he knew anything about Judaism, or took an interest in the church. He simply wanted to obstruct me in whatever way he could, in the same way that he challenged every decision I made about her from what to do on her birthday to which school she attended. But this upset me more than anything. The trouble was he knew that, and so he was determined to make things as difficult as he could out of sheer spite.'

In cases such as the above, it means that the new family is a mixed-faith household, with the mother and step-father being one religion and the child being another. With the increase in divorce and remarriage, there may be step-brothers and sisters also of different faiths from each other. In such instances, it means that more than one tradition is acknowledged within the home and there can be a blurring of distinctions between the faiths. Thus Ram recalls his father leading Diwali celebrations at home, while his step-mother would take responsiblity for the Christmas tree which she put up every year for her son by a previous marriage. 'It was sometimes hard to remember which rituals belonged to which faith, while the belief system we had was pretty muddled. To this day I am not 100% sure which are the Hindu bits of my life and which the Christian.' The occurence of serial marriages can also lead to multiple religious identities. Darren was born into a Methodist home, but his parents divorced when he was three. Two years later his mother married a Catholic and he was baptized into the faith a few months afterwards. The marriage did not last and when he was nine, she married a Jewish man and both she and Darren converted. Now aged eleven he is is on his third religious affiliation and will soon begin preparing for his barmitzvah. Whereas once his religious odyssey would have been unique for someone so young, he is far from exceptional and serial marriages can sometimes also mean serial religion for the children involved.

In virtually all faiths, the conversion of a child means that the child is now a full part of the new faith. Indeed, were this not the case, the child's religious status would be in limbo until adulthood and his or her self-perception would be very confused. One of the few exceptions is in Judaism, in which it is considered that any conversion undertaken before the age of maturity – thirteen – is not entirely voluntary as it is under the influence of others. The child convert therefore has the option of annulling it on attaining maturity, although this privilege is forfeited if it is not exercised immediately. In theory all child converts to Judaism could renounce their Jewish status on the day of their thirteenth birthday; in reality this rarely happens, largely because they are unaware of such a right, but also because, having been brought up Jewish, most feel comfortable with it and would be surprised to think of themselves as anything else. However, one problem that some child converts of any faith may encounter is a degree of discrimination in certain quarters. This is more likely in faiths where conversion is less welcomed, such as in Judaism, or where there are strong ethnic components to the local religious community. Thus Paula often had jibes hurled at her by other Muslim girls at school, because her father had converted to Islam, and they refused to countenance the idea that a white-skinned girl could have the same faith as the rest of them.

Jill's daughter was unable to gain entry to the local Jewish primary school because they had an admissions policy that refused to accept the children of converts from Jewish groups that were not Orthodox. Her parents tried to explain the reason to her rationally and spoke about the differences between different types of Jews, emphasizing that she came from one particular tradition – Reform – but they were all fully Jewish. However, that did not prevent her being greatly upset by a friend in the same street who attended the Orthodox primary school telling her that 'We didn't let you in because you're not a real Jew.' Such instances are very similar in nature to the personal and institutional prejudice that adult converts can face, as has been seen earlier. The only difference is that the adults consciously chose their own path, whereas children may feel that they are suffering because of their parents' decisions. They may also be less able to rise above the hurts and develop insecurities that can blight much of their life. They can also suffer from family tensions if the conversion of a parent has caused friction within the family. Carla's parents had objected on religious grounds when she converted from Christianity to Islam, but they had managed to maintain amicable personal relations. However, when Carla came home after her parents had been looking after her five-year-old son for the day, she was horrified to find that her parents had brought round an Advent calendar and were telling him stories about Jesus. They typify many grandparents who are saddened by the conversion of a son or daughter, and are determined to pass on elements of the faith to any grandchildren and ensure that at least they are familiar with its traditions.

In cases where the parents have decided to give their children some background knowledge of the converted parent's original faith, the grandparents can play a very useful and productive role. However, when they are deliberately avoiding any such information, surreptitious efforts by family members to provide it can lead to unpleasantness and sour domestic relationships. An extreme example of this applies to Gitta, who felt that she could not trust her Hindu parents not to indoctrinate her two children who were being brought up as Sikhs. 'Despite speaking to them about it several times, including some heated arguments, I just could not get through to them not to go on about how much better Hinduism is and how all the best people in the world are Hindus. It sounds ridiculous repeating all this to someone else, but that's exactly what they have been telling the children. The result is that we hardly ever see them – we certainly never go to their house, and if they come to us once or twice a year, my husband or I always make sure we are present in the room to make sure they behave. It's so sad, because I feel they are losing out, while the children realistically only have one set of grandparents. But that's the way they've chosen to play it.'

The religious future of the children of converts can raise dilemmas that other parents do not face in exactly the same way. Seema is very keen that her children should marry fellow Muslims 'partly because I believe it is such a wonderful structure for family life, and partly because, having made the effort to convert to Islam and worked very hard to integrate myself and my children into communal life, I would feel very disappointed if all that was to be for nothing and they married someone from outside the faith, or, even worse, converted to another faith'. However, she also realizes that she is open to the charge of hypocrisy, having rejected the religion into which she was she was born. 'Intellectually, I know I should give them the same right that I took for myself, but emotionally that is much harder to accept. I also appreciate the pain my own parents must have felt when I abandoned the church. I knew it hurt them at the time, but now that I am a parent myself I can understand what they must have felt.' Anne reckoned she would be upset for a different reason if either of her two children converted: 'Part of me would feel that I had failed to imbue them with a love of the Jewish way of life, and that would be my fault, either because I didn't have deep enough roots or because I simply hadn't put them over strong enough. I also worry that some people might make snide remarks about "what do you expect from a convert?" and so I would be reinforcing the worst stereotypes that some people have about proselytes.' Not all feel that way, and other convert parents would argue that what is important is that a person finds faith and the particular one they choose is entirely up to them. Thus Karina declared that 'yes, I am very happy as a Bahai and I will try to share that with my daughter and any other children we may have. But above all, I will teach them to be religious, and if one day that leads them to a different path, then so be it. It's the destination that counts, not the route.'

Special cases

Within the complex range of situations in which people decide to convert, a number of special circumstances stand out and which bring particular issues to the fore. They range from the dramatic, such as a minister of religion who has a religious change of heart, to the exotic, such as serial conversion. Some have been mentioned in passing in previous chapters, but now need fuller examination.

One instance is when a person in a same-faith marriage converts away from their joint faith – be it active or lapsed – and joins another religion. Ron was surprised when his wife wanted to join a different faith, but took it in his stride: 'Why not? I go off to the pub with my mates once a week, why shouldn't she go to her worship place without me? Anyway, what's the problem – it's all about honesty, charity and being good, so why should I object?' For other couples, the pressures that this can put on the marriage can be immense. For Cynthia it was a matter of acute religious pain: 'We met at a Bible study group and our lives had always involved a strong Christian element, including regular worship. I knew Chris was becoming disillusioned, looking elsewhere and finding answers in Buddhism. I know he needs faith, but it hurts terribly that he can't find it in Jesus, while I sometimes get sick at the thought of him losing the chance of salvation in the world to come. Religion isn't something to mess around with, and I feel he is really putting his soul in danger.' For others, such as Bernard, the worry was more about the consequences for the relationship: 'When Katie started getting interested in Judaism I became very nervous about what the effect would be on our relationship. I didn't like the idea of having all sorts of strange rituals at home, and I certainly wasn't keen on her developing a social life at the synagogue and in circles I wasn't part of. It just didn't seem healthy and resulted in a lot of arguments.' When she actually told him she wanted to convert formally, Bernard recalled that 'I thought the next thing she would say was that she wanted a divorce.' That particular concern proved unfounded, but there were fears about the effect on their children, who found that it was now only their father who took them to church, while their mother was sometimes absent at a synagogue on Saturday mornings. They were particularly surprised when, with a curiosity natural to all children, they asked if they could come along too and see what happened. Their father vehemently said it was out of the question and the two parents then stormed off to have a long and loud argument. With hindsight they now admit that they should have handled the whole situation differently, sat the children down and explained to them what was happening. Instead, their behaviour reflected Bernard's anger at feeling betrayed and Katie's resentment at not having her spiritual needs acknowledged. The message the children received was that religion, once a source of family unity, was now associated with tension, and it lost much of its attraction as far as they were concerned.

It is precisely because of such problems that some ministers treat very cautiously requests for conversion from one partner in a same-faith marriage. Much as ministers believe in the value of their own faith, they do not want it to be at the expense of the marital relationship. For many of them, domestic harmony is as important as religious truth, and there is no point increasing one's flock at the same time as multiplying the divorce rate. In such situations, for instance, it is the custom for rabbis belonging to the Reform Synagogues of Great Britain to meet with the non-converting partner to ascertain his/her feelings and ensure that the conversion will not cause tensions at home. Very often they will ask partners of prospective converts to give a written statement declaring that they have no objection to the conversion, while they will also be encouraged to attend the conversion course itself so that, although they themselves are not changing faith, they will understand what Judaism involves, not feel threatened by it and be able to support their partner's religious needs where appropriate. The reception given to the convert by the new faith can also be less welcoming if it is known that their partner will not be joining them or has reservations about the conversion altogether. In Katie's case, the rabbi initially refused to allow her to start classes on the grounds that it might cause unbearable frictions in the marriage and lead to domestic breakdown. Katie remembers that 'although I understood why he said that, the effect was to make me be even more cross with Bernard for causing obstacles to be raised in my path. In the end I convinced the rabbi that I was sincere and that matters at home would be okay, although he insisted on meeting Bernard first to be sure himself. By that time Bernard had come round to accepting it and so I went ahead.' It should be noted, though, that less scrupulous ministers of all faiths will actively encourage one partner to convert in the hope of gaining the rest of the family.

Problems of a much greater magnitude face a member of the clergy who comes to believe that he/she is in the wrong religion. In such cases, a change in faith involves the additional problem of losing one's job and completely revising plans for the future. Thoughts, for instance, of a career in the church and eventual retirement to a small rural parish combined with writing a book about the lives of the saints can evaporate overnight if the person no longer feels able to call themselves a Christian. Unlike other types of conversion which are motivated by a relationship or an unexpected experience, ministers are usually drawn to another faith through study. This usually starts without the slightest intention of conversion, but as an exercise in broadening their religious horizons or as a precursor to developing inter-faith dialogue. While such transformations are extremely rare and can in theory happen from one faith to any other, in practice there is greater likelihood of the case being a Christian minister who defects to Judaism. This is because Judaism is seen as the source of Christianity, the trunk from which the church branched out. It means that Judaism has an inherent fascination for some Christian clergy. Moreover, joining it can be justified as a return to one's true roots rather taking up an entirely new religion. In addition the knowledge of the Old Testament that most clergy possess means that it is familiar territory in which they already feel at home. However, whereas most converts can openly investigate the new faith and attend services or classes at leisure, clergy who are wrestling with their beliefs have to be much more surreptitious lest public questions are asked about their conduct. They are also much more likely to receive a hostile reaction from members of their former faith when they announce their desire to convert. As one such minister put it, 'For the first time in my life I realized how difficult conditions must be for closet homosexuals who are struggling with their identity and who eventually summon up the courage to come out. It was like that for me. I knew I was losing my faith but dare not admit it. I knew I was attracted to Judaism, but couldn't talk about that either. So it just bubbled away inside, causing enormous anguish and turmoil. But there came a point where I physically could not carry on my ministry any more. I knew I had to resign, but I felt I also owed people an explanation, so that was the time to come clean and reveal my intention to convert. I fully expected to be booed from the church. Instead I got stunned silence and a few muffled wishes of "God be with you" as I left. My future is a major problem, but at least I feel I can be honest to God and more at peace with myself.'

The minister's own family will also be acutely affected by his change of faith if he has not shared his doubts with them at an earlier stage, in which case they can feel badly let down by his sudden announcement. In one instance, the minister informed his wife only a week before he went public. She was horrified both at his personal volte-face and at the consequences for the rest of the congregation. She was determined to maintain her own churchgoing and continued attending after he left so as to show the parishoners 'that I still held to the faith and so should they'. However, the strain proved too much and she stopped going five weeks later, although she still attends another church where she finds it easier not being labelled as the wife-of-the-vicar-who-lost-his-faith. Pastor Wallace Wade, by contrast, kept his wife informed from the moment he began to have religious doubts. She sympathized with his misgivings and they both studied Jewish books together and eventually made a joint decision to convert. When the Lutheran minister told his church, the members were 'nonplussed', although Mrs Wade's parents were extremely distressed to hear the news. For those ministers who do change faith, their enthusiasm for the new religion often means that they wish to adopt it as fully and as full-time as their original faith. This in turn can help solve the question of their future employment, for they now become ministers within their new faith. Pastor Wade took this route, studying for the rabbinate and then working for an institute of Jewish learning, running seminars and counselling sessions. However, not all clerical converts receive such a warm welcome, for they can also provoke an ambivalent response. As another former cleric explained, 'Some people were suspicious on the grounds that if I could change my mind once, then I could change it again. They also thought I might be a bad influence as a speaker because audiences might think that they too could change faith just as I had done, and so rather than reinforce the religion, I might inadvertently encourage defections!'

The position of a convert who marries a cleric can also be

difficult. The wives of ministers are often judged harshly by the rest of the congregation, and are expected to live up to impossible expectations: be an ideal wife, perfect mother, excellent hostess, dress modestly but smartly, run a women's circle, handle all callers with sensitivity, be unpaid organizer of various communal activities, be knowledgeable without being too clever, and be a model of behaviour. However, this fierce scrutiny applies only to female partners. In instances where the cleric is a woman, and the partner a male, the same criteria are not brought to bear. If the wife of the minister has converted to his faith, then another layer of scrutiny is added, with questions raised over the sincerity of her beliefs and constant vigilance kept to check that she is punctilious in her devotions. Once again, much depends on the attitude of the faith to conversion. Thus the wife of a Pentecostal minister who converted was lauded as an example to all that their lives can be uplifted by 'finding Jesus', and was asked to go on lecture tours specifically aimed at outreach and missionary activity. Conversely, the convert wife of a rabbi was seen as an interloper and lacking true Jewish roots. Indeed, she was left under no illusion that it was wrong for him to have married a convert and that 'my husband, as a religious leader, should not have married someone from outside the community'.[1] In her case the criticisms came not just from the laity but from some of his colleagues, fellow rabbis who felt he was acting improperly and setting a bad example.

On the positive side, the convert wife of a minister can also become a role model for other women. This can apply both to those who are converts themselves and to those who believe strongly in a woman's right to map out her own path, religious or otherwise. As one congregant put it, 'My husband was horrified that the rabbi had married a convert, whereas I saw it the other way round: that it was great that a woman had chosen a new religious identity and had then decided to marry a rabbi.' Similar issues of propriety can arise if a convert marries the son or daughter of a minister. When Richard told his father, vicar of an inner-city church, that his Hindu-born fiancée wished to be baptized, his father was overjoyed: 'I was delighted as a father that my son would be marrying a fellow-Christian, and also pleased as a minister that another soul had been brought to Christ.' In complete contrast was Josh's father, an Orthodox rabbi, who was aghast that his son wished to marry a convert. 'As far as Dad was concerned, she would always be a non-Jew. However much she studied and however sincere she was, in his eyes she would never have a Jewish soul. It was actually very painful for me, stuck in the middle. Knowing my father, I understood what he meant and why he said it, but I was still angry with him for being so obstinate.' Jonas' father was even more distraught. He had been a Christian missionary and Jonas been brought up in a variety of different African countries where his father had been stationed. 'Both my parents were devoted to spreading the Gospel to people who had never heard the name of Jesus. You can imagine how devastated they were when I said I wanted to become Jewish. Here was someone who had read the New Testament every day of his life, yet was giving it up. But it wasn't just a matter of losing one soul to another faith. My father took it as a personal failure on his part. I tried to explain that I respected all the good work he had done but that I felt more at home philosophically with Judaism, but he saw it as undermining everything he stood for.' In such situations the conversion of a minister's offspring can appear not only a personal tragedy but also a professional disaster, casting doubts in their own eyes, if not in those of others too, on their ability to communicate the faith they are supposed to be preaching.

Another difficult situation is when someone perceived to be from the 'enemy camp' converts to that faith. When Jack converted to Catholicism, he knew he would receive some criticisms but was unprepared for the reaction of his sister in Belfast. Her husband had served in the Royal Ulster Constabulary for many years during the height of 'the troubles' and she accused Jack of 'selling out' and 'going over to the other side'. For her, the traditional rivalry between Catholics and Protestants was much more important than changing religious convictions: 'If I had become a Methodist or Baptist she would not have blinked an eyelid. But for her becoming a Catholic was like joining the IRA.' Gaynor experienced similar reactions in a different context. Her parents were ardent Zionists who supported a variety of Israeli charities and often went to Israel for holidays. They were horrified when she first expressed an interest in Islam and even more aghast when she converted to it. She tried in vain to persuade them that not all Muslims were gun-toting Palestinian terrorists, and that it was an ancient faith with a system of ethics and values that reached far beyond the current political problems in one corner of the Middle East. However, she found it impossible to dislodge decades of them associating Islam with Arabs and anti-Zionists. 'I know they would have been dreadfully upset if I had converted to any faith, but nothing could be worse for them than Islam. Of course, the argument is never about religious principles – they'd be very hard pressed to attack Islam if it was – but it's always political and emotional: me joining the murderers.'

Different ages have different enemies, and when Hugh Monte-fiore converted from Judaism to Christianity before the State of Israel existed, he was accused by family members of being a traitor. 'Although I was a bit lonely as a result of this, I cannot with hind-sight blame anyone in any way. For a Jew to become a Christian is to go over to the "enemy" . . . and to identify himself with a religion whose adherents have for centuries and centuries con-served an implacable hatred of their race.'[2] Muslims and Hindus in Britain whose families originate from the Punjab area can also find that a decision to convert to the other faith in the tolerant atmosphere of England suddenly plunges their family into a re-enactment of ancient rivalries the other side of the world. They quickly discover that religion is not just a personal matter but is identified with culture, family identity and nationhood – if not by themselves, then certainly by others, who then feel impelled to defend whatever honour they feel has been slighted. The convert finds that he/she is an apostate according to some members of their former religion and a traitor according to others, and it is not a comfortable position in which to be. It can also produce an angry backlash in the person themselves. After enduring weeks of sniping remarks about her new faith, Gitta angrily told her parents, 'Look, if I had become a drug addict or gone into porno-graphic films, then I could understand you being upset. But all I have done is joined a faith that believes in ethical standards and charity for others. I don't even claim it's better than your faith, just that I feel at home in it. What is the problem with that?'

In some cases, passions can be aroused from both of the faith groups involved. When the German Lutheran, Helga, converted to Judaism it was partly out of a desire to atone for the past maltreatment of the Jews by her own people. 'I found that the best form of contrition was to identify with the victims, so much so that I wanted to join them and uphold in my life what many of them died for.' Yet her gesture, which many would consider to be highly noble, involved her in considerable controversy. Her family were aghast at her decision, for although they knew it was not a rejection of them personally, they were fully aware of the larger implications and felt she had created a major divide between herself and them. 'It wasn't so much the change of faith that hurt them, it was me joining the Jews and all the political, social and moral consequences of that. They certainly found it hard to tell their friends. It would have been much easier if I had become a Buddhist or even a Hindu. That would have been very strange and outside their experience, but becoming Jewish presents them with unwanted memories and is a real challenge.' However, Helga also received much resistance from sections of the Jewish people. 'There were those who welcomed me, but equally those who were highly suspicious. They could not accept that a German could be genuinely pro-Jewish, let alone become Jewish. I thought that would just apply to the older generation, which I could understand, but it came from younger people too. That really upset me. Partly because my attempt to build bridges was being rejected, but mainly because they were indulging in the very same stereotyping that lies behind antisemitism. I had tried so hard to get away from racism but I was encountering it all over again.' Nevertheless, she recognizes how hard it is to change attitudes based on personal experience and she still possesses a letter that she received from a member of the synagogue she joined which tried to explain why her presence there was resented: 'I left Germany as a child shortly before the war, but my parents were unable to get out and subsequently died in the concentration camps. Please understand, therefore, that I do not want to go to synagogue and pray next to someone whose direct relatives may have been those who killed them.'

Those who are in the category of 'enemies who convert' often find that special sensitivities apply long after their conversion. A few weeks after Helga gave birth, her husband asked her would she mind not singing a German lullaby to the child. Although he personally did not mind, his parents had overheard her and had taken great offence. Helga was astonished. 'I had not consciously decided to sing a German lullaby. It was simply what I remembered from my own childhood, and the words came flooding back now that I was a mother. In principle I have no objection to English lullabies, but they won't come as naturally and I will have to ask my husband to teach me them.' Gitta's problem came with the naming of her son. Now that she had joined her husband's faith and become a Sikh, she felt it appropriate for the boy to have a Sikh name that would reflect the family faith and the circles in which he would largely mix. Her Hindu family were horrified and told her that they could not possibly call a grandson by a Sikh name. That in turn upset her in-laws who resented the idea of her parents editing the choice of their grandson's name, especially as he was their first grandson. 'What should have been a wonderful event, the birth of our first baby, became an absolute nightmare. In the event we compromised and decided to have an English forename, which was not what any of us wanted but which at least prevented a religious war breaking out in the family.'

Religious reunions can also present a problem. Gaynor's parents had always put much pride in the extended family getting together for the Passover meal and narrating the triumph of Moses over Pharoah as the Israelites made their exodus from Egypt. Moreover, it was always the tradition that everyone would interrupt the narrative with comments and questions. Her mother and father had been unsure whether to invite Gaynor after their rows over her conversion to Islam, but they did so and to their surprise she accepted. Despite their pleasure at her presence, problems erupted when, discussing Moses' cry to Pharoah to 'let my people go', Gaynor remarked that now the scenario was being repeated in reverse, with the Palestinians saying same thing to modern Israelis. However accurate her political analogy may have been, her parents took her point as a religious attack and embarked on a lengthy defence of the entire system of Jewish ethics. The result was a burnt meal and frayed tempers. But Gaynor was acutely aware that 'if anyone else around the table had said what I said, it was have been debated as an interesting point with arguments for and against it. But because it was me who said it – "the Jew who went over to the other side" – it was transformed into a one-sided religious crusade to prove the superiority of Judaism against the infidel. Next time I'll keep my thoughts to myself.'

Homosexuality is not usually a motivating factor for conversion, but for some proselytes it is a major concern. This can happen in one of two ways. For some, their sexual orientation is the trigger that prompts a religious change. Roy was a twenty-eight-year-old practising Orthodox Jew who took its tenets seriously and whose involvement in synagogue life was central to him. However, he was painfully aware of the discrepancy between his own homosexuality and the biblical teaching that it is an abomination and is regarded as such a heinous sin that it carries the death penalty (Lev. 20.13). 'The more I was sure of my own sexual orientation, the more I began to question Jewish teaching. I knew that my homosexuality was not an evil perversion but my God-given natural state. It made me think that if Judaism had got this one so badly wrong, then what else was incorrect? Unfortunately there was no one in my own circle who was prepared to discuss this, and so I carried on being an observant Jew on the surface but increasingly disillusioned underneath. I felt I was suffocating under the strain. The break came when I saw a meeting advertised for gay Christians. I was astonished. Here was a faith that proclaimed you could be yourself openly and still be loved by God. The meeting was led by a gay vicar, and listening to him speak, I felt years of repression and deceit fall off me. The following Sunday I attended a church service and I haven't been in synagogue since. My family hardly have any contact with me now, although I am not sure if that is because I have "come out" or because I converted. Certainly the combination has proved too much for them, and although that's something I regret, at least I feel I am being true to myself and I can breathe properly again.'

A similar situation led Anthony to come to the exact opposite conclusion, using faith to fight his condition. He had been aware of his latent homosexuality for some time and was frightened of its consequences. This was strengthened by an unsatisfactory homosexual experience that made him deeply ashamed of his sexuality. 'I know that many people are very open about being gay, but I don't find it appropriate for me. I felt I needed help to turn my back on that aspect of my life and concentrate on everything else. I had never had a religious upbringing, so when I came across a pamphlet on Catholic views about modern issues it was a welcome surprise. The teaching of the Catholic Church on homosexuality is quite unequivocal, acknowledging the tendency but condemning the act, and I found it gave me the structure and support that I needed. That by itself didn't make me a believer, but once I plucked up the courage to go to church I found that the liturgy spoke to me in so many other ways that I started going regularly. Three months later I was baptized. I have also taken a private vow of celibacy, which is unusual for a lay person, but it's helped put everything into context and I feel it's freed me from the burden I was carrying before.'

There are also those whose sexuality plays a secondary role in adopting a new faith. Amanda had felt unhappy with Christian life for reasons totally unconnected with her lesbianism. She found church services suffocating and also had problems with theological concepts of original sin and the resurrection. Her strong sense of God led her to look for a spiritual home within Judaism, which she found more appealing. She was aware of Orthodox Judaism's condemnation of gay relationships and therefore decided to approach a Reform synagogue which she had heard would be more accepting of her as it claimed the right to re-interpret biblical teachings in the light of modern knowledge. 'At my first interview, I never told the rabbi I was a lesbian because it was irrelevant as to why I wanted to become Jewish and I didn't want it to muddy the waters. I did mention it later when we discussed what sort of Jew I wanted to become, because that's where it was relevant. To my relief he didn't raise any objections, although by then I was fairly sure that he was going to be open-minded about it.'

If sexuality can play a role for some people in choosing a religion, then so can colour. The example has already been cited of Amos who found that despite the Christian injunction to love your neighbour as yourself, 'when your neighbour is coloured like I am, then you are less likely to be loved'. The gulf between theory and reality eventually led him to seek a religious home elsewhere, which he found in Islam 'in which I could still follow the teachings of Christ but not have to put up with Christians'. Amos' view does, of course, reflect his own personal experience and it was precisely the church's teachings on the common humanity of all people that brought Lee to God. He had left school without qualifications and had largely been unemployed ever since, save for intermittent spells as a casual labourer. He was, by his own admission, lucky to have avoided prison for various instances of petty crime. 'I felt I didn't have any purpose, nothing to aim for, and that as a black in a white society I was definitely at the bottom of the heap.' When he was handed a leaflet with the heading 'God loves you' in his local High Street inviting him to come to church, he challenged the distributor as to whether that applied to blacks too. To his surprise, the person grasped him by the shoulders and assured him that God loved him as much as anyone else. 'Then he suggested we go for a coffee in a nearby cafe and he abandoned his post in the High Street and sat down with me for two hours. I was bowled over. But it wasn't just him. I was a bit wary that others in the church would be different and would just see the colour of my skin. I was used to being judged at twenty metres. But when I went along I got more handshakes than I'd had all my life. They saw me as Lee, not as a black, and it was wonderful to be treated as somebody that counted. If I hear anyone say that "Jesus is a white man's God" I put them straight right away.'

It should also be noted that some converts have to persevere in their faith despite problems that arise over colour. Derek had to endure a number of unpleasant remarks about Islam when he converted to the faith, but he put that down to ignorance and prejudice. What hurt him much more were derogatory comments from some Muslims, especially references to him being one of the 'White Muslims'. 'I can't tell you how much I loathe that term. It's doubly awful, with the implication being firstly that I am not a real Muslim, but a special type that needs to be qualified and explained, and secondly that the reason is my colour. Fortunately I know enough about Islamic teaching to know that such attitudes are totally at odds with the faith. There is only one type of Muslim and we are all equal in the sight of Allah, but it is profoundly annoying to come across opinions like that, while I also feel that it gives the faith a bad name.' Geraldine felt her commitment tested in a similar way, albeit to Judaism. She had been told by the rabbi that her being black made no difference as far as he was concerned and that Judaism was colour-blind. 'That may have been true of him, but I'm not sure if it applied to everyone in the congregation, because although some people welcomed me warmly, others quite obviously kept their distance. There were times when I wondered if it was me being self-conscious, but there was another woman who converted at the same time, and she was white, and there's no doubt that she fitted in much better. Perhaps it was silly of me to think that Jews weren't colour-conscious, and I know that Jews have faults like everyone else, and it's the ideals of the faith itself that really counts, but I still find it disappointing.'

The final word in this chapter must be about those who engage in serial conversion. Shula was born into a Catholic family and attended a Catholic school until the age of sixteen. It had the effect of giving her a deep sense of spirituality although she could not reconcile her belief in God with Catholic dogmas. It led her on a spiritual search which resulted in study of the Jewish roots of Christianity and her eventual conversion to Judaism. 'I felt I had arrived at a purer understanding of God, but unfortunately I found synagogue life didn't sustain my interest. It was far too concerned with "committee-itis" and discussion over the state of the carpets. I wanted to talk about spirituality and the state of my soul. I wandered away, started reading about eastern faiths, got involved with Buddhist teachings and decided that was for me. I certainly did find it answered my personal needs, although as time went by, around ten years later, those needs changed and I wanted something less inward-looking and more to do with family and community. I was impressed by Islamic values and so eventually became a Muslim and here I am.'

Her story is unusual but not unique, as there are other individuals whose religious yearnings not only change over the years but are sufficiently strong to motivate the person to find a new home. They differ from those who also go through changes of religious attitudes, but either do not have sufficient interest to do anything about them, or feel they are locked into a faith because of family circumstances. The result is either that they simply ignore those religious impulses and carry on with their existing allegiance, or they quietly drop out of religious life altogether. It highlights the fact that there can be a strong element of luck to conversion. As has been seen in earlier chapters, many people became attracted to a particular faith through a chance meeting with a member of it or by coming across some of its literature. Very often the person was ready for a religious change, and the coincidence of their need and the faith's presence led to a relationship. However, just as emotional relationships are often based on chance meetings and a mixture of need and availability, but may not be appropriate for a long-term commitment, so too with religious relationships. The faith that was right for one stage in a person's life is not always appropriate for later stages, and the religious equivalent of divorce and remarriage can take place for those who have the energy to try again.

A variant pattern is for some individuals eventually to return to the religion in which they first started. One example is Stuart, who was brought up Jewish in a Reform synagogue, but felt it did not answer the major questions he was asking about life and death. His quest for self-knowledge led him to Buddhism, which he adopted during his early twenties. 'However, there was always part of me that believed in an actual God, and as that grew stronger, I felt less at home in Buddhism. So I began to look elsewhere and, through a friend of a friend, came across Sufism and found it tremendously exciting. It was great for a number of years, but then, perhaps it's age, or maybe it was meeting some old friends, I began to miss my Jewish roots. I started to read a bit about Hasidic Judaism and realized that it offered the same religious fire as Sufism but in a Jewish context. There was an awkward transition period to begin with, but it sorted itself out and now I'm really happy as a Jew again.' It is hard to know whether people in Stuart's situation would have been content to remain in their own faith if they had been exposed to more satisfying aspects of it to begin with, or whether they needed to make a religious journey far away before they could appreciate the value of their own home. For some, all that is important is the destination; for others, it is the journey that has been the most worthwhile part of their search.

8

The Balance Sheet

Types of conversion

The enormous range of individual situations that have been examined indicates how varied and complex is the act of conversion. In summary, though, they fall into four main categories. The first is Acquiring Faith, in which a person who previously had no religious allegiance at all suddenly discovers faith and joins a particular group. The second is Born Again, in which someone who was nominally attached to a faith but was not committed to it comes to see it in a new light and pursues it wholeheartedly. The third is Denominational, which involves conversion from one denomination to another within the same faith. The fourth is Transference, in which a person converts from one faith to an entirely different one. In each case, the experience can be totally unexpected for the person concerned and poses many challenges for his/her family and friends.

The actual way in which the changes occur also vary greatly, but can be characterized in six main types, each of which can apply to any of the four main categories above. One is Intellectual. Conversion comes because the person has read books or attended lectures on the faith, and has come to the conclusion that he/she agrees with its tenets and now wishes to formally adopt them. Although there may well be contact with other worshippers, it is not necesarily the case, and sometimes it is only when such individuals decide to convert that they come into contact with actual members of the faith. The second type of conversion is Mystical. The person has a religious experience that is 'out of the blue' and comes as a great surprise. It might also be very inconvenient, although it cannot be ignored, and it can cause them to reassess other aspects of their life, including career and relationships.

The third type is Experimental. The person has initiated contact with the religion and asked to attend services, so as to 'see what it's like.' It is motivated by a desire to have a faith and find a spiritual home, but the result depends on whether the person considers that what the faith has to offer matches his/her requirements. The onus is on the faith to 'prove itself' and belief in the faith gradually develops as they become more committed to it. The fourth type is Affectional. The person is drawn into the faith through a personal relationship with an existing member of the faith, or through social contact with members. It is the attachment to believers that leads to their own personal belief. Although the greater importance of personalities rather than dogmas may be thought to be less than ideal, the effect can be that the person is bound more strongly into the faith and becomes a practising member.

The fifth type is Revivalist. This involves an active process of outreach by a faith to win new adherents. It can involve open meetings or street parades or specific targeting of individuals, through house-to-house calls, visits to new neighbours, setting up social centres for teenagers or providing welfare to those in need. There is often an element of pressure, whether social, emotional or financial, and a deliberate attempt to encourage the conversion of others. The sixth type is Coercive. In such instances, the wishes of the individuals targeted are of little consequence compared to what the missionary believes is right for them. The gentle pressure of Revivalist situations is replaced by a much more extreme pressure that is highly manipulative, and often seeks to separate the individuals from their family and previous lifestyle.[1]

Whilst the particular route may differ widely, for the majority of people conversion is a long process. This might be either in the length of time that they take to admit that they are not happy in the faith in which they are born, or until they summon up the courage to turn passive interest in a faith into active involvement, or in the period it takes to feel that they have assimilated properly into it. The transition from being a wide-eyed visitor to feeling that they are fully at home can be a long one. Many find that adopting a new set of beliefs is relatively easy; it is adapting to the new way of life or interacting with a new set of co-religionists that proves the more difficult. Nevertheless, it can be argued that from a religious point of view, many come to their faith on a higher spiritual plane than those born into the religion. This is not just a general observation as to how converts lead their lives, but applies to the actual act of commitment that is demanded of converts. Thus when an adult is baptized into Catholicism and makes a profession of faith, they promise to obey the laws as promulgated by the successors of St Peter, which binds them completely, whereas most cradle Catholics never have to make that statement and never have to confront that issue within themselves. As Anne Widdecombe pointed out after her conversion, 'It is possible to become a semi-detached Catholic, but you cannot become a semi-attached Catholic'.[2] Similarly, converts to Judaism have to promise to take upon themselves 'the yoke of the commandments' whereas born-Jews have to give no such undertaking to justify their status. It was recognition of the unique ability converts have to make public their religious enthusiasm that led Albert Einstein to declare 'I am sorry that I was born a Jew, because it kept me from choosing to be a Jew.' The remark also highlights both the fact that converts are often admired for their conviction, and that a change of faith is seen as a personal matter purely for the individual concerned. This contrasts with past ages when converts were liable to be punished by those in power for crossing a religious divide which was not only seen as heretical but politically dangerous and against the interests of the ruling power.

The fast flowing current of those exchanging one faith for another in order to find a religious home acts as a mirror of society as a whole, in which religious trends are undergoing a profound change. There are two religious curiosities in Britain today. One is the clash between the statistics concerning those who attend church and the figures for those who say they believe in God; the former are decreasing yet the latter are stable. It indicates that religion is not in decline, but changing. People still have religious inclinations but are seeking to express them in new ways. Beneath the vast growth in New Age religions in recent years lie very old-fashioned questions which they too are asking: What is the purpose of life? What is my own significance? Why does suffering exist? What happens after death? How can I achieve immortal life? Religious impulses are as strong as ever, but many find that the faith into which they were born seems much less appealing than religious expressions elsewhere. The second curiosity is that the mainstream faiths which are attracting new members are also losing members. At the same time that born-Christians are deserting their pews, turned off by, as they see it, the church's outdated belief in miracles and the supernatural, non-Christians are discovering the wonder of God through Jesus Christ. In a similar way, many born-Jews are rejecting what they consider to be Judaism's oppressive adherence to meaningless rituals, while non-Jews are finding the faith bubbling with joy and cameraderie. This simultaneous pattern of loss and gain makes it seem that modern clergy are trying to fill a bath by running the taps yet leaving the plug-hole open. Very often this involves an element of transferred benefit, in that those brought up in one faith may reject its outer forms but still have imbibed the religious sensibility that it sought to promote. Having found a new faith, they then take it as seriously as they were expected to take their original faith but never did. It is a form of delayed response to early religious teachings that may appear to be ignored at the time but often surface in the new faith.

Religions also face another difficulty. The new climate of both ecumenicism and inter-faith dialogue militates against missionary activity. It is a condition of dialogue that neither party seeks to convert the other, and although technically that applies just to those participating in the inter-religous discussion, it carries much wider ramifications about respecting the integrity of other faiths and refraining from attempts to steal its members. It is not just a practical limitation, but a theological challenge: acknowledging the validity of other paths to God undermines the legitimacy of evangelism. This is particularly difficult for Christianity, which has traditionally held that 'I am the way, and the truth, and the life; no one comes to the Father but by me' (John 14.6). Some have decided that surrendering the mission of Christianity is too high a price to pay for the benefits of religious dialogue, especially those on the charismatic and evangelical wing of the church. Others have tried to reconcile the two, saying, for instance, that evangelism should be applied to acts of mercy and justice, but not to conversion. Alternatively, Christianity can be redefined as significant but not unique, with the equal role of other faiths being accepted. Another option is to maintain that even though Jesus is the exclusive path to God, it is possible to have a genuine encounter with God outside the Christianity without realizing that it is a manifestation of Jesus.[3] Whatever solution is adopted, though, there is no doubt that even those actively promoting their faith do so much more circumspectly and without gratuitously offending the sensibilities of other faiths. Even the most committed missionary knows that it is politically much safer to target those without a belief of any sort than those who are members of another faith.

The question may be asked: what makes a successful convert? Much depends on who is asking the question. From the point of view of the individual concerned, the answer is probably a mixture of the religious and the social: whether they feel spiritually uplifted by the new faith, as well as welcomed into a caring community by existing members of the faith. From the perspective of the faiths themselves, the answer is more complex and can vary considerably according to the different emphasis they each have. For some, it is the relationship with God that is paramount. Thus for Christianity, the successful convert is one who comes to know God through Jesus and gains salvation. Other faiths concentrate on the development of the individual. Thus for Buddhism, success can be measured in terms of achieving a state of enlightenment. Other faiths put considerable weight on the social context. Thus for Judaism, the successful convert not only observes the commandments but has to integrate into the community itself in order to perform many of them, whilst equally important is handing on the faith to the next generation. It could even be said that the litmus test of a good Jew is one who has Jewish grandchildren, and so the success or failure of the conversion can only be calculated much later in life or even posthumously. This is a heavy burden to bear and means that judgment of the conversion has to be suspended for several decades.

The long-term view is vital, and conversions that descend into indifference a few years later must raise questions as to either how sincere were the individuals concerned or how supportive was the religious environment into which they went. However, this has to be set beside the fact that levels of religious intensity can change over the course of a person's life. This is a common process and therefore does not necessarily reflect on the suitability or unsuitability of the faith they have chosen to adopt, which they may still value deeply. As Judy admitted, 'I don't go to church nearly as often as I did after I converted – maybe once every two months whereas once it was every week. But I still very much consider myself a Christian and still try to live by the example of Jesus. I suppose attendance isn't so important to me as a way of expressing that, although I know my vicar wishes it was!' Ideally, religious belief and practice should be a constant, but other circumstances such as age, family dynamics, work pressures, personal crises, economic circumstances, and health can all have an effect on a person's religiosity. Moreover, it makes it hard to select any one moment in a convert's life as the point at which overall judgment can be made, as their religious involvement might rise or dip soon afterwards owing to other factors.

Consequences

An equally important question is the consequences of conversion for the faiths themselves. Whilst each individual conversion can have a major impact on the life of those concerned and their wider family, collectively they can also affect the different religions in a variety of ways. First there is the numerical aspect. At a time when many faiths are complaining about the younger generation becoming secularized and increasingly irreligious, the influx of adult converts can help redress the loss. It should also be borne in mind that converts can also mask the internal decline as their addition to the overall figures can obscure the scale of defection by those born into the faith. The lack of statistical data kept by most faiths makes full analysis almost impossible, but certain figures are available. The comparison between conversions to Catholicism and marriages in Catholic churches may be of interest:

	1974	*1984*	*1996*
Conversions	5,253	5,146	5,180
Marriages	36,566	28,061	15,522

If it can be assumed that a significant number of conversions are undertaken as a prelude to marriage to a Catholic, then those converting have both added to the marriage figure and also prevented an even steeper decline than would otherwise have occurred through the dropping out of born-Catholics.[4]

A similar result can be deduced from the the few Jewish records of conversion. From 1948 to 1998 the number of adults converts to Judaism through the Reform Synagogues of Great Britain was 4,831. This was over a period when the estimated Jewish population of Britain fell by approximately 100,000, owing largely to a combination of assimilation, falling birth-rate and emigration. The period also witnessed a rise in the size of the Reform community at the expense of the Orthodox community. The significance of the converts is twofold. First, although there was a great disparity between the number becoming Jewish and the overall decline, those converting helped minimize the loss somewhat. Secondly, the number of converts was one factor in shifting the balance between the different denominations within Judaism. This was partly by the converts themselves adding to the Reform numbers, but also by them bringing into the Reform community Jewish partners who had previously belonged to the Orthodox and so depleting the Orthodox numbers. 89% of the converts were engaged or married to a Jewish partner, the vast majority of whom came from Orthodox synagogues, but as conversion via Orthodoxy was generally much harder than via the Reform tradition, it was more common for converts to choose Reform as their route to Judaism and to bring their Jewish partners with them.[5] In addition, 92% of the converts were aged below 40 – and thus of the group most likely to have children – and that in turn helped increase the number of children born within Reform, whilst at the same time Orthodoxy was denuded of the Jewish partners of child-bearing age and its natural growth rate in the next generation decreased accordingly.

Alongside the increase in numbers that converts make to any faith, a second consequence is the personal contribution that they bring, for many are keen to be involved in the organization of the local community. A study of one synagogue, for instance, revealed that three out of the nine form teachers at its Religion School were proselytes. As the head teacher commented, 'Whereas many born-Jews stop their Jewish education at thirteen and so are permanently going around with a spotty teenager's view of Judaism, proselytes have studied it at a sophisticated level and have a far higher level of knowledge. What's more they also have the enthusiasm to get out of bed on a Sunday morning and teach it while most born-Jews are still having a lie-in!' The synagogue librarian and the person running the synagogue shop – both part-time voluntary positions – are also converts, as is the organiser of the refreshments provided after services. Out of the past eight chairmen of the same synagogue, one was a proselyte and five more were the partners of proselytes. Their own sense of Jewish identity had been activated both by the enthusiasm of their con-verting partner and by attending the conversion course alongside them.[6] A similar story of converts taking an active role can be found in churches, mosques or Buddhist communities.

A third consequence of converts is the religious changes that they can introduce to the faith they are adopting. At first sight this may appear contradictory as the convert is attracted to the new faith because of what it offers. However, they inevitably bring to it religious influences from their own past as well as their own cultural education which may be different from that of many other existing members of that faith. One example is that a number of former Christians who have converted to Islam still celebrate Christmas for a variety of reasons: either to placate members of their family who would be hurt if they did not join in their tradi-tional festivities, or for their own sake because they so enjoy the season and are loath to relinquish it, or for the sake of the children who they feel should be allowed to enjoy what is so obviously going on in society all around them. Pauline also adds a theological justification by saying that 'Isa – or Jesus – is still a prophet in Islamic thinking, and so there is nothing wrong with celebrating his birthday and acknowledging his contribution to the world.' Whether or not she is right, it is not uncommon for other converts to Islam also to observe aspects of Christmas in some way – from eating a turkey at lunch, to bringing home Christmas crackers, to putting up Christmas cards, to exchanging gifts, to having a Christmas tree in the lounge. If they are married, they may thereby introduce such customs to their Muslim parents-in-law or brother and sister-in-law, while their children will grow up to regard the traditions as normal. The combined effect is to bring into Muslim homes Christian observances that would have been unthinkable in the previous generation and perhaps not even known about. Meanwhile the large numbers of Western converts to Buddhism have brought with them a very different perception of women from that within Tibetan culture, where they are often seen as inferior. Western Buddhists find this discriminatory and have effected various changes to give women a more equal role. Thus they omit prayers in which women ask to be reborn as men, they honour women Buddhist teachers and they have developed a notion of Buddhist 'foremothers'.[7]

At the same time, converts to the Greek Orthodox Church find that although they are enamoured with the spirituality of the music and liturgy, their children can find it very boring sitting through services in a foreign language. As a result some churches have started to hold services in English on a Saturday to supplement the main Sunday service. As this radical innovation becomes institutionalized, it may have profound implications for the content and shape of services in future decades. Similar changes are occurring within Islam under pressure from the large number of English converts to the faith. Koranic study groups that were previously conducted in Arabic are now held in English, while some mosques hold Friday worship in English. Another development has resulted from those Jews who have become involved with Buddhism but have decided to remain within the Jewish fold.

They have often brought back with them various insights and techniques from Buddhism that they have introduced at experimental services or Jewish retreats. These include meditational exercises in preparation for prayer or periods of silence and contemplation in the services themselves. Some might argue that these are to be found within Jewish tradition, such as some of the more mystical Hasidic circles, but there is no doubt that interest in them has been derived from Buddhist practices even if they happen to coincide with little-known Jewish ones. Another example of religious cross-fertilization of ideas is that a few Christian converts to Judaism have suggested the idea of a Passover Club modelled on that of the Christmas Club, by which weekly savings are made in preparation for the extra expenditure at Christmas, except that it would apply to Passover instead.

As well as these particular innovations, a more general effect of conversion is to break the link between faith and ethnicity that is common to many religions in Britain. This applies particularly to Hindus, Jews, Muslims and Sikhs who stem from a homeland, culture or language that acts as a binding force in addition to their faith itself. Converts from an entirely English background will therefore not share these extra bonds even though they may be totally devoted to the principles of the faith. The divergence in heritage and experience may lead them to different patterns of behaviour from those born within the faith. Thus converts to Judaism may not feel the same automatic loyalty to the Land of Israel as do most born-Jews. Whereas the latter tend to regard it as an ethnic homeland in which they have a personal stake, the former will see it merely as the geographical location of important religious events that has great interest but no direct relevance. This can also have repercussions for charitable giving, for whilst many born-Jews will give to charities in Israel simply because they are in Israel, converts are more likely to be motivated by the nature of the charity irrespective of where it is and whether or not it is Jewish-based. Moreover, they may feel guided in this by Jewish principles to help all who are in need and to see all people as equal in the sight of God. The same applies to other faiths, and the assumptions about levels of support previously taken for granted by the internal religious charities may need revision. Some fear that the gulf between faith and ethnic identity will mean that converts to any of the minority religions in Britain will not have strong enough roots within their various communities to maintain their own long-term commitment and certainly not that of their offspring. Thus Jonathan Sarna, a professor of Jewish History at the Hebrew University, warns that 'many of today's converts will be one-generation Jews – Jews with non-Jewish parents and non-Jewish children.'[8] Others would reject this view as alarmist and point to the personal commitment and practical involvement converts display towards their new faith, which are exactly the ingredients needed if their children are to grow up valuing the faith into which they are born. It is often said that 'religion is caught not taught'. In this respect, converts may succeed in enthusing their children in a way in which born members of a faith often fail to enthuse theirs. On a wider level, they bring many other benefits to the faiths that they join. However, as this book shows, the full extent of the joys, dilemmas, and sacrifices that they experience are rarely appreciated by those who take their birth-faith for granted.

Appendix

Guide for Those Considering Conversion

The following are offered as guidelines by the author based on his counselling experience. They are designed to ensure that individuals find long-term contentment and stability.

1. Explore your existing religious tradition thoroughly before deciding to abandon it. You may be surprised at how little you know it and how rich it actually is.

2. Investigate several different faiths to find out which has the values and lifestyle that appeals most to you. Be aware also of the different denominations within each of them.

3. Do not just read about a faith, but experience both its public worship and domestic ceremonies. Make sure you feel at home with both the practice and the theory of it.

4. Do not make your decision in a hurry. Give yourself time to feel comfortable at leaving your previous tradition and to feel at home in the new one.

5. Be fully aware of the demands your new faith will make on you, both in order to convert and what is expected after conversion. This applies particularly to changes in lifestyle and to any demands that will affect your relationship with your family.

6. Keep your family fully informed throughout the process of searching and converting, so that they do not feel alienated and so that you can benefit from any advice they may give.

7. Check whether your conversion will be recognised by all within the faith or be limited to certain denominations.

8. Be highly cautious when teachers tell you that they alone have access to the truth. Be wary of those who insist that joining their faith must involve surrendering control of your financial affairs.

9. Remember that the best teachers are those who encourage you to study the tradition for yourself and establish your own relationship with God rather than simply imbibe what others tell you about God.

10. Ensure that you are converting because you want to convert, and not out of pressure or to simply to please others. There has to be something in it for you. Nor should conversion be an attempt to escape aspects of your character or your past with which you have not yet properly come to terms. Conversion should a positive step, looking brightly to the future and bringing a sense of fulfilment.

Notes

1. Whose Soul Is It Anyway?

1. *Towards a Theology for Inter-Faith Dialogue*, Anglican Consultative Council 1988, p. 4.
2. For a fuller study see Jonathan A. Romain, *Till Faith Us Do Part*, HarperCollins 1996.
3. Lionel Blue, 'Insiders and Outsiders' in *Not By Birth Alone* ed. Walter Homolka, Walter Jacob and Esther Seidel, Cassell 1997, p. 133.
4. Ali Kose, *Conversion to Islam*, Kegan Paul 1996, p. 51.
5. William Abraham, *The Logic of Evangelism*, Hodder 1989, p. 12.
6. Ibid., p. 113.
7. For fuller discussion see Kose, op. cit., p. 145.
8. Ibid., p. 146.
9. William Shakespeare, *A Winter's Tale*, V i, line 106.
10. Adlin Adnan, *New Muslims in Britain*, MA thesis submitted to the Muslim College, London 1997, p. 2.
11. David Max Eichorn, *Conversion to Judaism* , Ktav, New York 1965, p. 172.
12. John Finney, *Finding Faith Today*, The Bible Society 1992; Alan Johnson, *The Psychology of Religion*, Abingdon, Nashville 1995.
13. Kose, op. cit., p. 47.
14. Jonathan A. Romain, *The Reform Beth Din*, Ph.D thesis submitted to the University of Leicester 1990, p. 171.

2. The Long and Winding Trail

1. Berkowitz, Allen L. and Moskovitz, Patti (eds), *Embracing the Covenant*, Jewish Lights Publishing, Vermont 1996, p. 53.
2. Brigid Marlin, *From East to West*, Collins Fount 1989, p. 13.

3. Abraham Carmel, *So Strange My Path*, Bloch Publishing Co., New York 1964, p. 17.
4. Gai Eaton, *Islam and the Destiny of Man*, Islamic Texts Society, Cambridge 1997, p. 5.
5. As reported in *The Times*, 14 January 1999.
6. *The Times*, 8 May 1999.
7. Eichorn, op. cit., p. 200.
8. Joel Allison, 'Empirical Studies in Conversion Experiences', *Pastoral Psychology* 17, 1966, p. 26.
9. Chana Uliman, 'Cognitive and Emotional Antecedents of Religious Conversion', *Journal of Personality and Social Psychology* 43, 1982, p. 187.
10. Ibid, p. 189.
11. Kose, op. cit., p. 83.
12. Lewis Rambo, *Understanding Religious Conversion*, Yale University Press 1993, p. 61; Kose, op. cit., p. 109.
13. D. Snow and C. Phillips, 'The Lofland-Stark Conversion Model: A Critical Reassessment', *Social Problems* Vol. 4, 1980, p. 433.

3. Different Routes

1. Rodger Kamenetz, *The Jew in the Lotus*, HarperCollins, New York 1995, p. 3.
2. Ibid., p. 12.
3. William Abraham, *The Logic of Evangelism*, Hodder 1989, p. 73.
4. Ibid., p. 106.
5. 'On The Jews', Documents of the Second Vatican Council, Rome 1965.
6. Roger Hooker, 'Mission and Salvation III', *Common Ground* No. 3, 1997; Hugh Montefiore, *On Being A Jewish Christian*, Hodder 1998, p. 173.
7. Hilary and Piers Du Pré, *A Genius in the Family*, Chatto 1997, pp. 337, 341.
8. Montefiore, op. cit., p. 14.
9. Peter Brierley, *Changing Churches*, Christian Research 1996, p. 7. It should be noted, though, that an almost similar number of people left the church, and so the net gain was virtually nil (p. 21).
10. Adnan, op. cit., pp. 3, 15.
11. Ibid., p. 11; this is reinforced by similar results from Kose, p. 112.

12. Malcolm X, *The Autobiography of Malcolm X*, Grove Press, New York 1964, p. 340.
13. Eaton, op. cit., p. 7.
14. Quoted in Lawrence Epstein, *Readings on Conversion to Judaism*, Jason Aaronson, New Jersey 1995, p. 141.
15. Abraham, op. cit., p. 113.
16. See Roger Sutton, 'The Seeker Approach', *Quadrant*, July 1999, p. 6.
17. Brierley, op. cit., p. 14.
18. In William Oddie, *The Roman Option*, HarperCollins 1997, p. 30.
19. Ibid., p. 1.

4. Taking the Plunge

1. Babylonian Talmud, Yebamot 47a.
2. Adnan, op. cit., p. 5.
3. Walter Homolka, Walter Jacob and Esther Seidel (eds), *Not By Birth Alone*, Cassell 1997, p. 134.
4. Rom. 6.3-4.

5. Reactions – Expected and Unexpected

1. Hilary and Piers Du Pré, op. cit., p. 195.
2. Eaton, op. cit., p. 11.
3. Father Oliver McTernan, quoted in Oddie, op. cit., p. 166.
4. Ibid., p. 174.
5. Adnan, op. cit., p. 19.
6. Ibid., pp. 23–25, 34–35; see also Philip Lewis, *Islamic Britain*, I.B.Tauris 1994, p. 210.
7. Adnan, op. cit., p. 27.

6. After Conversion

1. Kose, op. cit., pp. 130ff.
2. David Lamb, *Keys to the Harvest*, Hodder 1997, p. 145.
3. Eaton, op. cit., p. 16.

7. *Special Cases*

1. Dorothea Magonet, 'The Experience of Conversion to Judaism', *European Judaism* Vol. 22, No. 1, 1988.
2. Montefiore, op. cit., p. 15.

8. *The Balance Sheet*

1. These categories are based on those used by J. Lofiand and N. Skonovd in 'Conversion Motifs', *Journal for the Scientific Study of Religion* 4, 1981, pp. 373–85.
2. In *The Times*, 23 April 1993, p. 15.
3. For a fuller treatment of the impact of dialogue on evangelism see Abraham, op. cit., pp. 209–33.
4. Figures taken from the Catholic Bishops' Conference of England and Wales.
5. From 1948 to 1965, only 8% of the Jewish partners of converts to Reform Judaism came from Reform synagogues; for further details, see Jonathan A. Romain, *The Reform Beth Din: its influence on the growth of the Reform Movement and its significance for Anglo-Jewry*, Leo Baeck College 1992.
6. The synagogue in question is Maidenhead Synagogue in Berkshire.
7. For further description, see Kamenetz, op. cit., pp. 217–19.
8. Epstein, op. cit., p. 128.